Progress
in Educating
the Library User

Progress in "Educating the Library User

Edited by
John Lubans, Jr.

R. R. Bowker Company
New York & London, 1978

To Benjamin Carl Wells Holley

Published by R. R. Bowker Company
1180 Avenue of the Americas, New York, N.Y. 10036
Copyright © 1978 by Xerox Corporation
Printed and bound in the United States of America

Library of Congress Cataloging in Publication Data

Main entry under title:

Progress in educating the library user.

Bibliography: p.
Includes index.
1. Libraries and readers.   I. Lubans, John.
Z711.P77   021   78-12758
ISBN 0-8352-1102-9

Contents

Foreword

Educating the library's clientele in the principles of bibliographic organization and their practical application to the information-seeking process is becoming a dominant concern of a growing segment of the national library community. Library instruction, long the neglected stepchild of librarianship, now seems likely to develop, along with networking and resource sharing, as a focus of professional interest and activity in the next several years.

The growing centrality of library instruction and library networks reflect a more basic change in the character of libraries and librarianship away from an almost exclusively materials-centered orientation and toward a client-centered mode of operation. The client-centered library evaluates its accomplishment and institutional stature not in terms of collection size or circulation statistics, but in the at once more subtle and far more significant measures of document delivery capability and capacity to facilitate the information transfer process. The overriding objective of the client-centered library is to make the universe of recorded information effectively accessible to its clientele. To achieve this objective, it is clearly essential that library users be able to interact easily and effectively with both manual and mechanized information storage and retrieval systems. At a minimum, the client needs to be familiar with the range of human, technological, and bibliographic resources that are available to access knowledge records. Thus, to inform or *educate* the library user becomes a matter of critical importance to librarians.

The increasing concern for and activity in library instruction make the appearance of this volume singularly timely. It is eminently appropriate that it should be edited by John Lubans, Jr., a dedicated, effective, and widely respected advocate for user education at the national level. It is equally appropriate that the extensive and varied efforts in library instruction both in this country and abroad should be subjected at this time to the kind of penetrating review that is generally characteristic of the fifteen papers that comprise this collection.

What is most striking about the contents of this volume, taken as a whole, is the substantial evidence it offers of the development that has occurred over the past four years in our collective thinking about the problem of library instruction. It is apparent from the work of the eighteen contributors to this book that the spirit of missionary evangelism has been tempered and strengthened by a new tone of tough-minded realism characterized by a willingness to ask the hard, self-critical questions. Betty L. Hacker and Joel S. Rutstein, examining the problem

vii

of library instruction in large universities, report that "In the cold practicality of the 1970's, academic librarians . . . have, in many situations, adapted their sights to the possible," while Sheryl Anspaugh suggests that "If public libraries are working with library use instruction, it is being kept a secret." There is a consistent recognition here that an acceptable generalizable conceptual model for library instruction is needed, and that user education programs ought to be conducted in a climate of rigorous evaluation and accountability.

Given the significance of and the high level of current interest in library instruction, a state-of-the-art review as wide-ranging and thoughtful as *Progress in Educating the Library User* is obviously a valuable addition to the literature. This book is that, and considerably more. It reflects a genuine effort to address fundamental issues and to arrive at a collective statement of basic principles in an area of major importance to the improvement of library and information services to all. This book merits wide attention, and the issues identified by the editor and his contributors deserve thoughtful consideration by the entire library community. It is a privilege for me to have a small part in bringing this collection to the large audience who share a concern for the problems and a responsiveness to the opportunities that are identified in these pages.

Thomas J. Galvin
Dean
Graduate School of Library
and Information Sciences
University of Pittsburgh

Preface

Progress in Educating the Library User is meant to complement and bring up to date the 1974 volume, *Educating the Library User*, by analyzing, in original papers, recent international trends, innovations, and new directions in the field. Chapters discussing school, academic, and public library programs in user education again emphasize the seemingly obvious, yet often ignored, fact that we all share the same users. *Progress* does differ from the 1974 volume in its raising more critical questions for discussion about *where* we are and *why* we are where we are in library use instruction. It is hoped that those who have come to refer to *Educating* as a *vade mecum* in library instruction will use *Progress* similarly.

The reader familiar with the user education movement knows of the continuing and growing interest in this public services effort in all types of libraries. Among numerous conferences, seminars, and publications two significant events culminated almost simultaneously in 1977: the establishment of the American Library Association's Library Instruction Round Table and the Bibliographic Instruction Section of ALA's Association of College and Research Libraries. The coming about of these two national groups confirms the professionwide concern with the subject and the acceptance by many librarians of the importance of interpreting the library to the user in order to effect more and better use of a library's valuable resources.

My appreciation is expressed to numerous colleagues who have provided ideas, sometimes unknowingly, for this book. Special thanks are extended to the contributors for their willingness to create and to share their work with the profession at large through this publication.

JOHN LUBANS, JR.
Assistant Librarian for Public Services
Downtown College Library
University of Houston
Houston, Texas

INTRODUCTION: SEEKING A PARTNERSHIP BETWEEN THE TEACHER AND THE LIBRARIAN

JOHN LUBANS, JR.
Assistant Librarian for Public Services,
University of Houston, Downtown College

The progress of library instruction is being influenced by the same changes developing in education at large. For example, the dramatic decrease in the population of school-age children does affect a library skills instruction program, if only in that fewer children pass through our programs. In this recent trend the optimist sees more time for librarians *and* teachers to spend in planning higher quality programs and with the students than was available during the expanding and pressurized 1960s. The pessimist fears for his or her job—and with some justification. Staff and book budget cuts in all types of libraries are not merely chimerical apparitions. Some universities, it is forecast, are entering the dinosaur age: they are doomed unless they are able to entice students to enroll in their courses. Such is the state of affairs on most campuses except, for example, those that attract numerous students for nonacademic reasons, such as desirable location. The response of universities to this type of change has been encouraging. Continuing education, once the campus stepchild, is now described as "lifelong learning" and has, like Cinderella, been promoted out of the dustbin into a full partnership with traditional campus-based programs.

Typical of the changing times is a midwestern university that had a high enrollment of 13,000 on-campus students in the 1960s. Enrollment is now down to 10,000 and a further plummet to 5,000 students on campus is anticipated. This school, in order to survive, has created a flexible school calendar and continuous registration, but most importantly is *bringing* degree programs to students off-campus. This pursuit of the "lifelong learner" (or the nontraditional student) should require a high level of library support so that the student does not get short shrift in his or her education. Clearly there is a danger here of programs being watered down, of less than even minimal support being provided in the area of information finding and use. (Can master's degree–level students living in a rural area served by a 3,000-volume bookmobile be expected to write a paper on recent issues in federalism?) Campus administrators and academic librarians are

1

faced with having to create methods to support a quality education off campus. For me, the need of students to know how to find and use information *on their own* in a variety of libraries (or data banks) is just as great (perhaps greater) off campus as on. The question here is whether librarians will be up to the challenge.

It is fair, in a volume entitled *Progress in Educating the Library User*, to expect some measurement of where we are, of how far we have come in our efforts since the publication of *Educating the Library User* in late 1974. Several chapters address this issue, some more quantitatively than others. My personal standard has been the degree to which we have been able to convince the teacher or faculty member that library instruction is good *and* the degree to which, as a result, the teacher works with the library in inculcating this bit of wisdom into the heads of students.

If there is one subjective indicator of progress, it is the general acceptance by librarians of not having to go it alone. The realization at the grass roots level that teachers are crucial to library instructional successes or failures does appear to be more prevalent than in previous decades.

If we have realized the importance of the faculty-librarian connection, what is it that impedes the next phase of a wholehearted acceptance by teachers of the benefits accruing to themselves and their students from information finding and using skills?

The roadblock to change was best pictured in Perkins's study from the early 1960s.[1] There is, upon rereading it, startling and even unnerving currency to his viewpoint.

His research was based on the underlying hypothesis that teachers across the country do not have an adequate understanding of how to find information in libraries; in short, that teachers do not *know* how to use libraries. His findings bore out this hypothesis. For example over 1,400 respondents (all future teachers) to the *Peabody Library Information Test* did not score well—on a scale of 100 for each of the eight sections in the test, Table 1 shows the percentage of correct responses received.[2] The grade equivalent for these percentages would be one C-, one D, and six Fs.

The results from the 2,466 students taking the Feagley *Library Orientation Test for College Freshmen* were equally discouraging. Perkins concludes that "no evidence was gained from this test to contradict the hypothesis that prospective teachers, as a group, cannot make intelligent use of library facilities."[3]

I suppose what worries me most is the overpowering suspicion that if we were to redo this study today the results would be the same. It is professionally distressing to continue contemplating such a landscape as that depicted in Perkins's research.

Faced with this self-perpetuating problem, one can understand that, while there is an unabated tide of interest and activity in library skills instruction among librarians, those most intimately involved in the movement have begun to sound some disquieting notes on the state of the art. Their frustration stems from our apparently small impact on the way people use libraries. In our missionarylike zeal, we appear to be convincing the converted and *not* the great unwashed of users/misusers/nonusers, including the key individual that possesses the greatest ability to make changes in the use of libraries: the teacher. But then, perhaps I

Table 1
Percentage of Correct Responses by College Seniors, Peabody Library Information Test

Section	%
The book	70.5
Arrangement of books	61.3
The card catalog	66.3
The dictionary	43.7
The encyclopedia	26.6
Periodicals and indexes	43.6
Special reference books	52.8
Bibliography	37.6

am too critical of this condition; that is, of librarians "turning on" other librarians to educating the library user. There is something to be said for the fact that librarians denigrating library instruction efforts are a little akin in numbers and acceptance to those in the profession publicly supporting censorship. As well, we have made giant strides forward in the rationalization, creativity, and service-mindedness of promoting library use.

What I am proposing is that we not mire ourselves in the frustration of talking only to ourselves but establish the next phase with the clear objective of convincing those in power of the value of effective information use.

There is something of a dilemma facing us: (1) if we were all to achieve success for current programs in convincing faculty members about more and better information use we probably could not handle the demand for our services, and (2) if we stay at the same level of activity, progress will appear to be slight, and disillusionment might set in with a downturn in our teaching efforts.

What is needed is the frequently called-for partnership between the teacher and the librarian. Librarians would still have a teaching role (in class situations at a specialized subject level and outside of it on a tutorial basis) but in tandem with the instructor, so that students could achieve and maintain a basic proficiency in library use throughout and beyond their in-school years.

To realize this we must change attitudes and policies of politicians and educators (including librarians), school boards and state boards of education, about the value of information, both finding it and using it efficiently.

We have yet, in a *marketable* way, to identify those desirable qualities of libraries that can change the present condition under which the nonuser can yet do quite well in course work, the lecture/textbook syndrome still prevails, and 1978 graduates are blissfully ignorant of information-use skills. People do not *have* to quench their thirst with diet drinks, or play tennis, or brush their teeth, or read *TV Guide*, but they do so by the millions. They do so because they have been convinced they should. Although library use is on a different plane, some work needs to be done on "selling" the idea that information plays an ever-increasing role in a person's life, and that possessing skills that enable one to find and use information is as important as being literate. (Keep in mind that it is not the way people *imagine* libraries that has to be changed but the way they *use* or, better yet, *consume* them.)

One could argue that the user does not need to be burdened with such skills because an intermediary—either a "personal librarian" or an "interactive data bank"—will be there to handle information needs. To suggest that the self-service concept in libraries will soon become outmoded belies current and future levels of tax support, reduced employment of librarians, and costs of computer terminals and data bases, not to mention the difficulties in using the contents of these data bases both before and after the computer search.

To get to the point, how *do* we convince teachers of 20 years' experience that a new method, involving their students' solving problems in the library, is better than the lectures they have so carefully written and rewritten? Very likely the same way that many schools faced with tenure decisions and cutbacks in budget are working on "faculty development" programs. When programs involving the library in instruction do come into existence, librarians should be involved in making some changes for the better. Perhaps convincing the entrenched is a lot more difficult that proselytizing new or prospective teachers about creative ways to use the library in teaching—that effective use of information sources will provide students with a wider understanding and appreciation of their studies. One thing is clear—the concept of "information use" has to *replace* some other aspects of a teacher's method rather than be *added to* the existing curriculum.

The National Commission on Libraries and Information Science and its forthcoming White House Conference are inordinately concerned with the technology of information delivery, especially in conceptualizing networks. These concepts are venerable with age and indeed admirable, but they are far from the users' and front-line librarians' immediate concerns. Networks or other "mechanical" approaches to improving libraries serve only to facilitate present levels and styles of information use and do not improve the quality of use. The White House Conference attendees (largely laypersons) should have one overriding concern: the need for intelligent information use as part of the nation's educational program. The other issues of computers, copyright, funding, etc., follow this premise and do not precede it.

This conference would then serve as a base for librarians' realistically mounting a challenge to the enormous waste of resources through nonuse and misuse in all types of libraries.

RESPONSE TO QUESTIONNAIRE ON LIBRARY USE INSTRUCTION

In early 1978 a questionnaire was sent by Patricia Wally, a library science student at the University of Denver, and me to a selected group of library skills instruction veterans.[4] The simple object of this study was to gain a general opinion of the current status of library use instruction.

Here are the results* from the 28 respondents with some representative comments in response to each question. (The name in parentheses is that of the individual speaking.) Because the questions were broadly worded individual respondents in some cases gave more than one category of response per question.

QUESTION A: *From a national viewpoint, would you say that during the last five years students have improved their abilities in using libraries?*

A1. The most frequent answer, "Yes, progress is evident" was given in 11 responses.

> The opportunity and exposure to library use instruction is definitely offered and is expanding (Kirkendall).

> [Yes] Unquestionably, since more libraries have made the teaching of research skills a priority. The day is approaching when bibliographic instruction will be considered as much an integral facet of library service as reference is now. (Burton and Poole).

> I am aware of many fine programs of library instruction which have been developed over the last five years and I assume that those students who have had the opportunity to take these courses have improved their abilities in using libraries (Dudley).

A2. The opposing view, "No, no progress nationally," was given in nine responses.

> Students seem to have lost the ability to think for themselves as more and more faculty "spoonfeed" them needed information (Sherby).

> We see more students who have not had adequate preparation to do college level work (Willar).

A3. Eight respondents felt that they had no basis for a national viewpoint.
There were common threads among responses in all three categories. First there is the idea that while there may be no progress nationally (or national progress cannot be determined), individual institutions have made strides.

> ... the number of students with improved abilities to use them [libraries], on a percentage basis, has probably not changed significantly. In those institutions which have sound programs of instruction, greater numbers of students and faculty are better informed about the library and more capable of approaching it for information (Cottam).

The second focuses on the lack of research in this area and a call for better methods of evaluation so that questions such as this can be answered more authoritatively.
Finally, the idea that there has been an increase in the number of library instruction programs thereby improving the opportunity of students was expressed by many respondents.

*This summary is largely the work of Ms. Wally and used with her permission.

QUESTION B: *What do you think needs to occur before one's ability to find and use information becomes as routinely assumed as the possession of "survival skills" such as literacy and rudimentary mathematics?*

B1. The majority of responses (19) called for increased responsibility for change on the part of the entire educational community including administrators (both library and school), teachers, and librarians.

> [There is a need for] a fundamental rethinking by the educational establishment of what it means to be educated, and how the educational establishment views the process of educating one's self (Kirk).

B2. An additional six respondents felt that the first need was to have library skills recognized as survival skills.

> Some dramatic comparison needs to be made repeatedly and systematically apparent between the "haves" and the "have nots," to the extent that the bibliographically disenfranchised might demand "equal opportunity" (Cammack).

B3. Five respondents felt that "one's ability to find and use information" could not be considered survival skills on the same level with literacy and rudimentary mathematics.

> Information gathering in the sense it is used here will never be as basic as the need to complete an employment form or any other form for which rudimentary literacy is essential (LoBue).

> The assumption that everyone should know how to use libraries as a "survival skill" has never been tested and presently cannot be placed on a level with literacy. People need libraries and librarians at the time of need, just as they need other professionals and services at certain times (Cottam).

QUESTION C: *Do you think library schools should provide the basic training for newly graduated librarians to be effective in front of a class and in the design of an instructional methodology for the purpose of library skills instruction?*

C1. Of all the questions asked, respondents were most in agreement in answering this one. Twenty responses favored "library schools' providing the basic training for newly graduated librarians to be effective in front of a class."

> They should also have some practice in preparation of programs, particularly in subjects about which they know nothing. This preparation should include the compilation of selective reference sources on a subject at a specified class level, lecture outline, and aids used in actual class presentation (Werner).

> The establishment of behavioral objectives and the application of modern systems of evaluation are perhaps the least understood among the many skills involved in the creation of an effective instructional program (Cammack).

> Yes—my survey in 1975 clearly showed that librarians with previous teaching experience were 50% more likely to be engaged in an instructional program than those without (Galloway).

C2. Six respondents had some reservations about library schools' taking this responsibility.

> Training should not be left to the library schools alone, since a year or two in graduate school is not enough time in which to become proficient in library use instruction (Nielsen).

> I believe this should be provided in an elective course for those planning/hoping to enter public service positions in all types of libraries or information centers (Parr).

> It should possibly be required for those students intending to work in academic or school libraries and an elective course for all others (Sherby).

C3. Two respondents felt that library school was probably *not* the place to teach this information.

> They could, but I see it as a dilution of library science and a duplication of effort from other disciplines. There are already powerful programs to train teachers. There is time-tested instructional development methodology available from such teacher education programs. Would it not be more efficient to tap that expertise? All librarians are not and should not be teachers, but they should be experts on the complexities of information and bibliographic control (Cottam).

QUESTION D: *What general improvements, if any, do you think should be made in the ways (methods) we teach library skills?*

D1. The idea presented most often (eight responses) was that of relevance; i.e., librarians taking care to tailor the type and extent of instruction to actual need.

> More emphasis needs to be placed on tailoring what we teach to users' needs. Given the opportunity to teach, many librarians attempt to convey too much detail, jargon, and tangential information (Burton and Poole).

> Methods must be more carefully matched to (1) objectives, (2) clientele, and (3) capacities of institution. Methods should not be chosen because the librarian likes them, but because they best serve the three enumerated conditions . . . (Kirk).

D2. The second most frequent answer to this question (seven responses) was that library instruction be more course related.

> Active pursuit of course-related instructional opportunities has proved the most effective channel for library use instruction. Teaching actual *library use*, as opposed to teaching *about* library use is, in my opinion, the most hopeful development to have occurred in the recent past (Cammack).

> Less lecture! More worksheets and integration into the class requirements of instructors (Galloway).

D3. Four respondents felt that before improvements can be made, research is required on present methods and better standards of evaluation are needed.

> Before we can effectively teach library skills we need considerable research on existing techniques and methods employed and a way of testing whether our approaches to information gathering are better . . . (LoBue).

D4. Two respondents felt that there should be more use of instructional aids.

I feel that there should be more development of audio-visual programs and "packaging" of basic instruction; greater attention given over to exploration of CAI programming for individuals (Cain).

D5. Two respondents expressed some reservations regarding the use of technology.

I think there is sometimes a tendency to become so involved with educational theory and technology that we forget the content and the student, the former in knowledge of reference sources and the latter as a person (Werner).

It is rather a matter of emphasis. There is real value in spreading information through audiovisual, etc., means but those forms of communication can lead to superficiality of knowledge absorption. They must not be a substitute for thinking (Gourde).

D6. Ten responses did not group into any of the above categories.

We need to devise a method(s) that would reach more students. Most attempts at instruction reach relatively few students. We also need to find better ways to show students how to adapt the information they learn for one subject area to another. They often don't make the connection that the technique stays the same even though the index may change (Sherby).

I think it is a matter of commitment, making it an integral part of library work, recognizing that library instruction is not only vital to the student, but possibly to ourselves as well. Many good ideas have been tried, advanced, and accepted, but most of us are still on an ad hoc basis . . . (Toy).

Acknowledge, and believe, that we are teaching as vital a survival skill as reading and computation. We need not apologize for having to teach library use, nor can we deny or minimize library knowledge in relation to other skills or subject areas (Ellis).

QUESTION E: *How much value do you place on cooperation in skills instruction among types of libraries: school, public, academic? Is there need for our cooperating?*

E1. Eighteen agreed, "Yes, cooperation among types of libraries is valuable and there is a need for it."

I place great value on establishing clear definitions for levels of ability or proficiency, as this is what enables instruction to be a building process and not a repetitive one (Willar).

Whether academic libraries can cooperate with school libraries will depend on everybody's coming to an understanding of what the college bound high school student needs, and what the noncollege bound student needs (Nielsen).

Academic librarians, especially, should cooperate and help the others using some of the experience accumulated in the academic area (Rader Delgado).

E2. Five respondents felt there was only some benefit to be gained from cooperation.

From my perspective as an academic librarian, I find this goal somewhat unrealistic. Without standardization among schools in bibliographic instruction programs there will never be a point where the academic librarian can safely assume "all" patrons have "equal" education (Cain).

E3. Another five respondents said they placed only a little value on cooperation among libraries.

QUESTION F: *What limiting factors are there in our establishing a "continuum" of library skills instruction and achievement from kindergarten on up?*

F1. There was no answer given most frequently to this question. Two answers had seven responses each. The first is the opinion that the great differences in facilities and personnel from institution to institution limit the establishment of a continuum of library skills instruction.

> Many of our small rural schools have no libraries and no school librarians. Our public libraries may not have the staff time (Fowler).

> Some limiting factors are: (1) not all elementary schools have libraries; (2) not all school librarians have master degrees in librarianship; (3) some school libraries have excellent resources with which to teach, others have not; (4) some school administrators value the library and encourage use and instruction, others do not; (5) some librarians value library skills instruction, others do not (Cain).

F2. The second group of opinions with seven responses depicts the diversity of professional opinion on establishing such a continuum.

> [There is] a lack of understanding on where we are and where we have to go (LoBue).

F3. The next most frequent answer (six responses) was that a lack of accepted definitions and standards limits progress.

> If the public schools would develop distinctive "college-bound" and "noncollege bound" tracks in their library programs, means might be made for quality teaching of information-handling skills. This is an unlikely event, and thus adequate definition of levels of appropriate skill is difficult below the college level, at least for those skills deemed important by *academic* librarians (Nielsen).

> [There is a] void in existing standards for separate levels (Kirkendall).

F4. Lack of funds was seen as the next most limiting factor (four responses).

F5. Three types of answers had three responses each. The first regards making library skills instruction more course related.

> The limitations can be avoided by proper planning. These limitations consist of repetition, boredom, teaching in a vacuum and such (Rader Delgado).

> Unless such a program is tied into the writing and research of the curriculum at each level it is a meaningless exercise (Galloway).

The second regards the need to place more emphasis on bibliographic instruction and the training of personnel.

> A major job of educating teaching personnel to student need and the potential of librarians to fill that need must be undertaken before access to students themselves is possible (Cammack).

The third cites a lack of communication among librarians.

F6. Two types of answers had two responses each. The first presents the opinion that training should begin only at the college level.

> For the academic librarian, it is almost better to approach a student who has had *no* exposure to library instruction. The ghost of years of "the library tour" unit or experience is hard to overcome. The continuum should commence with freshmen college students and proceed through Ph.D (Birdsall).

> In my opinion nonprofessional people do more to turn students "off" when they *think* they are teaching them to use libraries. Teachers *force* students to do exercises in libraries that are a waste of time. I'd rather receive them as innocents than as bitter and negative about the library (Fowler).

The second area of response questions the desirability of establishing a continuum of library skills instruction.

QUESTION G: *Do you believe the nationally "shrinking" educational budget has had an impact on programs of library instruction? Do you think this has improved the political climate for implementing library skills instructional programs?*

G1. Seven respondents believed that, "Yes, the nationally 'shrinking' educational budget has had an impact on programs of library instruction, and, yes, it seems that the political climate has improved."

> There is a trend toward more highly visible services. Library administrators can point to this as visible evidence of what the library can do (Freeman).

> I believe the "shrinking budget" has caused libraries to develop user services in place of developing the collection. That is to say, as collection building becomes increasingly expensive and therefore is cut back the library must encourage patrons to make a greater/better use of materials on hand (Cain).

G2. Five gave no as the answer to both questions.

> I feel that budgets great or small, are not as significant a factor as the will of academic librarians to undertake a teaching function which traditionally could be avoided without criticism. Good library instructional programs are not necessarily expensive; they do, however, require initiative and large amounts of labor (Cammack).

G3. Five respondents felt that the shrinking budget has negatively affected library instruction programs and that the political climate has not improved.

> The "shrinking" educational budget has certainly had an impact on library instruction programs. It is much harder now to get support for instruction programs in terms of money and personnel. I don't think the political climate has improved at all; in fact, it seems to me to be much tougher since the competition for any program, new or continuing, is much sharper than ever before. Each department is concerned primarily for its own programs and unless the library has support from a broad spectrum of the faculty and administration, library instruction programs will often be the loser in the fight for funds (Sherby).

G4. Three categories of response were given by two respondents each.

Two had no opinion on the first question and felt the political climate had not changed.

Two believed that declining funds *should* have an effect.

> I think a diminishing dollar should have an impact on programs of library instruction. I think it is incumbent upon instructional librarians to press the point that we cannot afford to have our vast resources unavailable to our users because our users are unaware of our resources, that it is our responsibility to instruct our users in methods of effective use of our resources (Dudley).

> It should, if budgets shrink the emphasis must shift from collections to people—it is relatively easy to find some information in the largest libraries but where there are fewer resources the need for information search skills increases (LoBue).

Two respondents felt that "library use instruction may increase" and that it "depends on the library administration."

> It makes sense for patrons to know how to use collections intensively, when libraries can no longer buy extensively (Galloway).

G5. Four responses were of a general nature:

> The political climate has improved but few librarians have become politicians. Little use seems to have been made of the argument that in view of shrinking book budgets, students need to be taught to use existing resources more effectively and intensively (Burton and Poole).

NOTES

1. Ralph Perkins, *The Prospective Teacher's Knowledge of Library Fundamentals* (New York: Scarecrow Press, 1965).
2. Ibid., p. 75
3. Ibid., p. 193
4. The following are thanked for their participation in the opinion survey: Douglas Birdsall, Susan Burton, Patricia S. Butcher, Melissa Cain, Floyd M. Cammack, Keith M. Cottam, Howard Curnoles, Mimi Dudley, Virgina R. Ellis, Jane Fowler, Michael S. Freeman, Sue Galloway, Louise P. Gerity, Marc Gittlesohn, Rev. Leo Gourde, Thomas Kirk, Carolyn A. Kirkendall, Benedict LoBue, Brian Nielsen, Virginia H. Parr, Anne Passarelli, Jay Martin Poole, Hannelore Rader Delgado, Louise S. Sherby, Donald R. Smith, Beverly Toy, James E. Ward, Joyce Werner, and Arline Willar.

BIBLIOGRAPHIC INSTRUCTION: A REVIEW OF RESEARCH AND APPLICATIONS

ARTHUR P. YOUNG
Assistant Dean for Public Services, University of Alabama Library

EXIR B. BRENNAN
Coordinator of Library Instruction Programs, University of Alabama Library

Like Sisyphus, proponents of bibliographic instruction have been engaged in an uphill struggle to attain recognition for their point of view. The proposition that instruction in the use of library resources is needed in order to cope with the library's complex bibliographic apparatus is not a new phenomenon. By the last quarter of the nineteenth century, librarians were arguing the case for familiarizing patrons with library resources. However, it has been only during the past dozen years that bibliographic instruction has achieved a measure of acceptance as an important component of library service. Perhaps bibliographic instruction, unlike Sisyphus, has secured a foothold near the summit. It is therefore appropriate to review the progress and problems of bibliographic instruction at this rather critical point of development.

The literature pertaining to bibliographic instruction that has been published during the period 1973 to 1978 will be examined here. Major topics selected for inclusion are bibliographies and surveys of the literature; research studies; organizational trends within library associations; library instruction clearinghouses; and the design/evaluation, instructional strategies, staffing, and financial aspects of selected instructional programs. All types of libraries are included, but literature dealing with the formal education of librarians and orientation to automated retrieval systems is specifically excluded. Obviously, such expansive parameters preclude reference to all of the relevant literature. Compression and interpretation rather than exhaustive coverage is our objective.

LITERATURE REVIEWS AND BIBLIOGRAPHIES

The literature on bibliographic instruction has proliferated. In the six years from 1972 through 1977, 491 citations under the heading "instruction in library use" appeared in *Library Literature* index. This figure represents a considerable gain over the preceding six years when 309 entries were recorded. Most of the literature is still of the testimonial variety, but two encouraging trends are evident.

More attention is being given to bibliographic instruction in the elementary and secondary schools, and proportionately more doctoral-level research has been completed than in prior years. Further evidence of maturity is reflected in the appearance of the proceedings of the Annual Conference on Library Orientation sponsored by Eastern Michigan University, and the inauguration, in 1976, of a regular column on bibliographic instruction in the *Journal of Academic Librarianship*.

For a summary of literature reviews and bibliographic compilations published before 1974, see the essay by Young.[1] A major retrospective bibliography on library instruction in academic libraries has been prepared by Krier.[2] Spanning the years 1931–1975, the list is arranged chronologically, and supplemented by author, subject, and institutional indexes. Since citations were drawn from *Library Literature* and *Library and Information Abstracts*, several important research reports and theses/dissertations were not recorded. The annotated bibliography of library instructional literature, which has appeared annually since 1974 in *Reference Services Review*, is a helpful distillation.[3] A topical list of 259 books, articles, theses, and research reports on the use of educational technology in "information handling instruction" has been compiled by Crossley and Clews.[4] Accompanying the bibliography is a brief, incisive literature review and a section on research needs.

Two excellent surveys of the literature add perspective and delineate trends. Givens examined the extensive literature on bibliographic instruction from the 1930s to 1973.[5] Following a lengthy summary of early approaches to user education, she analyzes contemporary curricular patterns and librarians' responses to them. Rounding out the review is a proposed "systems approach" to bibliographic instruction and an assessment of various organizational structures that might facilitate the delivery of library instruction. Somewhat disappointed over the progress to date, Givens bemoans the fact that many projects have not built upon past experiences and that a cumulative body of knowledge has not been codified and validated. Future librarians will need to be more conversant with instructional technology, educational psychology, and management theory. This account of prior strivings and accomplishments is recommended as a sobering corrective for the presentists among us.

Another review, by Malcolm Stevenson of the University of Sussex, analyzes the research findings and practical applications from 167 citations.[6] Emphasizing instructional activities in the United States and England, his paper covers orientation sessions, separate courses, staffing, cooperation with faculty, design/ evaluation, and alternative approaches. Among the perceived trends are disillusionment with orientation, more practical skill exercises, and small-group and seminar teaching. Faculty are acknowledged as the impelling factor governing student use of libraries, and librarians have not yet convinced most faculty that successful library use competence must be a collaborative effort. Stevenson reported that the personal qualities of instructional staff, such as enthusiasm and approachability, may be even more important than professional qualifications.

RESEARCH: TRENDS AND IMPLICATIONS

Research, the process of testing ideas, refining concepts, and generalizing from objective data, is a vital component of scholarly inquiry. Without the identification of causal factors and interrelated variables, knowledge cannot be systematically advanced. Library research, until quite recently, has not matched the rigor and sophistication of the research conducted in more established disciplines. This observation may explain, but certainly not excuse, the paucity of significant research on library user education. To qualify for inclusion in this section, a research study on bibliographic instruction must reflect a serious attempt to test hypotheses, to generalize from reliable survey/experimental data, or to examine past experiences from a structured historical framework.

The need for systematic exposure to library resources and bibliographic organization has been amply documented in many studies. One recent, carefully executed study of student utilization of university business libraries again demonstrates the low level of usage.[7] Responses were obtained from 261 undergraduates and 70 M.B.A. students from the University of Delaware, the University of Maryland, and Wright State University. Fewer than 30 percent of the undergraduates used the library for pleasure and fewer than 50 percent of the graduate students rated themselves as regular borrowers. Nearly 75 percent of the students indicated that knowing how to use the library was necessary for academic success, but fewer than 50 percent viewed library use as important for career success. Low use can be explained, in part, by the lack of faculty example. Over 50 percent of the undergraduates and 75 percent of the graduate students claimed they rarely saw a faculty member use the library. Not surprisingly, the students' awareness level of many periodicals and indexes was extremely low. To overcome deficiencies in student knowledge of the library, the authors recommended tutorials for faculty, imaginative library assignments, and an earlier introduction to information-seeking skills.

For nearly 50 years, librarians have attempted to document a positive correlation between library use and/or proficiency and academic performance. Validation of this desirable relationship, an implicit motivation for providing library instruction programs, has proved to be elusive. In one of the few studies that have centered on secondary school students, Mitchell was unable to confirm a relationship between circulation and academic achievement.[8] Subjects for the study were 614 high school students from Tasmania, Australia. During the six-week test period, subjects borrowed 1,349 books. The library, a modern facility with a collection of 10,000 volumes, was considered an "inviting" educational environment. Although a statistically significant relationship was not found between use and academic achievement, the author reported that "a greater proportion of students of high academic achievement tend to borrow more books than do students of lower academic achievement." An unexpected finding resulted from an analysis of the types of materials borrowed and their effect on academic performance. A positive correlation was reported between the circulation of fiction and scholastic excellence. For a related study that confirmed a predictive relationship between library proficiency (as tested by the Feagley test) and grade-point averages in a university setting, see the investigation by Corlett.[9]

The relationship between high school library instruction and subsequent library knowledge was explored by McDowell.[10] One hundred freshmen at the University of Michigan were given the nationally validated Feagley test for college freshmen. Forty-four percent scored below the passing grade. Student perceptions of their library knowledge and actual test scores correlated, but dissonant perceptions were reported by students and their former high school librarians regarding the quality of library instruction received before college. No statistical relationship was observed between types of library instruction (formal, informal, none) in high school and performance on the Feagley test. The author correctly attributes this disturbing conclusion to untested variables relating to motivation and self-education. Long-term retention of library skills was analyzed by Cole.[11] Although her conclusion is not generalizable because of the extremely small sample size (20), Cole found no difference in library competence, when students were retested in high school, between those sixth grade students who had received instruction and those who had not.

Much of the hortatory literature extols the virtue of integrated library instruction and close librarian-faculty cooperation. Until recently, there have been few attempts to validate these propositions. At Brooklyn College, Breivik conducted an instructional experiment with disadvantaged students.[12] A three-treatment design was utilized: weekly, course-related instruction; brief orientation; and no instruction. She found that students who received weekly instruction achieved higher grades and dropped out of school less often than the control group, which received no instruction. One unanticipated finding was that students exposed to the three-hour library orientation scored lower than the control group. Breivik's study is important for its analysis of how to relate bibliographic instruction to the needs of disadvantaged students. However, the lack of statistical analysis in the text and the use of nonrandom selection techniques do not allow for generalization beyond the test site.

In a methodologically superior study, Smith investigated the gains in library knowledge recorded by 428 Alabama elementary school pupils who were exposed to integrated instruction offered by the classroom teacher compared to traditional instruction provided by the school librarian.[13] A control group, which received no instruction, was also monitored. Neither experimental treatment was statistically superior to the other, and only the students receiving instruction from the school librarian scored significantly better than the control group. Smith's candid discussion of the survey's limitations and her section on preparing apprehensive teachers to present library lessons increase the value of this research study. In a related investigation of 20 California high school students, Reveal failed to confirm a significant difference in library proficiency between students who were team taught by a librarian and teacher and those who were taught by a teacher.[14] College student reaction to instruction by a librarian compared with instruction by a library instructor who also exposed students to library staff was evaluated by Tucker.[15] Cognitive, attitudinal, and library use data indicated nonsignificant gains for each group.

Three studies of self-instructional approaches have produced mixed results. Hardison attempted to determine if community college students could be taught library skills more effectively by means of a videotape presentation than by traditional classroom instruction.[16] No statistically significant findings were reported. Sellmer experimented with programmed learning materials to teach the card catalog to fourth grade children. Subjects exposed to the programmed approach achieved higher post-test scores than a control group that was taught in the traditional manner.[17] Competency-based instruction was compared to the traditional lockstep, group-paced approach by Wilbert.[18] Although statistical significance was not achieved, the competency-based group displayed an improved self-image and a greater enthusiasm for learning. For another study that indicates favorable student reactions to self-instructional modules, consult the report by Dale of the program at Southern Illinois University.[19]

The theoretical and practical heritage of library instruction is illuminated in two historical works. For more than 40 years, the library-college concept as enunciated by Shores, Johnson, and others has provided a philosophical rationale for the integration of instruction, independent learning, and utilization of library resources. Terwilliger, in the first comprehensive examination of the library-college concept, has traced the evolution of the idea and identified the many scattered adoptions of various components of this idealized approach.[20] Her study, although not definitive, is enhanced by the inclusion of extended tape interviews with such library-college proponents as Louis Shores, Robert Jordan, and Howard Clayton. Rather expectedly, Terwilliger concluded that the library-college model has not been sufficiently tested due to the lack of operational definition. The early years (1876-1914) of bibliographic instruction in academic libraries are the subject of an excellent unpublished paper by Tucker.[21] Major themes of the period, still relevant today, included the instructional goals of independent learning and life-long education.

Two papers do not easily fit the categories delineated for this essay.[22] Drawing from epistemological principles and bibliometric analysis, MacGregor and McInnis have developed an instructional model based on the predictable relationship between substantive literatures and bibliographic sources. Classifying substantive knowledge—the research literature—as fluid, and bibliographic literature—the reference literature—as fixed, the authors argue that students must understand the nature of this continuum and the multiple functions served by each body of literature. This structural-functional approach to library research has been applied in an instructional setting through the use of graphic representations of citation analyses. The authors have fashioned an important conceptual model that should be refined and field-tested.

LIBRARY ASSOCIATIONS AND CLEARINGHOUSES

Library associations have been receptive to the intensified interest in bibliographic instruction. Cognizant of the heightened interest, the Association of College and Research Libraries (ACRL) of the American Library Association (ALA) appointed the Bibliographic Instruction Task Force in 1971 to investigate instructional programs, to promote research, and to encourage librarians' participation. Among the first undertakings of the task force was a survey of bibliographic instruction in academic libraries, which culminated in the publication of a status report.[23] Following the status report, the task force issued guidelines for library use instruction in academic libraries.[24] The task force also recommended the establishment of a bibliographic instruction section within ARCL, and the section was approved in 1977.

During the same period, another group of librarians gathered over 1,000 signatures to petition ALA for an association-wide library instruction round table. One of the primary purposes of the round table would be to provide a means of communication among divisions and committees of ALA, state clearinghouses, and other interested organizations.[25] The round table would also promote bibliographic instruction as a vital library service. At the 1977 midwinter meeting, the ALA Council voted to establish the Library Instruction Round Table, thereby permitting greatly increased participation by librarians from all types of libraries.

Just as bibliographic instruction has been an object of national concern, it has been a focus of regional and state activity. Committees on library instruction have been created by many state library associations and numerous workshops on instruction have been conducted. Surveys of library orientation and bibliographic instruction programs have consumed a large portion of time and effort at this level. Among the results of these surveys are published directories that delineate the features of bibliographic instruction programs and indicate the availability, and occasionally the usefulness, of these programs to other libraries. Published directories have been completed for the states of California, Illinois, New York, Ohio, Pennsylvania, and Wisconsin, and for the regions encompassed by the Southwestern and the Southeastern Library Associations.[26] Although, in some cases, there has been no provision for updating the published directories, they have provided an important vehicle for the communication of ideas and the promotion of bibliographic instruction.

Further evidence of the interest in bibliographic instruction may be seen by the rapid establishment of library instruction clearinghouses. Project Library Orientation—Instruction Exchange (LOEX), which serves as the national loan center for libraries interested in its holdings, has attracted institutional members from nearly every state, and has stimulated the introduction of similar services at the state and regional levels.[27] Four states and two regional associations have established clearinghouses for library instructional materials within their geographic areas.

Enthusiasm for this type of activity has not been confined to the United States. The Materials Bank, at the Loughborough University of Technology Library, is the British national clearinghouse. Interest is apparent in other European countries, notably in Scandinavia, where the work has been guided primarily by Fjällbrant.[28] The national unit in Australia, the Data Bank for User Education Materials, is located at the Caulfield Institute of Technology.

To ascertain the membership criteria, collection characteristics, and service activities of clearinghouses, the authors sent a survey questionnaire to 12 agencies identified as clearinghouses for library instruction. Three clearinghouses have been established since late 1977, and the oldest, aside from LOEX, originated in 1973. In spite of their relative youth and the fact that seven of them are staffed by volunteers, the clearinghouses have amassed collections ranging in size from 300 to 10,000 items. Academic libraries comprise the membership of the clearinghouses, but informal participation by other groups was reported. For example, some public libraries contribute materials to the California clearinghouses, while the Materials Bank at Loughborough invites the participation of all types of libraries. Five clearinghouses allow nonmembers to borrow materials regardless of the type of library.

All clearinghouses have collected some copyrighted items, and six are repositories for audiovisual materials. All except two clearinghouses prohibit the circulation of these two types of materials. Among the most-circulated materials are tests and excercises, and scripts prepared for slide/tape presentations. For materials of any type, the average loan period is two weeks to one month. Only one clearinghouse has no established loan period.

It is remarkable that the clearinghouses have managed to collect and disseminate hundreds of items, sponsor workshops, service as referral agents, conduct surveys, and promote membership growth without any membership fees, and with relatively little external funding. Three of them have no external funding, and none charge membership fees, although Project LOEX has notified members of future fee requirements. LOEX has benefited from a Council on Library Resources grant since 1971. Considering the rapid growth of the clearinghouses, it is reasonable to assume that additional units will be established in the United States and in other countries.

OBJECTIVES AND EVALUATION OF LIBRARY INSTRUCTIONAL PROGRAMS

Without the formulation of behavioral objectives for an instructional program, it is difficult, if not impossible, to determine what to measure and how to evaluate the effectiveness of that instruction. Yet, many programs of instruction are designed and implemented without identifiable objectives. Commenting on library orientation and instruction methods, Stoffle and Bonn observed that "most instructional programs are not based on objectives," and that "no quantitative measures of the results of instruction have been developed." They concluded that librarians were "at a loss" when it came to evaluation.[29] This situation remains relatively unchanged; and librarians, like Cervantes's redoubtable Quixote, continue to leap upon their steeds and dash off in every direction as they administer well-meant instruction. For example, in a 1977 survey of 337 southeastern academic libraries, only 12 percent of the libraries indicated that measurable objectives had been developed.[30] Only 24 percent reported the use of any type of evaluative instrument. An earlier statewide survey in Pennsylvania found that only 11 of the 67 responding libraries had developed written statements of objectives, while 12 of them reported some limited evaluation of their programs.[31] A recent national survey of 63 academic libraries revealed that some library instructors evaluated their work by a subjective assessment of student progress, and that most course-related instruction was given to meet immediate needs, with no long-range objectives in mind.[32]

Awareness of the needs for improved design and evaluation in bibliographic instruction has been reinforced by the work of Wiggins, Kirk, Fjällbrant, and others. Wiggins pointed out the futility of attempting to prepare and to evaluate instructional presentations without predetermined objectives. The experience of determining the relative importance of various instructional elements by means of a "task analysis" proved to be essential to the process of formulating objectives and planning instruction.[33] In his state-of-the-art review on library instruction, Kirk reiterated the need for objectives and the development of evaluation techniques that would measure not only students' skills, but also the product of their skills. He also called for an exploration of students' attitudes toward the library.[34]

One of the few librarians to evaluate bibliographic instruction in a comprehensive manner has been Fjällbrant. Her systematic evaluation was conducted at the Chalmers University of Technology Library, Gothenburg, Sweden. Because of the complexity of the teaching/learning environment in library instruction, exacerbated by the frequently divergent expectations of students, faculty, and librarians, she recommended several methods of evaluation.[35] Psychometric methods were used to ascertain student attitudes toward the content, teaching method, and organization of the library instruction courses. Performance outcomes were measured by examining student bibliographies. Approximately ten months after the initiation of the courses, structured telephone interviews were conducted with students to find out how well specific objectives had been reached. Detailed observation of student behavior during the courses also provided information that served to modify the courses under development. In addition to these approaches, a long-term program to measure the effects of the instruction was launched.

Some steps have been taken to rectify the lack of proper evaluation of instructional programs. Librarians committed to effective instruction have sought assistance from their colleagues in education, sociology, and psychology, and they have shared resources and knowledge in workshops and conferences. Two national conferences, as well as several regional and state meetings, have been devoted to the subject of evaluating library use instruction.[36] An avalanche of helpful literature has recently appeared surrounding what has been to many librarians, perhaps, a threatening topic.

To facilitate the design and evaluation of bibliographic instruction, a useful guide has been prepared by ACRL's Bibliographic Instruction Task Force.[37] Its guidelines introduce the concepts of general, terminal, and enabling objectives, and furnish illustrative material that explicates these concepts. The statement also provides a set of criteria by which instructional librarians can judge students' library research and the products of that research. This instrument is recommended as a starting point for the design and evaluation of bibliographic instruction. Additional guidance may be gleaned from the several humorous and informative books written by Robert Mager.[38] Not only does Mager demonstrate the importance of writing explicit objectives that will communicate the instructor's intent, but he offers advice about how to describe the criteria of acceptable performance, a factor not often considered in the writing of objectives.

Knowledge of the findings of library use studies can be useful in the design and evaluation of bibliographic instruction.[39] Before writing and implementing a program of instruction, librarians at the University of Texas worked closely with the university's evaluation center to formulate user surveys that would provide information useful to program design. They also examined surveys from other libraries to obtain useful ideas prior to constructing questionnaires.[40] A primary focus of Dougherty's study of document delivery at Ohio State University and Syracuse University was to identify how a researcher's subjective attitudes influenced his library usage.[41] It was found that user expectations regarding the location and retrieval of materials influenced library use patterns. The implications of this relationship should encourage the designers of instructional programs to delineate the nature of pertinent collections and to relate the probability of successful document retrieval. The recent volume by Lancaster is highly recommended as a convenient summary of evaluative research on all facets of library service.[42]

INSTRUCTIONAL APPROACHES OF PROGRAMS

Diversity of instructional approach has been the chief characteristic of library use instruction. A variety of methods, from mediated and computer-assisted instruction to self-paced modules and individual tutoring, have been attempted by librarians who realize they must cope with sometimes reluctant students who perceive bibliographic arrangements as unnecessarily complicated. The latter observation has reinforced the need to review the purpose of bibliographic instruction. Educating patrons to become self-directed, completely independent researchers is a laudable but often unrealistic goal. Recipients of bibliographic instruction should be apprised of this limitation and encouraged to seek professional assistance within a specified period of time. Perhaps the efficient negotiation of library resources, independently or with assistance, should become a more prominent objective of bibliographic instruction. Efficient negotiation is, in part, dependent upon the acquisition of transferable skills. And there is evidence that bibliographical instructors are now more concerned than previously with teaching generalizable search skills and emphasizing types of information sources.

Any approach to library user education must give careful consideration to the differences between orientation and instruction. Orientation should usually precede instruction, since it acquaints new users with the library's physical environs and with the personnel available to help them. Palmer has indicated that orientation is a necessary part of instruction at all levels because "the upper level transfer and graduate absorb it more eagerly," ostensibly because they, unlike freshmen who generally receive the orientation, must use the library's resources to support a large portion of their work.[43] Methods required to implement orientation programs will necessarily be different from those required for instruction in depth. Andrew emphasized efficiency in the approach to orientation, including adequate and effective use of signs so that the energies and time of librarians may be saved for instruction.[44] There is no clear evidence, however, that orientation by itself is a pedagogically defensible practice.

Formal instruction requires considerably more planning than orientation and should be directed toward those who have a demonstrated need. Instructional content should not only be based on the students' needs, but also be meaningfully related to the curricular program. Considerable debate has occurred over the merits of curriculum-integrated instruction as opposed to a separate library instruction course. Regardless of which approach is employed, the content should be specific to the needs of those who are supposed to benefit from it. The temptation to cover too many subjects in too much detail has plagued librarians and students alike.

The location for library instruction is a major factor in planning. A classroom location can legitimize the teaching role of librarians, whereas the proximity of bibliographic tools in the library has obvious advantages. Providing instruction to large groups of students generates a special locational problem. Institutions with large enrollments of undergraduates invariably face this dilemma. At the University of Alabama, library instruction for over 2,800 freshmen is delivered annually in the English classrooms to groups that average 25 students. The three-hour classroom presentation is a relatively simple instructional program designed to help students get started on the bibliography for a short paper. It is reinforced by the use of printed handouts containing the lecture information in a topical format. Instruction is provided by intensively trained graduate library students who are assigned duty in the library at regular hours. This approach allows for the simultaneous instruction of several thousand students and, more importantly, provides the opportunity for postinstructional assistance.

A library is only as effective as the people who represent it. A library instruction program is most effective when the library staff and administration are committed to it both philosophically and in terms of time, energy, and financial support. Dyson described four ways in which libraries organize for library instruction, and concluded that "the most effective library instruction programs are those that involve a large number of library staff" and that "the paramount factor determining the success of an instructional program is the extent of commitment to it by the library administration."[45] The experiment at Sangamon State University, where all librarians have teaching responsibilities, has received much notice in this regard.[46]

Support from the teaching faculty is a vital ingredient in any program of library instruction. As Reid noted, "No academic librarian will need to be told of the delicacy with which it is necessary to pick a path through scholarly pride, injured self-esteem and frequent bibliographic innocence."[47] It may be necessary to teach the teachers first, since only they can create the climate that will motivate students to seek bibliographic assistance and instruction. The issue of faculty involvement is so vital to successful instruction that much of the Fourth Annual Conference on Library Orientation held at Eastern Michigan University was devoted to papers and discussion concerning the matter.

MEDIATED PROGRAMS

Teaching aids for bibliographic instruction have proliferated, especially the nonprint variety. Printed handbooks, manuals, and search guides continue to be helpful, especially for the diligent researcher. However, in the nonprint age of the 1970s, audiovisual productions have been used extensively. Slide/tape programs alone have been so heavily used in libraries that Hardesty conducted a nationwide survey.[48] Film loop, slide/taped, and videotaped programs perhaps were usually most effective at point-of-use locations, such as at a particular index that needed elucidation before its use. Librarians, sometimes enthralled by the medium at the expense of the message, tended to produce verbose, overly detailed programs. Other observers have reported that reticent students and faculty did not approach impersonal audiovisual programs any more readily than they would approach librarians for assistance.[49]

The expense of producing mediated programs has been widely recognized, as has their lack of transferability to another setting. Although the British Standing

Conference on National and University Libraries (SCONUL) attempted to produce slide/tape guides useful to all libraries, Lubans reported that very few libraries used any of the 20 or 30 programs available.[50] Poor technical quality and/or lack of user interest were the main reasons. Hardesty implied that the same might be true in the United States, when he concluded that the slide/tape format demands expertise and time greatly in excess of what might be expected.[51] The complexities of videotaped productions and the development of computer-assisted programs would prove even more demanding.

Financing is an omnipresent consideration in the use of mediated instruction. Fjällbrant enumerated the advantages of the slide/tape medium, including flexibility of use, ease of updating, speed of presentation, and low cost, as opposed to filmstrips, films, and videotape.[52] These advantages notwithstanding, the initial cost of any mediated production might be more than already constrained library budgets could bear, especially if its potential use is fairly low. Worth considering, also, is the fact that anonymity in any educational program is questionable, even if mass education is promoted. Although audiovisual productions reduce expenditures and conserve staff time, they do not contribute to a personalized instructional approach. Stevenson agrees that the use of self-instructional material is sometimes effective at the point of need, but that "such materials and methods remove from the instruction the personal element generally agreed to be needed."[53]

Self-paced units of instruction and library skills workbooks (often the same item) have been successfully used in bibliographic instruction. Explaining the library's use of the self-paced workbook approach at the University of California at Los Angeles, Dudley praised its effectiveness with large numbers of students, and noted that it paid for itself. She also pointed out the fact that it complemented orientation and other instruction.[54] Hills endorsed the use of self-paced programs because they are "active methods of instruction which involve and interest the student," and because they are structured so that "the student progresses with full understanding."[55] The same caveat regarding the impersonal nature of self-paced instruction applies to mediated instruction. Exclusive reliance on impersonal techniques may reduce the amount and quality of subsequent student interaction with library staff.

FUTURISTIC MUSINGS

Prognosticating about the future of bibliographic instruction is a risky endeavor at best, and so it is with trepidation that we conclude with a few remarks about developments that may (or should) lie ahead. The research record has improved, but continues to be spotty. Generally, the continuing emphasis on the comparative evaluation of mediated approaches does not seem merited. A significant body of research literature already exists that delineates the virtues and limitations of various mediated strategies, but few studies have documented the instructional superiority of one form of media over another. More attention to evaluating the projected outcomes of bibliographic instruction would be desirable. Examples of this form of assessment are postinstructional analysis of students' research papers, negotiation efficiency, and retrieval effectiveness. Few studies have examined the comparative merits of different learning assignments. For instance, is it sufficient to explain the interdependence of reference sources and the research literature to students, or is it preferable for students to conduct a bibliometric analysis?

It is encouraging to witness the ascendancy of bibliographic instruction into the pantheon of accepted library services. However, we have all too often directed our efforts to preaching to the converted. As understandable as this tendency may be, proponents of bibliographic instruction should be devoting considerably more energy to reaching those outside the library's established clientele. Permanent acceptance of bibliographic instruction may well depend upon the creation of an enlarged library constituency. Few libraries have been immune to the demands for more accountability and to the erosion of services and collections due to inflation. Academic libraries, particularly, are beginning to conjure up apocalyptic visions of what the future may have in store. The retrogression of the 1970s may abate, but the period of unlimited growth has surely passed. Students of library history know that those innovative services that appear during expansive times tend to be the first casualties during periods of retrenchment. Securing the foothold will require gritty determination.

NOTES

1. Arthur P. Young, "Research on Library-User Education: A Review Essay," in *Educating the Library User*, ed. by John Lubans, Jr. (New York: R. R. Bowker, 1974), pp. 1-15.
2. Maureen Krier, "Bibliographic Instruction: A Checklist of the Literature, 1931-1975," *Reference Services Review* 4 (January/March 1976): 7-31.
3. Hannelore B. Rader,"Library Orientation and Instruction—1973," *Reference Services Review* 2 (January/March 1974): 91-93. For subsequent installments, see *Reference Services Review* 3 (January/March 1975): 29-31; 4 (October/December 1976): 91-93; 5 (January/March 1977): 41-44.
4. Charles A. Crossley and John P. Clews, *Evolution of the Educational Technology in Information Handling Instruction: A Literature Review and Bibliography*, OSTI Report 5220 (London: British Library, Research and Development Department, 1974).
5. Johnnie Givens, "The Use of Resources in the Learning Experience," in *Advances in Librarianship*, vol. 4 (New York: Academic Press, 1974), pp. 149-174.
6. Malcolm Stevenson, "Education of Users of Libraries and Information Services," *Journal of Documentation* 33 (March 1977): 53-78.
7. James D. Culley, Denis F. Healy, and Kermit G. Cudd, "Business Students and the University Library: An Overlooked Element in the Business Curriculum," *Journal of Academic Librarianship* 2 (January 1977): 293-296.
8. Rosemary Mitchell, "Academic Achievement and Use of the Secondary School Library" (Master's thesis, Tasmanian School of Education [Australia], 1973), pp. 1-53.
9. Donna Corlett, "Library Skills, Study Habits and Attitudes, and Sex as Related to Academic Achievement," *Educational and Psychological Measurement* 34 (Winter 1974): 967-969.

10. Sanford McDowell, Jr., "A Study of the Library Skills of Selected College Freshmen as Related to High School Library Orientation" (Ph.D. diss., University of Michigan, 1977), pp. 1–94, 96–103.
11. Jane B. Cole, "Library Skills Instruction and Retention: A Report on a Skills Program for Fourth, Fifth, and Sixth Grades with a Note on Its Relationship to Use of the High School Library" (Master's thesis, University of Chicago, 1977), pp. i–vi, 1–29.
12. Patricia S. Breivik, *Open Admissions and the Academic Library* (Chicago: American Library Association, 1977), pp. 40–72.
13. Jane B. Smith, "An Exploratory Study of the Effectiveness of an Innovative Process Designed to Integrate Library Skills into the Curriculum" (Ph.D. diss., George Peabody College for Teachers, 1978), pp. 25–81.
14. Arlene H. Reveal, "Library Instruction and Team Teaching" (Research paper, Brigham Young University, 1976), pp. 1–32, ERIC document ED144 604.
15. Ellis E. Tucker, "A Study of the Effects of Using Professional Staff as Co-Instructors in an Instructional Program" (Ph.D. diss., Florida State University, 1974; listed in *Dissertation Abstracts International* 35/10 [1976]: p. 6744-A).
16. Diana D. Hardison, "Library Instruction in a Community College: A Study to Determine the Comparative Effectiveness of Classroom Teaching and a Video Self-Instruction Unit for Developmental and Degree-Program Students" (Ed.D. diss., Virginia Polytechnic Institute and State University, 1977; Listed in *Dissertation Abstracts International* 38/03 [1977]: 1189-A).
17. Donald F. Sellmer, "Teaching Fourth Grade Children to Use a Library Catalog: A Programmed Approach" (Ed.D. diss., Ball State University, 1973; listed in *Dissertation Abstracts International* 34/05-6 [1973]: 2669-A).
18. Shirley S. Wilbert, "A Study of Competency-Based Instruction to Determine Its Viability as a Technique to Teaching Basic Library Skills to a Selected Sample of Seventh Grade Students" (Ph.D. diss., Wayne State University, 1976; listed in *Dissertation Abstracts International* 37/05 [1976]: 2617-A).
19. Doris C. Dale, "Mastering Library Research Techniques Through Self-Instruction," *The Journal: Technological Horizons in Education* 4 (November/December 1977): 44–46.
20. Gloria H. P. Terwilliger, "The Library-College: A Movement for Experimental and Innovative Learning Concepts; Applications and Implications for Higher Education" (Ed.D. diss., University of Maryland, 1975), passim.
21. John M. Tucker, "The Development of Bibliographic Instruction in Academic Libraries, 1876-1914" (Unpublished seminar paper, Graduate School of Library Science, University of Illinois, 1978).
22. John MacGregor and Raymond G. McInnis, "Integrating Classroom Instruction and Library Research: The Cognitive Functions of Bibliographic Network Functions," *Journal of Higher Education* 48 (January/February 1977): 17–38. For a similar article with examples from the field of history, see Raymond G. McInnis, "Integrating Classroom Instruction and Library Research: An Essay Review," Western Washington State College, *Studies in History and Society* 4 (Winter 1974-1975): 31–65.

23. Thomas Kirk, *Academic Library Bibliographic Instruction: Status Report 1972*, February 1973. ERIC document ED072 823.
24. "Toward Guidelines for Bibliographic Instruction in Academic Libraries," *College and Research Library News* 36 (May 1975): 137–139+.
25. *ALA Handbook of Organization 1977–1978* (Chicago: American Library Association, 1977), p. 70.
26. *Academic Library Instruction Programs in the Southwest* (SWLA Task Force, 1976); Kathy Coleman, *Directory of Library Instruction Media: Produced by California Academic Libraries* (San Diego: California Clearinghouse on Library Instruction, 1976); *Directory of Library Instruction Programs in Ohio Academic Libraries* (Project Team on Bibliographic Instruction, Shaefer Library, Findlay, Ohio, 1977); Melissa Cain and Lois Pausch, comps., *Library Instruction Programs in Illinois Academic Libraries: A Directory and Survey Report* (Illinois Library Association and Illinois Association of College and Research Libraries, 1978): *Library Instruction Programs 1975: a Wisconsin Directory* (Madison: Wisconsin Library Association, 1975); *New York Library Instruction Programs: A Directory* (New York Library Instruction Clearinghouse: Franklin Moon Library, SUNY College of Environmental Science and Forestry, Syracuse, New York, 1977); *Southeastern Bibliographic Instruction Directory: Academic Libraries* (Southeastern Library Association, 1978); Sara Lou Whildin, *A Directory of Instructional Programs in Pennsylvania Academic Libraries* (Pennsylvania Library Association, 1975).
27. Project Library Orientation—Instruction Exchange (LOEX), Center of Educational Resources, Eastern Michigan University, Ypsilanti, Mich. 48197. For descriptive information see Mary Bolner, "Project LOEX: The First Year," in *Planning and Developing a Library Instruction Program: Proceedings of the Third Annual Conference on Library Orientation for Academic Libraries, Eastern Michigan University, May 3–4, 1973* (Ann Arbor, Mich.: Pierian Press, 1975), pp. 53–58.
28. "Nancy Fjallbrant of Chalmers University of Technology Library at Gothenburg, Sweden, reports that her Library functions as a central collection for Scandinavian teaching materials, guides, etc., produced as aids for library use education" (*LOEX News* 4 [December 1977]: 3).
29. Carla J. Stoffle and Gabriella Bonn, "An Inventory of Library Orientation and Instructional Methods," *RQ* 13 (Winter 1973): 129–133.
30. James E. Ward, "Library and Bibliographic Instruction in Southeastern Academic Libraries," *Southeastern Librarian* 26 (Fall 1976): 148–159.
31. Sara Lou Whildin, "Library Instruction in Pennsylvania Academic Libraries: A Survey Summary," *PLA Bulletin* 31 (January 1976): 8.
32. Exir B. White, "Course-Related Bibliographic Instruction for Credit" (1977 survey conducted for *ACRL Status Report of Bibliographic Instruction Update*, in press).
33. Marvin E. Wiggins, "Evaluation in the Instructional Psychology Model," in *Evaluating Library Use Instruction: Papers Presented at the University of Denver Conference on the Evaluation of Library Instruction, December 13–14, 1973* (Ann Arbor, Mich.: Pierian Press, 1975), pp. 89–97.
34. Thomas Kirk, "Bibliographic Instruction—A Review of Research," in

Evaluating Library Use Instruction: Papers Presented at the University of Denver Conference on the Evaluation of Library Instruction, December 13- 14, 1973 (Ann Arbor, Mich.: Pierian Press, 1975), pp. 1-29.

35. Nancy Fjällbrant, "Evaluation In a User Education Programme," *Journal of Librarianship* 9 (April 1977): 84-95.

36. The University of Denver Conference on the Evaluation of Library Instruc- tion, December 13-14, 1973; and "Improving Instruction, Then Proving Its Worth: How to Teach and How to Evaluate," Eighth Annual Conference on Library Orientation for Academic Libraries, Eastern Michigan University, May, 4-5, 1978.

37. "Toward Guidelines for Bibliographic Instruction in Academic Libraries," pp. 137-139+.

38. Robert F. Mager, *Developing Attitude toward Learning* (Palo Alto, Calif.: Fearon Publishers, 1968); *Goal Analysis* (Belmont, Calif.: Fearon Publishers, 1972); *Measuring Instructional Intent: Or, Got a Match?* (Belmont, Calif.: Fearon Publishers, 1973); *Preparing Instructional Objectives* (Palo Alto, Calif.: Fearon Publishers, 1962).

39. Susan Edwards, "Library Use Studies and the University of Colorado," in *Library Instruction in the Seventies: State of the Art; Papers Presented at the Sixth Annual Conference on Library Orientation for Academic Libraries Held at Eastern Michigan University, May 13-14, 1976* (Ann Arbor, Mich.: Pierian Press, 1977), pp. 105-107.

40. University of Texas–Austin, The General Libraries, *A Comprehensive Pro- gram of User Education for the General Libraries, The University of Texas at Austin*, Contributions to Librarianship, no. 1 (Austin, Texas, 1977).

41. Richard M. Dougherty and Laura L. Blomquist, *Improving Access to Li- brary Resources* (Metuchen, N.J.: Scarecrow Press, 1974), pp. 76-86.

42. Frederick W. Lancaster, *The Measurement and Evaluation of Library Ser- vices* (Washington, D.C.: Information Resources Press, 1977).

43. Millicent C. Palmer, "Academic Library Instruction: Problems and Prin- ciples," *Tennessee Librarian* 25 (Winter 1973): 12.

44. Ann Andrew, "Getting Started: Designing a Program, Proposal Writing, Funding: A Conversation," in *Planning and Developing a Library Orienta- tion Program. Proceedings of the Third Annual Conference on Library Or- ientation for Academic Libraries, Eastern Michigan University, May 3-4, 1973*, Library Orientation Series, no. 3 (Ann Arbor, Mich.: Pierian Press, 1975), pp. 1-11.

45. Allan J. Dyson, "Organizing Undergraduate Library Instruction: The English and American Experience," *Journal of Academic. Librarianship* 1 (March 1975): 9-13.

46. Howard W. Dillion, "Organizing the Academic Library for Instruction," *Journal of Academic Librarianship* 1 (September 1975): 4-7.

47. Bruce J. Reid, "Bibliographic Teaching in French and Politics at the Univer- sity of Leicester," *Journal of Librarianship* 5 (October 1973): 293-303.

48. Larry Hardesty, "Survey of the Use of Slide/Tape Presentations for Orien- tation and Instruction Purposes in Academic Libraries," January 1976. ERIC document ED116 711.

49. Stoffle and Bonn, "An Inventory of Library Orientation," pp. 129-133; and Peter Fox, *Reader Instruction Methods in Academic Libraries* (Cambridge: The University Library, 1974), p. 42.
50. John Lubans, Jr., "Educating the Library User in England," *MPLA Newsletter* 20 (1975-1976): 3.
51. Hardesty, "Survey of the Use of Slide/Tape Presentations."
52. Nancy Fjällbrant, "Teaching Methods for the Education of the Library-User," *Libri* 26 (1976): 252-267.
53. Malcolm B. Stevenson, "Information Services in University Libraries," *Journal of Documentation* 31 (June 1975): 134-136.
54. Miriam Dudley, "The State of Library Instruction Credit Courses and the State of the Use of Library Skills Workbooks," in *Library Instruction in the Seventies: State of the Art*, Library Orientation Series, no. 7 (Ann Arbor, Mich.: Pierian Press, 1977), pp. 79-84.
55. P. J. Hills, "Library Instruction and the Development of the Individual," *Journal of Librarianship* 6 (October 1974): 255-263.

RECENT DIRECTIONS IN EDUCATING THE LIBRARY USER: ELEMENTARY SCHOOLS

Anne M. Hyland

Now District Media Coordinator for North-eastern Local Schools, Springfield, Ohio, formerly State Supervisor, School Media Programs, Ohio Department of Education

There are several current and positive trends in elementary school library skills instruction. An acceleration in the variety and quality of curriculum guides is now resulting in more guides at the elementary than at the secondary level; instruction has expanded from basic organization and selection of print materials to utilization, comprehension, and production involving all types of resources; and the growing inclusion of nonbook media in all areas of instruction has been additionally encouraging.

Many elementary schools are experiencing decreasing enrollments. As a result, once-crowded classroom space has now become available for enlarging school media centers and providing for unscheduled (vs. "fixed") time throughout the day. The new locations also provide appropriate areas for mediated and group activities. Where crowded conditions are still a factor, elementary schools have loosened fixed schedules and established various times as informal or unscheduled time.

Budgetary factors have fostered important trends in elementary school media programs. For example, "categorical aid" in urban areas gave an initial thrust to the development of school media in cities. Frequently, the funding has been used not only to establish facilities and provide adequate resources but also to provide personnel. The funds often provide a full-time aide for each of several buildings, one professional for a number of schools, and a district-level program director. But because of various inhibiting restrictions in categorical aid, especially in relationship to "local" school moneys, the hiring of aides and professionals for nonurban (but still impacted) schools continues to be neglected even within the same school district. This has often resulted in the use of volunteers to provide daily routine service, with a single professional serving as many as 5,000 students. The present fiscal problems facing many school districts may inhibit elimination of this problem.

The trend established by the urban schools with the help of federal moneys has provided a model for media staffing in developing rural areas. In the past a secondary school librarian provided the technical assistance needed to maintain federal Title II (now Title IV-B) funding in elementary schools. No particular program of library instruction was carried out beyond what classroom teachers were capable of providing. Rural districts now are beginning to hire professionals to supervise the elementary library program and are also providing some limited clerical assistance. A professional on the scene provides school staff with increased access to information sources, instructional television networks, statewide public library cooperatives, and other cooperative educational service agencies of which the professional is aware. Though unserved schools often felt their media programs were adequate, the availability of even one school library media professional usually has been enough to encourage further expansion. Unlike cities, rural districts generally do not have a district-level program director, but some recent appointments in rural areas hold promise for future expansion.

Suburban districts generally have been relatively small and relatively wealthy. They tend to provide a professional for each building, or one for two smaller buildings. Collections are diverse and adequate. There is usually a district-level program director and a district resource center where materials are available to others in the district. With the beginning of even limited staffing in urban and rural areas, it is encouraging to see that once programs begin, teachers are eager to take advantage of them.

CURRICULAR DEVELOPMENTS

Elementary teachers are becoming proficient in the use of instructional objectives, team planning, interdisciplinary approaches to learning, and student grouping for specific skill instruction. This has provided opportunities for library media personnel to work with smaller numbers of students over extended periods of time. Team meetings also provide times throughout the day when the librarian can meet with various clusters of staff members to discuss needs, instructional plans, and evaluation of materials.

The training and certification of school library media personnel in traditional educational courses has contributed to the success of joint curricular planning in elementary settings. Teacher certification has become more specific, and with enough teachers to meet current needs, standards are being met. This has brought to the growing number of new elementary positions school library media personnel who have been specifically trained to work with students, teachers, and curriculum in an educational setting. These professionals have encouraged the use of learning centers, prescriptive learning, individualized planning, and a full range of resources, and techniques and processes of applying these to the total design of instructional experiences.

It is logical to extend this training to the area of library skills instruction. Elementary library media professionals have given a serious look at the effect of library instruction on total student learning. In order to have the greatest impact, instruction must be given in a way that closely resembles how the skill will be used in the future. It must be directly linked to other curricular areas of the school in a practical approach. Instruction and exercises have begun to cover all aspects of the learning process and spring from science, social studies, and language arts curriculum rather than from the traditional field of library science. As skills are expanded and clarified, teachers can more easily see how the various skills are needed to successfully complete assignments in individual subject areas; and communication among librarian, teacher, and student becomes easier.

The challenges facing elementary library media professionals are twofold: What skills shall we teach? How can we best link them to curricular areas?

WHAT SKILLS SHALL WE TEACH?

The first challenge can in part be answered by examining—in state standards, professional literature, and published curriculum guides—the skills we say we should or do teach. Skills mentioned in the following were tallied. Ohio's *Minimum Standards*,[1] North Central Association of Colleges and Schools' *Policies and Standards*,[2] American Association of School Librarians' *Media Programs: District and School*,[3] six publications by persons noted in the field of school library instruction, and 86 kindergarten through college curriculum guides. Approximately two-thirds of the available guides addressed elementary programs. Guides that provided instruction in carrying out various activities but did not cite what skill the activity addressed were not used in the computation.

Table 1 displays the five basic skill groupings, individual skills identified within each area, and the percentage of guides for each educational level citing each skill area. The skill groupings view the library learning process from the student's perspective. *Organization* refers to the basic floor plan and workings of the school media center space. Once the student has arrived in a specific location, *selection* skills are needed to choose the most appropriate resources. *Utilization* skills are those needed to effectively use each type of material. *Comprehension* skills are those needed to gain meaning from resources. And, finally, any time a student is asked to take information from one source, translate it through personal experiences, and give it back to someone else, it is a *production*. A production might be retelling a movie seen last week, giving a speech to a class, building a sugar-cube fort, writing a paragraph, or taking slides. The student's mind must sift through everything learned, select the necessary details, and communicate a thought to someone else.

TRENDS

It is interesting to note the inclusion of nonprint resources in each of these five areas. This is a definite break with guides of the 1950s, which dealt exclusively with print materials. The relatively small percentages in production skills are noteworthy in view of the much higher priority given the same area in school media center standards. Perhaps this is a predictor of future emphasis.

As would be expected, the elementary guides place a heavy (51 percent) emphasis on the first two skills. Contrary to expectations, however, secondary schools place a heavier (57 percent) emphasis on these same two areas. This suggests a lack of continuity in K–12 skills. In fact, only three of all the curriculum guides covered the entire K–12 range of student learning needs. One would expect secon-

Table 1. Library Skills Cited in Standards and Guides

	Total % of:					Overall Skill Area Percentages
	Standards Tallies	Professional Tallies	Elementary Tallies	Secondary Tallies	College Tallies	
Organization	21	17	27	27	8	20
1. Library citizenship						
2. Acquaintance with other information agencies in the community						
3. Organization of the library						
4. Dewey decimal						
5. Dewey arrangement						
6. Alphabetical order						
Selection	18	30	24	30	32	28
1. Kinds of media available for use						
2. Parts of the catalog card						
3. Use of the card catalog						
4. Choice of type and level of materials						
5. Periodical guides						
6. Problem selection						

Utilization	13	20	15	19	24	19
1. Use of reference books						
2. Use of parts of books						
3. Use of government documents						
4. Use of equipment						
5. Information from sources other than libraries						
Comprehension	31	20	24	17	20	23
1. Self-direction in reading: literature appreciation						
2. Reading skills						
3. Listening and viewing skills: film/media appreciation						
4. Study and work skills: note taking, outlining, and synthesizing						
5. Judgment in the use of newspapers, periodicals, and indexes						
6. Student evaluation of own work						
Production	16	12	9	7	16	11
1. Bibliographic form						
2. Speaking and writing to communicate						
3. Production of graphics and other media						

dary students to be quite bored with the repetitive instruction they are receiving, and college librarians to be upset that students do not know how to use resources more effectively than they do.

The information displayed in Table 1 is "pure," that is, no judgment has been made about its appropriateness; it is presented here for reaction. Each district must develop a full scope and sequence of skills that best meet the learning needs of its students. Certainly there is no need to teach the use of government documents in the fourth grade if none are available for use. One panel of professionals seriously questioned the inclusion of the comprehension skills in the list. They did not feel they should be primarily responsible for such instruction, which obviously affects all aspects of a student's ability to learn. The reader is referred to an excellent example of a full K–12 scope and sequence of library instruction chart, which is available from the Calgary Board of Education in Canada and which can serve as a model to fit local needs.[4]

CURRICULAR CONSIDERATIONS

For whatever reasons, school districts do not generally publish lists of skills for their library programs. They generally do have such lists for every other subject area, however. It seems critical to establish the validity of the elementary library program by having it printed. A printed program not only gains a measure of status with administrators, but can also easily be used with other faculty members to: (1) identify the skills their students are weak in, (2) identify the skills that need to be mastered, (3) match with curricular skills in other areas in order to develop appropriate assignments, and (4) provide a document that clearly identifies the instructional range of the library program.

One word of caution. A curriculum guide is not a course of study. A course of study is a list of skills, similar to what is presented in Table 1, but also extending horizontally across the page with grade-level breakdowns. Each of these skills has levels of difficulty and will be introduced, reinforced, and mastered at various points along the way. A course of study changes very slowly because we have assigned values to the listed skills. A curriculum guide lists the skills, but also makes suggestions about which resources, filmstrips, magazine articles, guest speakers, and the like can be used to teach the skills at each of the identified grades. Clearly, these kinds of suggestions and available resources change rapidly. A curriculum guide should be in a loose-leaf notebook with divisions identified. It should be updated frequently. The course of study, manifested in a scope and sequence of skills, should be plainly visible to teachers, parents, and administrators.

HOW CAN WE BEST LINK SKILLS TO CURRICULAR AREAS?

There are no easy answers to this other challenge. The involvement of any aspect of the library program with any other portion of the school program is laden with variables. We must also realize that library instruction is only part of a total library program. All aspects of a program work together, and each affects the impact of the other. While a public relations program may not appear to be part of a library skills program, in reality it may be critical in changing attitudes of teachers and encouraging them to participate in such a program.

Successful programs of library skills instruction are based on the educational assumption that students learn best if the information is taught in a way that closely parallels the manner in which the skill will be needed in real life. Therefore, (1) assignments need to be made in subject areas by subject area teachers, and (2) assignments need to be constructed in such a way that students must employ one or more library skills in order to complete them. The key to the process is involving teachers in planning instruction.

Before program planning begins, individual building or district variables need to be considered and assessed. Variables such as space, availability and training of the library staff, resources, time schedules, school policies, school organization, staffing patterns, administrative support and/or concern, availability of bookmobiles or other resource collections, teacher expectations and attitudes, teaching styles, general program support from public libraries or other educational agencies, parental involvement, and funding must be examined for potential impact on the program. It is sound advice to assess what the variables of any given program are and to place a value on each of them, using a "+," a "–," or a neutral designation. As a rule, successful programs clearly exhibit their strengths and weaknesses.

Successful programs also plainly demonstrate the characteristics of a successful program. Ideas of success differ from program to program and person to person. Nonetheless, there are specific goals. A general list of desirable program characteristics is given in *Media Programs: District and School*.[5] The local program staff needs to consider these and decide, rather specifically, what each means in terms of the local school program. Example 1 shows how a regional group of school media personnel interpreted several of these program characteristics to meet their needs and program variables.

EXAMPLE 1. SUCCESSFUL PROGRAM CHARACTERISTICS APPLIED TO A LOCAL SCHOOL PROGRAM

Successful program characteristics from *Media Programs: District and School*	Specific successful program characteristics for local school
Defining the purposes of the school media program with proposed implementation and evaluation to achieve them	Curriculum guides, student handbooks, and teacher handbooks will be printed and will include the purposes, process, and evaluation plan for achieving stated purposes.
Planning media program activities and integrating them with other programs of the school	The media staff will meet at least twice with each staff member and will suggest library activities that extend content instruction.

EXAMPLE 1. (*Cont.*)

Successful program characteristics from *Media Programs: District and School*	Specific successful program characteristics for local school
Participating in instructional design, course development, and the creation of alternative modes of learning	The library media specialist will attend all meetings of the curriculum council.
Developing budget criteria and budget as required by the school administrator and the district media director	An annual budget will be prepared and discussed with the faculty. The revised budget will be submitted to the district director.
Developing and maintaining a balanced, relevant collection	The media staff will (a) scan four review periodicals for new publications; (b) weed a portion of the collection; and (c) consult with each teacher a minimum of three times regarding the purchase of new materials.
Providing maximum access to collections in the school district and community	Access to collections: (a) the school media center will be open from 7:30 A.M. to 4:00 P.M. each school day; (b) a book catalog of all nonprint holdings will be made available to each staff member; (c) brochures promoting the public and college library will be available; and (d) field trips to each will be conducted for all fourth and sixth grade classes.
Conducting orientation and in-service education in media for school media staff and teachers	Orientation and in-service education: (a) one media workshop will be offered for all aides and volunteers who work in the library; (b) each student teacher will receive a one-half day orientation of the library to include viewing a slide-tape presentation; and (c) five minutes at each monthly staff meeting will be used by the library staff to highlight new materials.
Building a public relations program that communicates the role of the school media program and its contributions to the goals of the school	Public relations: (a) monthly one page newsletters will be sent to each staff member; and (b) four persons in the community will demonstrate their crafts in the library during March, April, May, and June (crafts presented will be carving, weaving, cornhusk dolls, candle making).

TEACHER INVOLVEMENT

While all factors affect the success of a local school media program, teacher involvement and curricular ties are two critical considerations. As librarians become involved with teachers, teachers become involved with libraries. There appears to be a progression of teacher involvement that leads to meaningful curricular considerations. The process can be either librarian initiated or teacher initiated. However, if teachers are not asking for assistance already, it is incumbent upon the librarian to take the initial steps. Since teachers are not trained in techniques of effective selection and utilization of resources, they usually need guidance and assistance from the media professional. Teachers often do not seek assistance simply because they are not aware of the large skill area the librarian is responsible for, nor do they know that the librarian could be of assistance in this area. There are two tiers of involvement. That is, an actual library instruction program must be developing at the same time that teachers are becoming more cognizant of the library and its resources and of how this part of the school can increase student learning. Progressively the librarian plans the library instruction activities and does the teaching, while teachers become involved with the review and selection of resources. The librarian becomes involved with teachers in developing library instruction plans for students. The librarian does the teaching, while teachers select instructional resources to meet the instructional and learning needs of students. Teachers and librarians plan mutually for library skills instruction: (a) instruction is focused directly on library skills instruction that aims toward an end result project and (b) instruction is indirectly focused on library skills, but skills are apparent in all subject areas.

Librarians are almost always involved in the first level of a library skills program. The first thought of the teachers is to request that the librarian spend a given period of time to teach the students library skills, usually three to five days. The librarian is expected to do the planning and the instruction. Often programs do not develop beyond this point because the librarian does not have a conceptual model in mind of how library skills fit into the rest of the curriculum, and/or because the librarian does not involve the teachers in the planning or evaluation of the instruction. Involving teachers can be as simple as keeping them informed about what is being done, or as complex as actually planning the instructional goals and teaching strategies together. The librarian must strive for as much involvement as possible without consuming too much time.

The second level of librarian activity is generally apparent in interdisciplinary schools, where librarians are regularly involved in teacher team planning. The librarian is expected to do the actual teaching and to arrange the instructional activities. However, the teachers and librarian have planned together when the instruction should occur and have discussed the instructional units in which the students are presently participating.

Teacher Activities

The first level of teacher activity is with the review and selection of resources. An example of this is an elementary district of ten schools ranging in size from 65 students (two classrooms) to 350 students where there is one media professional for the elementary program. The media professional established a policy that nonprint resources would not be purchased unless each had been recommended by at least two teachers in the district, preferably with the assistance of students. The media professional identifies teachers who are likely to be interested in the content of the various resources that are ordered or sent for preview. The resources are transported to the various schools by the professional and are personally given to each teacher. The success of the program is based on the fact that when teachers are aware of the large numbers of resources available (1) they are not likely to order "everything in the catalog"; (2) they become more critical of published resources and make positive suggestions regarding strengths and weaknesses of resources; and (3) they begin to use the resources for instruction at an accelerated rate because they are familiar with the content of large numbers of purchased resources. The use of instructional resources in the district has increased 87 percent during the four years of the review and selection program. More importantly, teachers have become more aware of their own instructional objectives and are able to select resources for use that will meet those very specific objectives. The development of this awareness is the second level of teacher involvement and is a natural outgrowth of the first.

Another example involving teachers in the selection of resources is a K–6 building of 260 students. Once a month the teachers are invited to have lunch in the media center. The media professional uses this opportunity to preview new materials, to introduce older resources that have not been used well, to highlight special resources that may be pertinent for particular upcoming units of instruction, and to be accessible on an informal basis to teachers who do not have time away from their students during the day. Another school of 1,000 K–8 students invites one sales representative each month to leave materials for a two-week preview. Teachers are encouraged to select resources and review them. A printed review sheet is provided and purchase of these materials is considered along with other materials. The media professional has found that the teaching staff is now more aware of instructional materials and they tend to select materials that will help students meet specific instructional objectives.

The use of *learning centers* or stations is also an effective way to help teachers focus on student learning objectives. These can be developed by either the teacher or the librarian working alone, but they have been successfully used in a number of programs to focus the attention of a librarian-teacher team on the instructional needs of students. The needs are identified, resources and activities are planned, and follow-up evaluation is conducted. Essentially, a learning center is a "guided tour" through many resources useful in meeting instructional objectives. Resources are selected that permit students to select several activities. These activities have been preselected to focus student attention on skills or concepts, which can relate to any area of instruction, including library skills. *The Now Library Media Center*[6] provides detailed plans for setting up learning centers to teach library skills. Even if the selected learning center objectives are not library skills, students are still learning how to use resources, and are being directed to read, look, listen, or do as a result of interaction with various resources.

Curricular Tie

Mutual planning for instructional purposes is the basis for the most advanced level of teacher involvement. On this level students are learning library skills, being either *directly* or *indirectly* aware of the library instruction. Both modes of instruction assume that students learn best by applying the library skill in an actual situation.

In the *directly aware* mode the student's instructional objective is to grasp information finding and using skills that have been decided upon as necessary by the librarian and the teaching staff. The example outlined in *The Monteith College Library Experiment*[7] is an excellent conceptual model easily adapted to elementary schools almost as presented. Basically the model identifies skills students need in order to complete a project. Reasonable content assignments are made over a period of time. These assignments focus student attention and provide students with practice in using the identified skill in an actual situation. By the end of the three or four years, students have had practice in each of the prerequisite skills and are now prepared to complete a major project, the natural culmination of all the previous assignments.

For example, a reasonable sixth grade goal is the completion of a display at the science fair. The faculty and the librarian decide what characteristics they expect to see in a well-prepared project. These characteristics are arranged in a hierarchy of skills covering a period of four years, with the first skill being introduced in the later part of the third grade. Appropriate assignments are developed by the teachers and the librarian so that student attention is focused on the library skill presented.

Skills and accompanying assignments are maintained in a notebook or a learning center arrangement. As new students enter the school they can be instructed in these skills on an individual basis. Example 2 is an outline of a possible sequence of skills with sample assignments.

In the *indirectly aware* mode the student's primary instructional objective is to learn something about a subject area. While library skills are secondary in the student's mind, they are nevertheless used by the student in order to obtain subject information. These subliminal (if you will) skills are scattered throughout the curriculum in all subject areas and are presented all year. By the time a student leaves the school, the skills may have been included dozens of times in assignments from every subject area (see Example 3). In this type of program it is incumbent upon the librarian to work closely with teachers throughout the year to develop assignments that will address all identified skills. A chart for noting class completion of assignments in each skill area can be kept for each class or subject area. As skills are completed, Xs can be used to indicate the skills presented to each class; these typically would be organization, selection, utilization, comprehension, and production. The chart allows both the teacher and the librarian to keep track of the skills yet to be covered.

A distinct advantage of these approaches is that individual progress is encouraged because (1) assignments can be more or less complex according to the ability of the student and still meet the objective; (2) a variety of means can be built into the assignments allowing for individual learning styles. They can stress, in establishing a field of library content to be mastered, that the content is beneficial only to the extent to which it can be applied to the needs of the student. Example 4 lists some assignments that can be used by students of different ability to meet the same instructional objectives.

EXAMPLE 2.   SEQUENCE OF SKILLS
WITH SAMPLE ASSIGNMENTS

Fourth Grade Skills	*Fourth Grade Assignments*
Select specific appropriate information	From sample information sources, print and nonprint, select those sections that relate to an assigned topic
Identify materials that contain appropriate information	List three sources containing information on an assigned topic
Condense information from several sources into own words	Put the ideas from four sample information sources on the same topic into your own words

Fifth Grade Skills	*Fifth Grade Assignments*
Identify four possible topics	After looking over magazines, encyclopedias, and other selected resources, identify four topics that would be appropriate for a science project
List four resources available for a topic	From an assigned topic, locate four resources containing information on the topic
Summarize a topic	From a preselected set of resources on a topic, summarize in your own words the important facts of the topic

Sixth Grade Skills	*Sixth Grade Assignments*
Identify a problem	From a list of possible topics, either student or teacher selected, select one of interest to you, describe why it is of interest, and identify one question that relates to the topic
Outline a topic problem	Outline the selected question to include history, recent developments, problems, suggested solutions to problems
Graphic skills	Prepare a printed sign using lettering equipment; mount a picture using two techniques; construct a display according to one of five basic principles
Bibliography	Prepare a written bibliography that includes four types of resources
Display at science fair	Prepare a display to be considered for the April science fair

EXAMPLE 3.   EXAMPLES OF GENERAL ASSIGNMENTS FOR SUBJECT AREAS

Language Arts
1. Verbal report to class about how two myths are alike and different
2. Verbal or taped report about an author
3. Verbal presentation about published book review
4. Written report re: author, poetry, media form

Social Studies
1. Five facts added to a class chart
2. Map, graph, or chart of historical words and their current use
3. Written report on aspect of instructional unit
4. Verbal presentation with pictures to illustrate

Math
1. Five main points of a filmstrip
2. A percent chart
3. A math model, constructed and presented to class
4. Reading assignment: a thin book or a chapter in one book, with listing of main points

Science
1. Main points of a film loop
2. Bulletin board, set up and explained to class
3. Visual and/or oral presentation to class on selected area
4. Written report on positive and negative effect of an action of a person, including future prediction; oral report on main points

Career Development
1. Bulletin board of various aspects of one career possibility
2. Five- to ten-minute slide show detailing job functions of one career
3. Ten-minute oral report, outlining possible careers for a given set of characteristics
4. Written report—compare and contrast two careers

Art
1. List of resources on one artist
2. Verbal report—biography of an artist
3. Bulletin board of one artist's works
4. Picture in a style similar to that of an artist or a time period
5. Slide presentation of artist, types of art, period of art history, etc.
6. Slide presentation or bulletin board of historical development of a region as seen through its art

Music
1. Oral report about a musician, instrument, type of music
2. Written or oral report on uses of music in agriculture
3. Written or oral report on effects of music on people
4. Bulletin board display highlighting a musician, and pointing out some noted works
5. A short piece of original music

EXAMPLE 3. (*Cont.*)

6. A five minute audiotape, utilizing three types of music, with narrative explanation

Home Economics
1. A visual media form emphasizing recommended procedures for: budget preparation, house buying, consumer protection, etc.
2. A written report on: government food inspection standards, methods of assessing interest rates, antique furniture, etc.

Industrial Arts
1. Oral report on safety precautions when using a specific type of equipment
2. A visual display detailing procedures used to construct a specific project
3. Written report detailing available resources useful for quality evaluation of wood/tin/plastic products

Foreign Language
1. Visual media emphasizing irregular verb forms, traditional dress of country, foods of country, modern architecture, stamps, etc.
2. Written report on: economic policy, historical progress in language, holidays of country, etc.
3. A short folktale read to class in the language
4. An original story in the language
5. Verbal description of historical art, pointing out its significance to the history of the country

EXAMPLE 4. ASSIGNMENTS FOR STUDENTS OF DIFFERENT ABILITIES

Sixth grade, First Semester, Language Arts

Library Skill
Use of reference books

Content Skill
Critical evaluation of books

Possible Assignments
Low: Given instruction in the use of book review sources available in the school media center, the student will make a verbal presentation detailing the type of information included in a single book review.

High: Given instruction in the use of at least two book review sources and a

Sixth grade, First Semester, Social Studies

Library Skill
a. Use of the card catalog
b. Use of reference books

Content Skill
U.S. economy during World War I

Possible Assignments
Low: Given instruction in the use of the card catalog, specialized reference books, and almanacs, the student will create a chart showing the fluctuation in valuation of the U.S. dollar from 1900 to 1930.

High: Given instruction in the use of the card catalog, specialized reference

EXAMPLE 4. (*Cont.*)

Sixth grade, First Semester, Language Arts	Sixth grade, First Semester, Social Studies

list of suggested book titles, the student will make a three-minute verbal presentation to the class that (1) identifies the title of a book that has two published book reviews, (2) cites the general theme of the book, and (3) compares the overall evaluation of the book given by each of the reviewers to include why each reviewer did or did not like the book.

Affective: The student will: (1) bring to class the actual book to show to the group, or (2) present additional reports on other books, or (3) bring to class book reviews from sources not in the library (e.g., magazines).

resources, and almanacs, and a list of possible topics, the student will prepare a written report on a teacher-approved aspect (e.g., repatriation) of the instructional unit that should include: (1) definition, (2) facts involved, (3) implications for the overall unit content.

Affective: The student will (1) verbally evaluate the morality of repatriation, or (2) suggest alternatives to repatriation, or (3) bring current newspaper articles on the U.S. economy to class, or (4) verbally apply current economic practices to World War I conditions.

CURRICULAR CONSIDERATIONS

There are several curricular considerations that need to be explored by the librarian. First, one must become familiar with the curriculum. What is the overall philosophy of the district? Are curriculum guides available? Are they used? If not, why not? How are subject area skills interpreted and implemented in the school? The answers to these questions will be useful in selecting which conceptual model will best meet the needs of teachers and students in a particular setting.

Second, all students do not need to be taught all skills. One could develop a proficiency test that asks students to demonstrate various skills. Students who can complete the task are not required to participate. Instruction is given only to those students who need or can benefit from it. It may be best to develop the skill into a more complex concept for some of the students than to require them to attend an introductory unit of instruction.

Instruction should be organized according to a student frame of reference, using examples and words familiar to students. The librarian should consider what the student already knows and develop the lesson from that point by building in small steps of thinking or activities—for example, introducing utilization skills before comprehension skills, requiring verbal reports before written reports, making sure basic skills have been learned before introducing higher-level skills.

Finally, while library skills are important, they are not the key to all the world's information. Individual subject areas do not necessarily organize themselves in ways that neatly fit into library classification. One should alert students to the exceptions, such as that: All information in the library is not in the card catalog; *all* information is not in libraries; government documents are arranged differently from the rest of the collection; what happened (history) and why (sociology) are not located near each other in libraries; and the terminology of standard subject headings in card catalogs or automated data banks does not necessarily keep pace with changes in the language.

CONCLUSION

There are many positive developments apparent in educating the library user in an elementary school setting. The increase in the number of curriculum guides alone is encouraging. Of greater importance, however, is the very real effort to involve teachers in every aspect of the school's library media program. This, coupled with increased awareness of how children learn, has placed library skills instruction in a position of importance equal to other areas of the school curriculum. When the entire instructional staff and the administration realize the potential impact that a properly carried out library skills program can have on total student learning, then school library instructional programs will be as basic as reading, writing, and mathematics.

NOTES

1. Ohio Department of Education, *Minimum Standards for Ohio Elementary Schools* (Columbus: Ohio Department of Education, 1970).
2. North Central Association of Colleges and Schools, *Policies and Standards for the Approval of Elementary Schools, 1975–1976* (Chicago: North Central Association of Colleges and Schools, 1975).
3. American Association of School Librarians, Association for Educational Communications and Technology, *Media Programs: District and School* (Chicago: American Association of School Librarians, 1975).
4. Calgary Board of Education, *Research Skills: A Scope and Sequence Chart of Library and Information Skills* (Alberta, Canada: Calgary Board of Education, 1976).
5. American Association of School Librarians, *Media Programs: District and School*, pp. 13 and 14.
6. Mary Margrabe, *The Now Library Media Center: A Stations Approach with Teaching Kit* (Washington D.C.: Acropolis Books, 1973).
7. Patricia B. Knapp, *The Monteith College Library Experiment* (New York: Scarecrow Press, 1966), ch. 5.

THE HIGH SCHOOL LIBRARY AND THE CLASSROOM: CLOSING THE GAP

JO ANNE NORDLING
formerly Librarian, Newberg High School
Newberg, Oregon

> Between the idea and the reality
> Between the motion and the act
> Falls the shadow.
> > *From* "The Hollow Men"
> > *by* T. S. Eliot

According to most school district library skills curriculum guides, students should be able to intelligently use nearly all the basic reference tools in the school library by the time they enter high school. The assumption seems to be that students will learn the essential steps of library usage in elementary and middle school, and that in high school they will have at least the rudimentary ability to independently apply this knowledge so that the high school library media center can serve as an extension of the classroom.

In my experience, this is seldom the case. Even in a school system that provides elementary librarians, librarians who work hard at their jobs, too many students enter high school unable to utilize the library as a working tool for their personal and academic needs. As one high school teacher said, "The poor students know how to copy out of the encyclopedia; the good students know how to use the *Readers' Guide*, look up books in the card catalog, and copy out of the encyclopedia."

How come? What happens? How can it be possible that after all the lessons on biographical reference books, specialized indexes, atlases, yearbooks, and dictionaries, not to mention the Dewey decimal system, so little insight into how to actually apply those lessons has been acquired along the way? Why, after eight years of library use instruction in the elementary school, do so many students seem unable to integrate what they have learned about the library media center into their research and study needs? And why, after four more years in the high school, do so many students continue to understand so little of the basic skills of library research?

WHAT HAPPENS

The high school library media center is a unique kind of library. It exists to support the curriculum of the school. Unlike the public library, which attempts to meet the broad spectrum of needs of the entire community, the school library must focus on those resources that reinforce the needs of the school curriculum. Limited resources and the stringent demands of the budgeting process dictate this reality. Ideally, the high school library does not sit apart and function as a separate, optional entity within the school, but acts as an integral part of the classroom experience, as necessary to the student and teacher as textbooks or chalkboards.

Within the school curriculum, there are three broad areas the school library is intended to support. First, the library media center enhances the efforts of the classroom teacher to teach the skill and pleasure of reading. Second, the school library provides a collection of subject matter materials that broaden and deepen the range of information in the classroom textbook. Third, the library is a laboratory in which the process skills of asking questions, gathering data, and independently drawing conclusions may be acquired. The last two school library functions—subject matter support and process skills acquisition—are inseparable. In order to learn the application of research skills there must be subject matter materials to investigate; in order to investigate subject matter there must be research skills.

The school library–media center is a great success in its first function of supporting the school reading program. Throughout the school years, the library serves an indispensable role by providing a wide variety of relevant reading materials. In nearly every school, the librarian performs enthusiastically and skillfully, in partnership with the classroom teacher, the task of enhancing the reading process. In this area, the librarian, the student, and the teacher are all clear as to the role of the school library. Students know that their teachers consider reading library books important to their progress and growth as readers. Students are given grades by their teachers on this "outside" reading, which is actually "inside" reading, because here the school library and classroom function as one.

The process breaks down in the later years of high school if the community is unwilling to allow the school library collection to keep pace with the interests of its maturing, young adult population. Then the reader is forced out into the bookstores or the corner drug store. If he is lucky, he has access to a public library. Still, the partnership between classroom teacher and librarian is as strong as ever, sometimes stronger when they face the common foe of censorship. In the area of teaching reading, the classroom and the library media center function interdependently and in the process each serves the student well.

The teamwork, the integration, the polar magnetism that exists in the reading curriculum, somehow disintegrate in the attempt to teach the student subject matter and research skills. Here, a deep chasm exists between the classroom and the library media center. From elementary school on through the high school years, the classroom is separate, self-contained. The classroom seems not to need the school library for teaching and learning history or geography or science. Classroom sets of textbooks take the place of library use. Unlike the teaching of reading, where the school library makes the task easier for both teacher and student, teaching subject material through library use seems a laborious and uncertain task best left to university scholars.

The school system acknowledges the importance of learning research skills by making library research an independent and isolated part of the curriculum. Library use becomes a separate subject taught by the librarian; library research becomes an end in itself instead of a means to an end.

Such a situation fosters the myth that the library media center is somehow the exclusive province of the librarian, with the library serving as the classroom in which the librarian teaches a subject known as "library skills." Since students are expected to learn their basic library skills in the elementary school, elementary librarian media specialists especially are caught in the trap of teaching research skills with nothing in particular to research. Making the best of it, elementary school librarians go to incredible lengths to make their library skills classes worthwhile to the students.

Jean Rappaport, a creative elementary librarian, has written of her disenchantment with her own attempts to integrate the teaching of library research skills with regular classroom studies. She tells how she finally gave up and launched instead into her own compromise means of teaching library skills based on Mary Margrabe's individualized stations approach.[1] The results of this experiential involvement in the library media center have obviously been successful for her in teaching students about the library and its resources. Still, the fact remains that optimum use of the library requires teacher involvement and curriculum-related library use. Without this key element, the library media center remains isolated from the classroom and actively supports the curriculum only in the area of personal reading growth.

The high school librarian, on the other hand, who is not expected to offer regular, scheduled classes on library media center use, gives orientation sessions to incoming students, attends to the myriad tasks of administering a large high school library media center, and acts as a resource/reference person to students and teachers at their request. The expectation in the high school is that the library exists for its role of research facility and as a source of reading pleasure. The "trap" of a separate classroom facility for the teaching of research skills has apparently been left behind in the elementary school.

But here, exactly as in the elementary school, there continues to be a wide gap between the library media center and the classroom. A sense of frustration over the difficulty of integrating library resources with classroom teaching prevails. Every group senses it; the librarian, the teachers, the students, are all faintly dissatisfied with the library. It is a frustration succinctly summed up in the perennial student lament "This dumb library doesn't have anything."

HOW COME

One of the earliest and most obvious reasons for the split between classroom and school library media center is scheduled library class time. This insidious invention, used widely in elementary schools, sets the stage early for learning some misguided assumptions about the nature of library use. It is generally recognized, and properly so, that each classroom teacher needs a certain amount of preparation time throughout the day. Even in the traditionally scheduled high school, it is relatively easy for the administrator to provide preparation time by the expedient of setting aside one period a day for each teacher. During this so called "free" period, the students are scheduled into other classrooms, leaving the freed teacher open to plan, correct papers, or recharge drained energy batteries.

In the elementary school, however, the problem of finding adequate preparation time is much more difficult, since each teacher is responsible for the same students all day long. The elementary administrator must juggle the schedule to provide preparation time for each teacher by counting the time each teacher's class is in physical education class or music or library. Library visits become inflexible, for the schedule must mesh perfectly with times set aside (for every classroom in the school) for the music teacher, the physical education teacher, recess times, and lunch time. In this way, library media center visits are scheduled for an entire class at one time and *without the teacher.*

This process is not lost on the student, who sees clearly that library research skills are not related to classroom study. The fact that teachers seldom accompany their students to the library and that library skiils are taught in isolation by the librarian and seldom used in classroom work prompts most students to interpret the situation by deciding that teachers think library research is not very important. The damaging outcome of the rigid library schedule is not just that it is an irritation, but that the children learn very early in their school careers that library research is unrelated to either their teachers or to the lessons they are learning from textbooks in the classroom.

A second component in the split between school library and classroom is the process by which teachers learn to teach. Most teach as they were taught. And most teachers were educated in elementary and high schools where the textbook was the ubiquitous arbiter of subject matter, where the school library (if one existed) was primarily used to support the reading program.

Going on to a university does not significantly change matters, since most teacher training institutions do not require a course in how to integrate the school library into the teaching of a subject or even require an introductory course in the use of the university library. The best most college students receive is an orientation to the library. As in high school, the orientation is generally based on the assumption that somewhere down the line one has learned how to use the library as a reference tool. And even here the textbook, especially in undergraduate classes, reigns supreme.

Teachers, when asked: "In college, were you required to take a course in how to use the library?" almost always answer no. In some courses professors would mention certain reference tools that might be useful in researching a paper, but mostly these future teachers used the card catalog (often ineffectively) and the *Readers' Guide,* and browsed. Not until the senior year and graduate school did the vast resources of the university library begin to become apparent, as professors insisted on some independent scholarship and relied less on a common set of textual materials to teach their subjects, and advanced students gradually stumbled across and learned about a growing number of reference tools.

This came about too late for most prospective teachers to figure out how the process of research relates to high school teaching. Thus ill equipped, the late library use bloomers keep going into the elementary and high school classrooms, not understanding exactly how the school library can be utilized to teach. During my own years as a high school teacher, I, who loved libraries, continued to make assignments requiring library research only to receive piles of papers dutifully copied out of *Reader's Digest* or the encyclopedia. Neither my students nor I knew what to do about it. The librarian and I taught them to use the *Readers' Guide*, but I ended each teaching year increasingly frustrated over our inadequate use of the library. With 130 students, all of whom are studying the same period of history at the same time, and a finite number of reference materials, what *does* one do? And how does one do it?

The third element in the force holding apart the school library and the class-room has to do with the expectations and duties of the high school librarian. Usually, there is one library media specialist in a high school. This is true despite American Library Association standards that since 1969 have recommended one librarian–media specialist for each 250 students.[2] Even in a high school of 2,000 students with a faculty of 65 teachers, one librarian remains the norm. Depending on the size of the student body, the librarian is generally helped by two adult aides—or perhaps three if a strong committment to the library exists—and by students who staff the circulation desk, reshelve books and magazines, and perform other necessary library chores. The student staff varies widely in mastery of skills and ability to work responsibly. There is also a high rate of turnover each semester necessitating an ongoing training program for student staff members. In some schools there is an attempt to provide an audiovisual specialist to deal with the nonprint materials. If the audiovisual collection is small, or handled mostly through district interschool loan, the librarian will also be in charge of the nonprint materials. Keeping this in mind then, here is a job description listing duties most high school librarians are expected to perform.

The head of the school library media program:

Has responsibility, subject to administrative approval, for planning and implementing the media center's program of services to students and faculty, for the formulation of the media selection policy, and for the selection, organization, and administration of all materials and equipment in the school media center.

Has responsibility for training and supervising the media center staff, including paraprofessionals and student helpers.

Plans the expenditure of funds allotted to the school media program and keeps records of these disbursements.

Makes available to the faculty, through the resources of the professional collection, information about recent developments in curricular subject areas and in the general field of education.

Assumes responsibility for providing instruction in the use of the library media center and its resources that is correlated with the curriculum.

Works with teachers by serving on teaching teams, acting as resource person in the classroom and serving as instructional resource consultant to students.[3]

A natural order of priorities arises out of the elemental need to keep the library doors open and materials in some semblance of order for use. The nitty-gritty jobs take precedence: reading book reviews and ordering books, cataloging materials, administering budgets, training and supervising an ever-changing student staff, supervising record keeping for catalog cards and shelf list, and acting as reference librarian.

There is little energy left for working with faculty members in a team situation, helping to plan specific integrated research sessions to facilitate the teaching of art, or speech, or child care. The part of the high school librarian's job description that recognizes the role of team teacher, the component essential in closing the gap between classroom and library media center, becomes relegated to the shelf of regrets and half-forgotten dreams.

WHAT TO DO

Assuming that the case, as stated so far, is a reality in a majority of our public schools, how can the situation be remedied? For until it is remedied, the school library will continue to fall short of its potential as a learning tool. Students will continue to leave high school knowing little of the skill and joy of research.

In the search for solutions, the beginning must come in the elementary school, for it is here that unintended affective learning regarding the use of the school library first becomes entrenched in the mind of the student. The elementary school library must be freed from the rigid scheduling that separates teachers from students and results in the creation of the library as a separate classroom. The change from rigid to flexible library scheduling will ensure that classroom teacher and librarian can plan library use in conjunction with the needs of classroom study. It is far more effective to have four daily consecutive sessions in the library once a month than once-a-week library lessons unrelated to what is happening in the classroom. In this way, students will realize early that research in the library is an important and normal part of learning.

It is true that those teachers who feel uncomfortable working in the library will avoid signing up for such experiences. Or, if they do sign up, they may be tempted to use the time as preparation time. The alert administrator can make suggestions and let these hesitant teachers know that integrated library research experiences are considered an important part of their teaching skill. The librarian–media specialist has a key role in helping these teachers learn to use the library with their classes.

Solving the problem of inadequate teacher training in the use of the school library at the university level is more difficult than rearranging the elementary school schedule. It is obvious that teachers who feel comfortable and competent in the library milieu are likely to want to provide significant school library experiences for their students. It is essential that teacher training institutions require a basic class in bibliography and reference as a prerequisite for admission to the teacher training program.

A further requirement for future teachers should be a methods course in which they learn specific ways of using the school library as a teaching tool to enhance not just the reading program but the entire subject matter curriculum. Such a methods course should be required before prospective teachers go into the field for supervised practice teaching so they may further experiment with this integrated method of using the library media center to teach subject matter.

Such a class need not be just another advanced bibliography and reference course, but may become an opportunity through which each teacher can learn to become more questioning, more independent of the textbook-dominated classroom, more creative and more powerful in using the wide variety of resources available in the high school library. The librarian remains the person who can provide the skills for using specific library tools and finding needed data. The teacher needs especially to hone skills as a seeker and a questioner. Together the librarian–media specialist and the classroom teacher form the team necessary to integrate library use into the acquisition of knowledge and values. Neither can do it alone.

Finding the college staff to teach such classes to future teachers may not be easy. Nancy Fjällbrant argues that the same gap exists at the university level.[4] College instructors have been criticized for their own lack of adequate knowledge of important sources.[5] In one survey done in 1975, out of 47 American Library Association–accredited library schools in the United States, only four offered courses specifically on library instruction, and only four others planned to set up such courses by 1977.[6] Evidently, even the people whose profession it is to teach librarians do not consider library use instruction important enough to divert resources for its support. No wonder librarians so often are mere keepers of the flame, instead of teachers of the use of fire.

Only when university trustees and high-echelon administrators begin to look past the sheer bulk of materials and begin to ask "What are we doing to assure the optimum use of these materials?" will the university library be able to assume its rightful role as intellectual center of the university. Only then will there emerge significant numbers of high school and elementary teachers who will be able to use the school library in their teaching as easily as they now use textbooks.

Finally, consideration must be given to that part of the solution having to do with the role of the high school librarian. It has already been pointed out that the nature of this job description is so all-encompassing it ensures that only scraps of time and energy remain for the job of team teacher. Yet the librarian is probably the single most important missing component in the process of closing the gap between classroom and school library media center.

Nowhere is there a better argument for implementing the standards calling for one librarian for every 250 high school students. Until this is understood by those who make up the school budget, they will be deceived by the fact that the library media center continues to function, warm bodies study and whisper at the library tables, books that supplement the reading program are checked in and out, audiovisual materials are checked out by teachers for classroom use, monthly new-materials lists are distributed, and an occasional young scholar haunts the bookshelves. All seems in order, sometimes in very impressive order, but until teachers are using the library to help them teach their subjects, the school library is not being used at anywhere near its potential. School board members and school administrators as well as university officials need to look past the bulk of materials to the crucial question, "What are we doing to assure the optimum use of these materials?" It is time to expand the notion of the high school librarian's role, to give its team teaching function proper recognition and fiscal support.

All over the country school budgets are in trouble. How is it possible to convince a school board and administrators struggling just to maintain services to hire at least one more librarian? Even the teachers on the staff often do not understand the benefits that would accrue to themselves and to their students through the addition of one more librarian–media specialist. In one study conducted by the National Education Association, only 27 percent of the teachers polled considered the library important, and a whopping 34 percent stated that it was of limited or of no importance to the school![7]

It is, of course, the high school librarian, with those leftover scraps of time and energy, who must carry the burden of proving the worth of the team teacher-librarian concept. To aid in the task of integrating subject matter with library research, there is a small but growing body of information available. All annotated items in the bibliography following contain specific ideas and examples that will be helpful to both the librarian–media specialist and the classroom teacher.

Much has been written on the importance of the librarian as a member of the curriculum committee. Serving on the curriculum committee is certainly desirable, but what is even more important is that the librarian know the material being used by the classroom teacher. Whether the librarian–media specialist likes textbook materials or not, the information in these books is what the teacher is interested in teaching. A librarian who does not know what the classroom teacher is teaching has no chance of being accepted by the teacher as a fellow team member.

Realistically, maybe all one librarian can manage is to focus on one subject each year. Choosing a subject already familiar, the librarian can then find one teacher in the chosen subject field who likes the idea of using the library for research. Together the two of them can create a research experience for their students that is directly related to classroom learning and that will furnish a peek into the possibilities of the library media center as an extension of the classroom.

It is important to make up an evaluation questionnaire for each student to fill out before and after the library research. Administrators and school board members may be impressed by those students who say things like "I really learned a lot about the library. I even figured out from that history research project how to look up articles about cam shafts!" And they will give useful feedback on what did not work—"That sheet on atlases where we looked up stuff on the Soviet Union was really confusing because . . ." The next time that section will be more effective.

When more teachers come requesting similar help in their subject areas, the librarian—overworked and alone—may have to refuse. But a record can be kept of these requests so that when a formal proposal for that second librarian is written, there are more data to support the arguments.

This is not to denigrate the teaching of library skills as a separate subject whenever there is legitimate reason. It is certainly logical to offer a reference and bibliography course to any high school students who recognize that learning the use of specific reference tools is related to their academic needs. College- bound seniors especially tend to become interested in the process of library search as they contemplate their college careers. Unfortunately, the lone high school librarian has neither time nor energy to teach such a class. Here is yet another bit of information to include in the proposal for the second library media specialist.

Closing the gap between high school classroom and library, then, is dependent upon effecting changes in these three areas: elementary school scheduling practices, teacher training procedures at the university level, and the role of the high school librarian–media specialist. It is a slow and patient work in which a few dedicated supporters of library media center use are now engaged. It is a task that falls most heavily on librarians at all levels, elementary, high school, and university. Without their leadership and perseverance, there is little chance that the break between classroom and library will be mended or that the school library will assume the role it was intended to have in the education of children.

NOTES

1. Jean Rappaport, "SLJ/Letters," *School Library Journal* 22 (February 1976): 3.
2. American Library Association and National Education Association, *Standards for School Media Programs* (Chicago: American Library Association, and Washington, D.C.: National Education Association, 1969), p. 12.
3. Compiled from recommendations in ibid., pp. 7–12.
4. Nancy Fjällbrant, "Planning a Programme of Library User Education," *Journal of Librarianship* 9 (July 1977): 199–211.
5. Robert Vuturo, "Beyond the Library Tour: Those Who Can, Must Teach," *Wilson Library Bulletin*, May 1977, p. 736.
6. Susan Galloway, "Nobody Is Teaching the Teachers," *Booklegger Magazine* 3 (January/February 1976): 29.
7. Ralph Perkins, *The Prospective Teacher's Knowledge of Library Fundamentals* (New York: Scarecrow, 1965), p. 18.

BIBLIOGRAPHY

American Library Association and National Education Association. *Standards for School Media Programs.* Chicago: American Library Association, and Washington, D.C.: National Education Association, 1969.

Anderson, Margaret C. "The Use of the Library: A Unit for Business Students." *Business Education World* 37: (April 1957): 35–36. Describes a way of introducing business students to basic reference tools for looking up rules of etiquette, rules of parliamentary procedure, how to type certain legal forms, how to compose invitations, etc.

Bates, Louise. "Card Catalog Game." *Wilson Library Bulletin*, April 1955, p. 659. A fun way of gleaning information from the card catalog. The idea was originally conceived for elementary students, but could easily be adapted for older students.

Carter, Robert R., and McLellan, Magarete S. "Library Use Program." *Science Teacher* 36 (January 1969): 66–67. A librarian and a science teacher join forces to investigate science material using a wide variety of library reference tools.

Davies, Ruth Ann. *The School Library Media Center: A Force for Educational Excellence*, 2nd ed. New York: R. R. Bowker, 1974. A book aimed at the librarian but well worth any teacher's time to explore. The teacher/librarian team will be especially interested in the examples of Shirley Pittman's learning guides on pages 108–110, 158–159, 190–192, 215–216, and 229. The sample resource units on pages 356–365 (Contemporary American Culture) and 368–381 (The Civil War and Reconstruction) are also helpful. Chapters 6–9 discuss ways in which the library can support the teaching of English, social studies, science and mathematics, and the humanities.

Elza, Betty, and Maslar, Isobel. "REFECOL." *Science Teacher* 42 (November 1975): 31–32. Describes a project designed by a librarian and an English teacher to acquaint tenth-grade students with a wide variety of reference materials. The project uses ecology as subject matter.

Fjällbrant, Nancy. "Planning a Programme of Library User Education." *Journal of Librarianship* 9 (July 1977): 199–211.

Galloway, Susan. "Nobody Is Teaching the Teachers." *Booklegger Magazine* 3 (January/February 1976): 29–31.

Gruner, Charles R. "A Library-Research Assignment." *The Speech Teacher* 22 (March 1973): 158–159. A college speech teacher describes his method for introducing beginning college students to basic speech reference sources. Could be easily adapted to fit the resources of the high school library.

Janeczko, Paul B., and Mendala, Ruth. "Interpol Case #101: Getting Students to Use Reference Works." *English Journal* 61 (October 1972): 1048–1050. Two teachers set up a James Bond, spy-counterspy situation that can only be solved by tracking down clues in reference tools. Imaginative and fun.

Leopold, Carolyn. "Beyond the DDC: The Teaching of Library Skills Can Be an Intellectual Adventure." *Library Journal* 93 (October 1968): 3930–3931. A high school librarian explains how she uses the teaching of library skills as a way to explore the history of ideas and to foster a spirit of inquiry about how those ideas are communicated. Excellent ideas here for all history and English teachers who are interested in an interdisciplinary approach to learning.

Nordling, Jo Anne. *Dear Faculty: A Discovery Method Guidebook to the High School Library.* Westwood, Mass.: F. W. Faxon Co., 1976. A collection of specific class projects designed to guide the interested but uninitiated teacher through the process of integrating the teaching of subject matter with library research. Chapters are devoted to: specialized magazines and possible career choices; U.S. history; indexes of books and the Dewey decimal system as access to almost any subject in the curriculum; literature reference tools; finding information for speeches, articles, and debates; the geography, culture, and historical background of a country; researching ethnic backgrounds: backgrounds for creative writing and literature; foreign language; the public library. Covers a wide range of subject areas in the high school curriculum.

Perkins, Ralph. *The Prospective Teacher's Knowledge of Library Fundamentals.* New York: Scarecrow, 1965.

Rappaport, Jean. "SLJ/Letters." *School Library Journal* 22 (February 1976): 3.

Sawyer, Byrd Fanita. "We Can Use Our Library!" *Wilson Library Bulletin,* February 1958, pp. 432–434. A high school librarian outlines in detail three book-writing projects that involve students in the use of library resources. The sophomores write a book on an interesting vocation, the juniors write on some facet of state history, and the seniors write on the life of an author. Any subject matter taught in the high school could be substituted for the suggested topics.

Sayles, Lois. "Teaching Library Skills through Subject Matter." *Education* 86 (March 1966): 412–416. Gives an example of learning library skills through the study of English literature.

"Team Teaching Used." *California School Libraries* 44 (Summer 1973): 27–30. Describes how teachers at Acacia middle school successfully incorporated the librarian into their team teaching approach.

Vuturo, Robert. "Beyond the Library Tour: Those Who *Can*, Must Teach." *Wilson Library Bulletin*, May 1977, pp. 736–740.

INSTRUCTION IN JUNIOR AND COMMUNITY COLLEGES

JOHN LOLLEY
Director of Library Services, South Campus,
Tarrant County Junior College District,
Fort Worth, Texas

A self-proclaimed goal of the American community-junior college in the latter part of the 1970s is to prove that nearly all people are educable.[1] If nearly all are educable, then it must follow that most are capable of succeeding in college—if (1) they are let in, (2) they pursue the right program, and (3) they are taught in a way best suited to their individual needs. In order to reach this goal the two-year college has evolved from a single-purpose junior college to a multipurpose community-junior college with an open-door admissions policy offering low-cost instruction ranging from the remedial to the highly technical. Admirers note the many community-junior college graduates who have succeeded in four-year colleges or those who have upgraded their present occupational skills or found a new occupation as a result of their instruction. Detractors question whether nearly all people are educable, noting the alarming attrition rates and the prevalence of traditional instructional techniques where nontraditional techniques are needed, and in general feel that the community-junior college has failed to live up to its stated promises.

Regardless of one's point of view, most will agree that an institution with few admission restrictions, offering a variety of programs that may include remedial courses, general education courses leading to a two-year degree, college-parallel courses for transfer students, and vocational-technical courses for one- and two-year degrees, will attract a wide diversity of students. Most will also agree that these students present a formidable challenge to the librarian attempting to design a library instructional program.

THE STUDENTS

Since the early 1960s, two-year college students have been characterized as being different, that is, different from four-year college and university students. Four-year college students were considered to be a homogeneous group "moti-

vated to engage in abstract intellectual activities and related academic exercises . . .
to have a background of training and competence in linguistic, quantitative and
conceptual tools required for advanced academic work . . . to be largely in
harmony with the requirements of the educational program so that college teaching could be focused almost exclusively on the knowledge and skills."[2] Because
of their wide ranges in age and educational, social, and economic backgrounds,
however, it was assumed that on the whole junior college students did not possess
these abilities. Today many four-year college teachers and many community-
junior college teachers would seriously challenge these assumptions about their
students. The truth is that both institutions have students who fall into each of
the characterizations.

The tendency still persists, though, to compare the students, particularly in
terms of academic ability. There are numerous studies confirming that
"community-junior college students compared to their counterparts in four-year
colleges and universities score significantly lower on all current measures of
academic ability."[3] O'Banion argues, however, that community-junior college
students are representative of the total population of the community whereas
four-year college and university students usually represent a more narrow segment of the community. "Compared to the general population, the academic
skills of community-junior college students appear quite normal. It is only when
compared to four-year college and university students that community-junior
college students appear academically disadvantaged."[4] Rather than describing
community-junior college students according to their tested academic ability, one
can obtain a better picture by focusing on their academic backgrounds and subsequent reasons for coming to college. Medsker identifies eight types of students
who traditionally enroll in community-junior colleges:

1. The high school graduate who enters a community-junior college right after high
   school as a full-time student with the intention of transferring to a given institution with a particular major.
2. The low achiever in high school who "discovers" college quite late and then becomes highly motivated to enroll in a community-junior college transfer program for which he is not equipped, yet who may be a "late bloomer."
3. The high school graduate of low ability who enters community-junior college
   because of social pressure or unemployment.
4. The very bright high school graduate who could have been admitted to a major
   university who may have low scores on measures of "intellectual disposition" or
   "social maturity."
5. The intellectually capable but unmotivated, disinterested high school graduate
   who comes to a community-junior college to "explore," hoping it will offer him
   what he does not know he is looking for.
6. The transfer (in) from a four-year college who either failed or withdrew after an
   unsatisfactory experience in a semester, a year or more.
7. The high school dropout who probably comes from a minority group and a cul-
   turally disadvantaged family with only grade school level skills and a strong interest in securing vocational training.
8. The late college entrant (over 25) who was employed, in military service or in the
   home for a number of years after high school and who now is motivated to pursue
   an associate (and perhaps a baccalaureate) degree, however long it may take.[5]

Add to these the over-30-year-old students who are seeking to upgrade their present occupational skills, such as police or fire-fighting personnel, or those who were previously unemployed and need to learn a marketable skill, such as newly divorced mothers.

Many of these students fit into Patricia Cross's classification of "new students," that is students "new" to higher education only because of open admissions. Originally, new students were those who "ranked in the lowest third of the high school graduates on traditional tests of academic achievement." The term now embraces "all learners who were previously underrepresented in higher education, adults, students from lower socioeconomic levels, ethnic minorities and women."[6]

There are some commonly held misconceptions among certain members of the educational community regarding new students. The first is the tendency to think of them as predominantly in the 18–22-year-old bracket. The fact is, their average age is 28 and climbing. A second image is to view them as students only. In reality, the overwhelming majority are part-time students, with college demands coming in a distant third in their priorities, ranking behind family and job. A third misconception is that most new students are members of a minority group.

> This is not true: the majority of high school graduates ranking in the lowest academic third are white. Concern about the lack of academic preparation of ethnic minorities, however, is well justified. Black Americans are overrepresented among the new student population; about two-thirds of the blacks entering two-year colleges fall among the lowest academic third of the entering students. Mexican Americans and American Indians are also overrepresented.[7]

Faced with such diversity, one begins to wonder at the levels of library experience and skills in library use that these students will bring to their first day of class. Unfortunately, there are few published studies that document entrance-level skills in library use. However, one such study, of 101 full-time day students of a large urban community-junior college, tends to confirm the worst suspicions. Forty-eight percent of the students did not know how books were arranged on the library shelf (that is, by subject); 74 percent did not understand the use of call numbers; 67 percent did not understand the basic author, title, and subject entries in the library catalog; 82 percent could not identify the elements in a *Readers' Guide* entry; 73 percent could not list at least one method of locating a biographical sketch; and 98 percent could not identify a book review source.[8] It is safe to conclude that, without extensive instruction, the majority of these students could not perform the simplest of library skills.

These then are the students. To some, learning to use the library is about as interesting as translating Egyptian hieroglyphics and probably just as difficult. Others can take it or leave it. They will take it, however, only if they can be shown that library instruction has an occupational value. Still others would welcome library instruction if they were convinced that using the library would help them to obtain a magical college education. Their only problem is that they are "deficient in the traditional language arts (reading, writing, listening, spelling, speaking, grammar) and mathematics."[9] And there are some whose ability and desire to learn library use would make even the most jaded university professor smile.

But how can they be taught, all of them? How can a library instructional program be designed for low-aptitude, educationally disadvantaged students who require "drastic modifications in traditional instructional techniques?"[10] What about high-aptitude, educationally advantaged students who may be capable of independent study or older students who "thrive" on the more traditional teaching methodologies that younger students tend to neglect? Perhaps a better question now is, how *are* they being taught?

HOW THEY ARE BEING TAUGHT

The following analysis of library instructional programs in 302 community-junior colleges is largely based on state and regional surveys supplied by Project LOEX (Library Orientation—Instruction Exchange).[11]

The first impression one receives in analyzing the surveys is the tremendous variation among the programs, ranging from simple to complex. For instance, in one survey a library described its program as:

Methods: Conducted tours; individual instruction
Publicity: Personal contact with faculty
Evaluation: Questionnaire presented to the various departments
          Present orientation viewed adequate

Another library in the same survey described its program as:

Methods: Conducted tours, cassette self-guided tours; point-of-use instruction; course-related instruction; and community groups; 16mm self-instructional film; individual instruction, separate credit courses—three one-credit hour courses; use of individual small group projects, lectures, films, slides, field trips, handouts, readings, tapes, etc., all three on general library use
Print Materials: Library Newsletter circulated throughout institution each term; subject bibliographies—in classes and pick-up, point of use; subject guides; guides to tools; exercises or assignments—classes; student handbooks. Nonprint Materials: Films—locally produced; Filmstrips; videotape—in planning; slide/tape presentation, locally produced; transparencies—for lecture illustrations
Publicity: Personal contact with faculty and students; letters to faculty; announcements in faculty and student news
Evaluation: Required student evaluation questionnaire of faculty and courses

Table 1 shows the methods and instructional materials used by the reporting libraries.

As the study reveals, the much-maligned guided tour still plays the predominant role in most instructional programs. Eighty-two percent use some form of the tour; 70 percent combine the tour with an orientation lecture. The major advantage of the required tour and lecture appears to be that students must visit the library at least one time during their college career. Most community-junior college librarians recognize the disadvantages of tours: disrupting noise, distracting traffic,

Table 1. Library Instruction in Community-Junior Colleges

Area:	SW Lib. Assn.	SE Lib. Assn.	Ohio	Mich.	N.Y.	Pa.	Total	Total Libs.[a]	%[b]
Number of Libraries:	75	131	21	22	39	14			
Methods									
Tours	60	108	16	19	34	12	249	302	82
Term-paper clinics	6	—	—	2	6	3	17	150	11
Orientation lectures	61	83	10	12	31	13	210	302	70
Credit Courses	12	21	2	4	13	—	52	288	18
Course-related instr.	33	109	8	14	9	3	176	302	58
Point of use	33	37	—	13	29	11	123	281	44
Print									
Textbooks, manuals, guides	—	40	—	1	4	2	47	206	23
Handbooks	48	95	—	12	5	11	171	281	61
Self-paced instr.	21	8	—	6	4	3	42	281	15
Nonprint									
Slides	22	10	3	4	7	1	47	302	16
Slide/tapes	19	26	3	9	11	3	71	302	24
Videotapes	9	6	3	3	—	—	21	249	7
Films	7	1	2	3	—	2	15	263	6
Filmstrips	29	16	2	6	—	2	75	263	29
Audiotapes	27	10	3	2	7	3	52	302	17
Computer-asst. instr.	—	—	—	2	—	—	2	—	—
Evaluation									
Formal	30	31	4	9	—	2	76	263	29
None	45	95	17	13	—	12	182	263	69

[a]Total participating libraries in each special area.
[b]Percentages figured on participating libraries only.

difficulty in hearing the guide, inattention, lack of motivation, etc. According to one librarian,

Our students are herded through the building by an ingratiating staff member, who fleetingly points to the scenic book stacks, the imposing card catalog, the colorful periodicals and the ever-amusing microfilm readers. The rest of our staff stands around like so many rest-home attendants eager to cater to the students' every need. Clutching their handbooks and floor plans, the students shuffle off to the library lecture room where for thirty minutes they are told how and why they should use library resources and services.

Perhaps the cruelest blow of all is the evidence that, for some students, the tour may do more harm than good. Patricia Breivik describes a controlled experiment structured to measure the value of library-based instruction in the academic success of educationally disadvantaged students in developmental English classes. Three groups were studied: (1) students who were provided weekly instruction that acquainted them with "information resources" and allowed them to acquire "information-handling skills," (2) students who were given a library tour and lectures, and (3) students who had no exposure at all to the library. "The experiment established that the weekly instruction produced the highest academic gains as measured by the best improvement in ability to produce a research paper defending a chosen proposition over a semester's time, and, rather surprisingly, the traditional library instruction [tour and lectures] produced lower results than no library instruction at all by the same measurement."[12]

In an attempt to overcome the intrinsic disadvantages of the tour and lecture, many libraries use a printed, cassette, or slide/tape self-guided tour. Even with these devices, however, a major extrinsic disadvantage is still there—the lack of students motivated to use them. Unless required to do so, it is doubtful if most community-junior college students would take the tour.

Why then do so many community-junior college libraries continue to cling to an admittedly ineffectual instructional method? The primary reason is that it is quick and easy, requiring little preparation and expense and conductable by almost any member of the library staff including student aides. Of the libraries that reported staff time devoted to instruction, few could afford the luxury of even one staff member assigned full time to it. In most cases, instruction is a part-time affair. The program is typically assigned to the reference librarian with the rest of the staff assisting when the need arises. Where the staff of the library is small, this situation is understandable. (In 1971, the median number of professional staff of two-year institutions was only 3.0 and "clerical and other staff" was 2.6.) The "part-timeness" of the instructional activity, however, is not limited by the size or even by the type of institution. Of the 337 academic libraries in the Southeastern Library Association survey, "practically all of the reporting libraries indicated that personnel assigned to orientation and instruction was on a part-time basis, with only six libraries (2 percent) providing full-time persons for the program, three of them being in junior and community colleges."[13] Similarly, of the 216 libraries in the Southwestern Library Association survey, only "twenty-eight libraries (13%) reported one or more librarians working full time on instruction."[14] It is ironic that in a time when academic libraries are recognizing and employing innovative business and management practices, they all but ignore one of the most very basic of business practices—advertisement. One of the explicit purposes of advertisement is to communicate to consumers "(1) the existence of want-satisfying products and services; (2) where they can be obtained; and (3) the qualities possessed, expressed in terms that will enable the consumer to make an intelligent choice."[15] Most academic librarians appear to be engaged in management or in providing services; few are engaged in instructing consumers in the location, use, and benefits of those services.

Fortunately the picture is not all bleak. Many community-junior colleges do offer formal instruction in locating and using library materials. Instructional methods utilized most often are: course-related lectures by library staff for specific courses, 58 percent; point-of-use instruction, 44 percent; credit courses, 18 percent; and term-paper clinics, 11 percent. Even though the majority of community-junior college librarians do not have faculty rank and privileges, such formal instruction represents an important gain in the library's attempts to become an integral part of the college instructional program. As Thomson states, "staff responsible for learning resources seemed to have become significantly more involved in the instructional program of community colleges than staff in traditional libraries in four-year colleges and universities."[16]

Most of the instruction, however, is geared primarily toward one segment of the students. Except for a few courses in the vocational-technical areas, course-related lectures are in the humanities and pure sciences, useful only to college transfer students. Some examples of college credit courses are: Library Skills, Use of Books and Libraries, Finding Information, Introduction to Research, Principles of Learning Center Utilization, Special Projects in the Learning Center, and Enjoying American Magazines.[17] Although enrollment figures are not given for these courses, probably few vocational-technical or remedial students took them.

When questioned as to the types of instructional materials used in their programs, the majority of community-junior college libraries, as Table 1 reveals, are still primarily print oriented. In addition to the library tour and lecture, over 60 percent distribute a student handbook. Even though many are cleverly done, it is doubtful whether typical community-junior college students read student handbooks. In addition to handbooks, 23 percent of the libraries use a library textbook, manual, or guide and 15 percent use some form of printed self-paced instruction.

The dominant form of nonprint instructional materials used by the libraries is the filmstrip, with slide/tapes, slides, and audiotapes used less extensively and videotape and motion pictures used hardly at all. Finally, as shown in Table 1, only 30 percent of the libraries formally evaluated their programs.

What does all this mean? It appears that the majority of instructional programs in community-junior colleges are not really instructional at all, but fall into the category of library orientation, that is, an introduction to the library building, facilities, collection, and staff. They require a minimum of resources and planning and rely on outside interest rather than library initiative. These methods are cheap in the short run but expensive over a period of time. Perhaps the supreme irony is that the library and media staff of many of the colleges produce for other disciplines innovative instructional programs involving sophisticated advances in educational technology, yet rely on the most traditional methods for library instruction.

Further, there is little evidence that the unique instructional needs of community-junior college students have been dealt with. While there are some excellent examples of individualized self-paced "packages," most of the instruction is on a group basis.

Most of the instructional programs do not take into account the different curricular pursuits of the students. Except for a few course-related lectures, vocational-technical students, a large segment of the student body, are overlooked. Remedial students are almost universally ignored.

HOW THEY SHOULD BE TAUGHT

In designing an instructional program for students, it may be necessary to look beyond teacher colleagues for inspiration. For example, according to Cohen, "it is paradoxical that an institution which purports to offer educational opportunity to all who come through the open door is beset with instructional practices [so] unfocused, they serve as major factors contributing to dropout rates which often approximate 30 percent per semester."[18] Roueche asserts that "new media are less likely to be introduced in the junior college than they are at any other level of education and the lecture-textbook get it or don't syndrome persists as it does in many four-year colleges and universities."[19] And to the horror of many college administrators, Bushnell intones: "Once considered to be the vanguard of innovative instruction in higher education, community-junior colleges are in danger of slipping behind their four-year counterparts."[20] If this is true, then one ideal area in which to help reverse the trend is the community college library, offering instruction that accommodates the diverse set of student instruction needs. Based on the experiment with educationally disadvantaged students, Breivik outlines six "Principles of Library Instruction" for teaching these students which suggest that: (1) students need instruction, not orientation, (2) instruction should be individualized, (3) instruction should be approached from the viewpoint of student needs, (4) all students should be required to take library instruction.[21] An expanded discussion of Breivik's principles as they apply to all community-junior college students follows.

STUDENTS NEED INSTRUCTION, NOT ORIENTATION

There is an oft-quoted, admittedly overworked analogy that describes the similarities of learning to drive a car and learning to use the library. While one may be loath to compare the rather mundane act of driving with the enlightened process of using the library, the fact remains that most students can drive and most cannot use the library. Discounting the very obvious motivational differences, one reason that students learn to drive is that they usually receive instruction. In the case of formal instruction, one would not expect a driver education teacher to gather a group of students at the new car dealer's showroom; show them the various models on display; tell them that the engine makes the car go, the transmission makes it go better, the brakes make it stop; and then step back waiting for them to jump in and drive merrily off. The expectation that students can learn to use the library with this type of orientation must also be abandoned. In the community-junior college, learning to effectively use the library means first mastering a set of skills. Smalley argues, however, that by concentrating on strictly technical skills "we may perhaps exclude or deemphasize the teaching of the more conceptually based search strategy skills, which would set the specific peculiarities of a particular research tool in context"[22] (that is, concentrating more on method than on content).

There are three reasons why the technical-skills approach is better for community-junior college students than the conceptual. First, according to Patricia Cross, "New Students learn gradually that they are 'below average' and many learn that they are failures. Research shows that they are more likely than successful students to adopt passive attitudes toward school learning, to state that they feel nervous and tense in class and to protest that teachers 'go too fast' with lessons."[23] It is very important that these students see, at an early date, a certain measure of success in their classes. Search strategy is conceptual, while the demonstration of skills is procedural, and it is easier and faster for new students to achieve success by using a particular library resource in an isolated setting rather than in an overall conceptual setting. A second reason is that for vocational-technical students, the mastery of skills in a step-by-step fashion is the predominant form of classroom instruction. Finally, the level of research and the resources available in many community-junior colleges simply do not require intensive search strategy.

INSTRUCTION SHOULD BE INDIVIDUALIZED

In spite of negative criticism, perhaps justified, the admission of new students and recognition of their individual instructional needs has brought about an "instructional revolution." The individualization of learning lies at the heart of this revolution as "dramatic changes in community college programs between 1970 and 1974 occurred in the instructional area. The use of programmed instruction increased from 44 percent of the colleges in 1970 to 74 percent in 1974; the use of self-paced learning modules increased from 31 percent to 68 percent; and skills centers spread from 36 percent of the colleges in 1970 to 67 percent by 1974."[24]

The teaching of library skills to community-junior college students lends itself to individualization. With such a wide range of academic abilities in the classroom, group instruction will obviously reach one segment—the more able, above-average students. By means of individualization, less-able students can learn at their own rates and in a style that better suits them. Further, group instruction is normally passive while the learning of library skills should be an active process. Regardless of the method, following instruction students are able to perform the skills or they are not, and performance should be the ultimate goal. Stating objectives before instruction is important because one cannot measure whether a student has reached a satisfactory level of performance unless the desired level is stated.

Keeping in mind that the same level of performance of library skills is required of all students, one might well establish a simple model of individualized instruction.

A. *Diagnostics.*   Diagnostics in the form of a pretest will tell the level of performance of library skills each student already possesses.
B. *Instruction.*
   1. Those students who score well on the pretest need only orientation to the facilities and resources, and exercises that allow them to demonstrate their ability. Successful performance of one skill is monitored by a librarian and then students move on to the next, independently finishing the complete set of library skills at their individual speeds.
   2. Students who fail the pretest need orientation, encouragement, instruction, exercises, immediate feedback, and evaluation. One individualized method that contains these features is the Personalized System of Instruction (PSI). It works as follows. The course is broken down into small, self-paced learning modules. The objectives of each module are clearly spelled out by the librarian and in a study guide. The student uses printed self-paced instruction to master the skills. Unlike other approaches, PSI stresses the written word. In our situation, however, any medium can be used for instruction. The advantage of printed instruction is that it is relatively inexpensive when compared with multimediated instruction and it is portable, allowing the student to carry his instruction to the actual library tool.
C. *Performance.*   The instruction is brief, followed by exercises that provide immediate feedback. When students feel they have mastered a given module—for instance, use of the library catalog—they present themselves to student proctors for testing. (The students who scored high on the pretest and demonstrated proficiency early would be ideal as proctors.) The test consists of demonstrated competency. In the case of the library catalog, exercises can be used followed by actual use of the catalog in locating specific materials.
D. *Feedback.*   If the student fails to pass, then the student proctor attempts to determine the difficulties, or may refer the student for further study or consultation with the librarian. There is no penalty for failing to pass the test but the learner may proceed to another unit only after demonstrating mastery of prior units. By the end of the course all students should have mastered the units. The pretest can then be administered as a post-test. Students are often astounded at the difference between the two test scores, before and after instruction. In PSI, librarians provide motivation rather than information. At the beginning of each course the librarian explains the procedures, distributes the study guide, administers the pretest, and selects student proctors. Librarians, however, should also always be present for consultation. There are many advantages in using PSI for library instruction. It allows a small library staff to instruct a large number of students; the instructional program is monitored by student proctors who often appear more approachable to fellow students than do librarians; it is relatively inexpensive if printed instruction is used; and—the greatest advantage—it accommodates different learning rates and abilities. PSI stresses performance rather than dialectics. There are of course disadvantages, such as disenchantment with student proctors and the failure of some students to complete the course. The disadvantages can be alleviated somewhat by application of the next two principles, making the instruction practical and requiring all community-junior college students to take the course.

INSTRUCTION SHOULD BE APPROACHED
FROM THE VIEWPOINT OF STUDENT NEEDS

If it can be demonstrated to students that instruction is beneficial, they are more likely to accept it. For instance, in the vocational-technical area, instruction should begin with the point that in most technical fields, reports must be compiled using data from books, journals, or reference works. If students expect to rise above the screwdriver and pliers level to a management level or perhaps to owning a business, they should know how to gather such data. It follows then that examples in the exercises and practical work should be from vocational-technical areas. The overall theme of a vocational student's instruction could be to gather data for a technical report. The direction for college-parallel students could be the term or research paper. Remedial students could gather information on a popular subject or figure. In each case, materials must be located using the three basic types of library tools—the library catalog, periodical indexes, and reference works. Some degree of search strategy would be necessary to complete the assignment. While there is no guarantee of success, it simply makes good sense that students will accept and respect instruction that contributes to their educational goals.

ALL STUDENTS SHOULD BE REQUIRED
TO TAKE LIBRARY INSTRUCTION

To many this is an unrealizable pipe-dream because of resistance from administrators and the lack of library staff. The fact is, however, that many community-junior colleges *do* require all freshmen to take such instruction. Eighteen percent of the community-junior colleges offer credit courses in library instruction.

If the instruction cannot be structured in a regular one-hour credit course, then it should be an integral part of freshman orientation, as is the case at Tarrant County Junior College. For the past ten years, from 70,000 to 80,000 students have received library instruction. The present program incorporates many of the fea-

Table 2. Comparison of Pre- and Post-test Scores of 101 Full-time Community-Junior College Freshmen[a]

Question	Pretest %	Post-test %
1. Understand arrangement of books in a library	52.4	93.1
2. Identify a call number	25.7	83.2
3. Understand how books are entered in the library catalog	32.7	87.1
4. Name a periodical index	16.8	87.0
5. Identify elements in a *Readers' Guide* entry	18.0	81.2
6. Locate a biographical sketch	26.7	78.2
7. Identify contents of an atlas	37.6	93.1
8. Locate a book review	2.0	38.6
9. Name at least one almanac	53.5	91.0
10. Use an encyclopedia	33.7	73.3

[a] Scores represent percentage of students who answered questions correctly.

tures of PSI. A color videotape (with student actors) is used for motivation and general orientation. The approach is a practical one with the opening scenes depicting reasons why students would need to use a college library. Then each situation is "solved" as the camera follows the student through the library, successfully locating needed information. After the videotape, instruction in library skill development is given through an individualized self-paced manual. Does it work? Table 2 shows the pre- and post-test scores of a group of students from Tarrant County Junior College.[25]

CONCLUSION

The time is ripe for library skills instruction in community-junior colleges. There is currently a "back to basics" movement in all education. Parents, educators, and employers are becoming more vociferous in their concern that students entering college (and often graduating) cannot read and write at the expected level. "General education designed to give students a broad range of skills is a 'disaster area' at most U.S. colleges and universities with English and math especially neglected."[26] Therefore many colleges, particularly community-junior colleges, have extensive remedial reading and developmental English and math courses to teach fundamental skills.

In the eyes of many, the ability to read and write *and* use the library are considered fundamental skills of college graduates. Citing a Carnegie Foundation for the Advancement of Teaching report, a recent newspaper editorial noted that "besides English and math such skills as statistics and using library sources are frequently ignored . . ." in colleges.[27]

Community-junior college librarians must renew or intensify their push for the required teaching of library skills. The time is ripe!

NOTES

1. James W. Thornton, *The Community-Junior College* (New York: Wiley, 1972), p. 65.
2. Ralph Tyler, "The Teaching Obligation," *Junior College Journal* 30 (May 1960): 526.
3. Terry O'Banion, *Teachers for Tomorrow* (Tucson: University of Arizona Press, 1973), p. 41.
4. Ibid., p. 41.
5. Leland Medsker, "The Junior College Student," in *Junior College Student Personal Programs: Appraisal and Development* (A Report to the Carnegie Corporation, November 1965), p. 21.
6. K. Patricia Cross, *Accent on Learning* (San Francisco: Jossey-Bass, 1976), p. 4.
7. Ibid., p. 6.
8. John Lolley, "Educating the Library User," *Texas Library Journal* 51 (Spring 1975): 32.
9. William Moore, *Against the Odds* (San Francisco: Jossey-Bass, 1970), p. 169.
10. John Roueche, *Time as the Variable, Achievement as the Constant: Competency-Based Instruction in the Community College* (Washington, D.C.: American Association of Community and Junior Colleges, 1976), p. 2.

11. The surveys supplied by Project LOEX are: *Academic Library Instruction Programs in the Southwest*, with 75 community colleges reporting; *Library and Bibliographic Instruction in Southeastern Academic Libraries*, with 131 community-junior colleges; *The Directory of Library Instruction Programs in Ohio Academic Libraries*, with 21 community-junior colleges; *Library Instruction Programs in Michigan, A Directory*, with 22 community-junior colleges; *A Directory of Library Instruction Programs in Pennsylvania Academic Libraries*, with 14 community-junior colleges; and *New York Library Instructional Programs, A Directory*, with 39 community-junior colleges.

12. Patricia Senn Breivik, "Resources: The Fourth R," *Community College Frontiers* 5 (Winter 1977): 49.

13. James Ward, "Library and Bibliographic Instruction," *Southeastern Academic Libraries* (Fall 1976): 152.

14. *Academic Library Instruction in the Southwest* (Dallas: Southwestern Library Association, 1970), p. 5.

15. C. H. Sandage, *Advertising: Theory and Practice* (Homewood, Ill.: Richard D. Irwin, Inc., 1967), p. 62.

16. Sarah K. Thomson, *Learning Resource Centers in Community Colleges* (Chicago: American Library Association, 1975), p. 4.

17. Doris Cruger Dael, "Questions of Concern: Library Services to Community College Students," *Journal of Academic Librarianship* 3 (May 1977): 83.

18. Arthur Cohen, "Credentials for Junior College Teachers?" *Improving College and University Teaching* 17 (Spring 1969): 97.

19. John Roueche, "Improved Instruction in the Junior College; Key to Equal Opportunity," *Journal of Higher Education* 41 (December 1970): 716.

20. David Bushnell, *Organizing for Change: New Priorities for Community Colleges* (New York: McGraw-Hill, 1973), p. 86.

21. Breivik, "Resources," p. 49.

22. Topsy N. Smalley, "Bibliographic Instruction in Academic Libraries: Questioning Some Assumptions," *Journal of Academic Librarianship* 3 (November 1977): 282.

23. Cross, *Accent on Learning*, p. 7.

24. Ibid., p. 10.

25. Lolley, "Educating the Library User," p. 32.

26. *Fort Worth Star-Telegram*, December 16, 1977, p. 6a.

27. Ibid., p. 6a.

SEEKING A USEFUL TRADITION FOR LIBRARY USER INSTRUCTION IN THE COLLEGE LIBRARY

JON LINDGREN
*Head, Reference Department, St. Lawrence
University Library, Canton, New York*

In the fabric of everyday life, satisfactory explanations for social phenomena can usually be found, and when the woof and warp of cause and effect weave an especially intricate and puzzling pattern, a social historian will usually step forth to help unravel the texture of that complexity. On the other hand, rarely, if ever, does our perception of a situation yield results equating with the experience of the small boy in the folktale who, with boldness born of innocence, declares that the emperor is naked, and thus illuminates reality for all of us in a stroke.

Yet it is simply apparent that the emperor of priorities in American education has been running around in a state of partial undress for a long time, for the priority asserted in behalf of educating the library user is of grotesquely small proportion. Historical analysis could probably unfold the particulars of the situation with considerable subtlety, but three brief observations can at least expose some dimensions of the problem.

First, students, faculty, and college administrators equate the mere addition of resources with the development of a better library. As they conspire to find more and more dollars for more and more resources on which to gorge, they rest apparently content to ignore the means by which those resources can be well digested. One can scarcely imagine, for example, that any chief officer at the college would not instinctively applaud the head librarian's submitting a library budget that projects a decrease in personnel costs and diverts the savings into library resources.

Second, scholars and would-be scholars assume that they can participate in the dialogue of educated persons (of all ages) without knowing how to consult the "memory of civilization," which is the library.

Third, students, faculty, and administrators embrace a myth, both actively and passively, that grievously wants exploding: that libraries are easy to use. That myth issues forth in a thousand expressions, all representing failure of the imagination. Two manifestations of the myth: the student who asserts with glib assurance that he has exhausted every route of access to resources on a topic; the faculty member who casually assumes that anything worth teaching about the library can surely be accomplished in an hour's time.

Hence an impasse to perceiving and understanding better the proper role of the library (and librarians) in the academic setting has bulked large among library users. Not only do they not know how to use libraries effectively, they do not know that they do not know. And instruction librarians, having assaulted that impasse, retreat with the vague certainty that there remains a new educational frontier out there, and that library user instruction deserves much more attention—devotion, even—from the entire educational establishment.

PRESENT STATE OF USER INSTRUCTION IN THE SMALL ACADEMIC LIBRARY

By what means, so far, have librarians attempted to focus that attention by creating a structure for educating the library user in small colleges? In what stage of construction does that edifice stand today, and how does it fit into the landscape of American education?

It is probably fair to characterize the efforts of user instruction librarians as having concentrated primarily on building, brick by brick, a structure that attends to certain details of solid construction. For example, instruction libraries have thoughtfully crafted various user performance objectives, specific techniques of instruction by which to reach those objectives, and means of assessing the outcome of that instruction. Furthermore, they have begun to learn the political role they must play in order to earn a permanent place in higher education. They have tried to build on carefully cultivated grass-roots support and not on the shifting sands of an empty rhetoric. Thus, they have aimed not to promise more than they could capably deliver.

In an attempt to gather concrete details of the present state of user instruction in the small academic library, a mail survey of 220 undergraduate institutions, primarily liberal arts colleges, was conducted during the winter of 1978. (For details of questionnaire and results see the Appendix to this chapter.) The expectation was aroused that from those details there would emerge generalized patterns of user instruction activity—predictors, possibly, of the shape of things to come.

To be sure, there are some encouraging signs in the survey results: the prevailing belief that the curricula of the graduate library schools must address the need for professional training of librarians for teaching, the tendency for evaluation of existing programs to exhibit positive results, widespread confidence that library administrators strongly support (at least morally, when dollars are few) the instructional efforts, and, indeed, the mere fact that most libraries do have some kind of instructional program going.

Just as surely, some evidence exists beyond the present survey that steady progress is being made against the tide of ignorance of effective library research strategies. Two potentially significant organs for the development and promulgation of library user instruction have recently been founded—the Association of College and Research Libraries' (ACRL) Bibliographic Instruction Section, and the

Library Instruction Round Table of the American Library Association (ALA). It is far too early to anticipate the eventual impact of these fledgling organizations, but surely the Bibliographic Instruction Section can broaden and extend the thrust of the ACRL Bibliographic Instruction Task Force; while the Library Instruction Round Table, with its broader role within the library profession, can be expected to push further the work of the ALA Instruction in the Use of Libraries Committee, and it may strive to emulate in quality the achievements of the Government Documents Round Table in so doing. The success of these organizations will be a measure of their cause.

Glancing elsewhere, current advertisements for professional staff in reference departments across the land now routinely include user instruction responsibilities in their job descriptions; Council on Library Resources Library Service Enhancement Program grants and National Endowment for the Humanities/ Council on Library Resources College Library Program grants have pumped valuable support into developing instruction programs; and the professional development of teaching librarians has continued to grow through numerous conferences and workshops, for example, those at Eastern Michigan University, Earlham College, and Pratt Institute (now transferred to the Columbia University School of Library Service). These are obvious emblems of concerted efforts now being made to advance library user instruction that were in scarce evidence, say 20 years ago.

Yet, looking to the survey tabulations for the kind of dramatic results in user instruction that would inspire confidence in the reliability of hopeful prognostications, one is likely to come away disappointed, if not confounded. The generalized patterns that emerge from an inquiry into the current state of user instruction in the college library are notable chiefly for their mildness and lack of dramatic import—no overwhelming trend toward the wedding of students' experiences in library user instruction with their actual course work ("integration"), no ground swell of participation and support by classroom teaching faculty and college administrations, an abiding sense that existing instructional programs are modestly developed and modestly successful, moderate use being made both of user performance objectives for instructional and subsequent evaluation of that instruction, tempered enthusiasm for conferences on teaching library use and the professional literature on the subject, little notion that the commitment of the library profession to instructing the user is overall very hearty, or that there is very much that is new under the user instruction sun. Do bland results, then, portend a bland future for instruction in the use of the small academic library?

Or is the situation even worse than that? For persistent critics of user instruction maintain that past efforts to teach library users the skills and habits for effective use has ended "not well, but miserably."[1] Apparently, in spite of encouraging signs, major problems persist.

FAILURE TO SOLVE THE USER INSTRUCTION PROBLEM

A clear measure of one problem is the widespread belief (a dominant theme clearly seen in the survey results) that user instruction has gained little cooperation and support from the rest of the academic community. Indeed, the gains have occurred chiefly within the library profession itself. Elsewhere—in dormitories, in faculty offices and clubs, in administrative executive sessions, in meetings of college boards of trustees—one may sense that the winds of change are shifting only slightly, at best; so what about the impact on teaching colleagues outside the library? Library instruction contributions to the academic enterprise will be severely limited if concentrated mainly within the library profession.

Part of the failure to solve the user instruction problem inheres, too, in the fact that good reasons exist why users' imaginations are stunted regarding library use, and why the myth has flourished that libraries are easy to use.

1. Many library procedures are, indeed, perfunctory in nature, and, as with amateur psychologizing, since everyone can do it a little, in no time at all one can feel comfortable as a self-styled expert.
2. Many of the library investigations users undertake are so ill chosen for their breadth of scope and lack of focus that random resources on a given topic practically fall off the shelves at users' feet, creating a false aura of success.
3. Reference librarians appear to function mechanically much of the time, as conduits between users and their required resources,[2] and do not always take time (or have time to take) with each user to weave a reference response into even the flimsiest fabric of instruction.
4. Users seldom ponder what resources they may have missed in the library, and unsought resources are like so many trees falling unheard in the forest—they make no noise.
5. Classroom teaching faculty do not generally enforce rigorous standards of quality for the library resources used by students in support of their research.
6. Library research is *always* auxiliary to other enterprises, and is therefore never the final object of the user's attention; nor should it become an end in itself.

The fact that reference librarians are commonly perceived to function as mechanical conduits has sometimes caused their teaching to appear mechanical as well, and instruction librarians have not always taken pains to overcome that liability. Occasionally, in fact, they must feel not a little like the bit character in the James Bond movie who customarily supplies Bond with an arsenal of gadgetry with which to confront his world. That long catalog of weapons is (one may note) of considerable survival interest to his client (Bond); but library clients, in their considerably less violent world of knowledge and ideas, are not nearly so motivated to assimilate lists of resources for not-quite-perceived future uses. The point is that effective use of the library is not a matter of life and death.

FINDING A SUPPORTIVE MODEL OR TRADITION

Given that fact, librarians have lacked a discoverable "body of theory" and a "methodology" by which to advance their instruction, to quote the responses of two librarians in the "open-ended" part of the survey. Viewed through this portal on reality, it seems that what contrives to hold them back is the lack of a useful, working tradition for library user instruction, encompassing both broad cultural support and a supportive "pedagogy," in the best sense of that word. When one casts about for evidence of the absence of a tradition for "learning the library," invidious comparisons between teaching library use and teaching, say, language skills, abound. The *New York Times* reports that Cornell University has appointed a "dean for writing"[3]; if a dean is appointed whose sole responsibility lies somewhere with the mustering of students' personal intellectual resources toward precise exposition, can one hope for a "dean for library instruction," whose charge it would be to ensure that students develop their capabilities to summon forth the intellectual resources and creative expressions of all human history? Can one imagine anyone lamenting, "The public schools just aren't teaching library research skills anymore"? Can one recall reading articles and books entitled "Why Johnny Can't Research"? Can one estimate the total annual financial expenditure in the United States for teaching composition, or even foreign languages, versus the amount spent for teaching use of the library? And how many professional journals exist for the sole purpose of improving instruction in language skills versus the number whose primary focus is the improvement of library user instruction? Instruction librarians lack a tradition that would furnish them with a philosophical base and a stability for their curriculum.

One cannot, of course, hope to spawn overnight a "new" tradition for library user instruction—the mere idea embraces a contradiction of terms, rather like spinning straw into gold. Yet it might be that the growth of a user instruction tradition could be hastened by an alliance with an existing tradition (projecting, of course, a marriage happy in conception and fruitfully productive). In so doing, one might learn useful lessons from a parallel model, and discover an identity that would help others perceive the usefulness of library user instruction in a new light.

IDENTIFYING WITH THE GENERAL MODEL OF LANGUAGE STUDY

It appears helpful, in looking around for useful models with which to identify, to view the library as belonging to the broad area of communications. The comparison is not gratuitous, for the role of libraries is to communicate "information" to users, and the role of user instruction is to facilitate that communication. Identifying with that tradition, one can explore the possibilities of further clarifying, refining, and articulating perceptions of what is being taught, and why and how it can best be taught. Even if the identification with that tradition turns out not to fit quite snugly (too early to say), one can at least use the tradition as a partial model for the teaching role.

The nearest models, then, are in the areas of language study, both written and oral. These fields are traditional to, and well represented in, every college curriculum; in spite of minor ebbs and flows of educational trends over the decades, it is obvious that they possess genuine stability. For example, after much erosion of required undergraduate courses in composition in the 1960s, the English composition teaching community is still busily exploring innovative ways of teaching writing. And although its heyday may have been before the turn of the century (when, at some institutions, every graduate was required to deliver a public oration), oral expression remains alive and well in many a college curriculum.

In addition to that broad cultural support, these fields of communications study own self-renewing pedagogies—inherited, used, and then built upon by successive generations of practitioners—and looking closely at the development of those pedagogies, one finds much to learn. For example, an examination of the struggles that have taken place on the battlegrounds of teaching composition (i.e., in the literature of the field over the years) reveals that composition instructors have groped for an identity as well as a methodology. Evidence is there of yearnings to escape the "service course" role and to locate the ultimate treasure—teachable subject content. In this endeavor they have largely failed, yet the importance of teaching composition, even without subject content, is clearly perceived.

Parallels with Teaching of Composition

In spite of some evidence that the teaching of composition has occasionally been held in low esteem, it appears that this sentiment has taken root in the reality that so few people know how to teach it well. Yet, useless techniques for teaching composition are being abandoned and new ones are evolving with renewed vigor. For example, though a few diehards may persist, most composition instructors have discovered that there is precious little point in trying to teach writing by exhorting students to master the intricacies of grammar as an abstract body of mechanics for writing, and —even outside the curriculum—"writing centers" are springing up at colleges and universities across the land, purveyors, in many cases, of new techniques of individualized instruction. Writing instructors are learning anew (if they ever forgot) that it can be as noble to teach process and craft as to teach subject content.

In generalizing a pattern from the preceding observations on the teaching of composition, three distinct elements in that tradition can be categorized.

1. *Existence of abiding philosophical support from the education community.* Cultural support for the teaching of writing has run broad and deep for a very long time. It dwells in the belief that the ability to express oneself effectively in writing is essential intellectual equipment for the educating person, and no educator needs persuading in that belief.
2. *Continual searching for a pedagogy—the theoretical and methodological base.* Efforts to establish workable principles for teaching writing have come nowhere near approaching ultimate development and universal acceptance. Indeed, attempts to solve the writing problem have been characterized by much trial-and-error bungling and many false starts. Yet, those efforts continue to receive unstinting support—never more so than now, in these days of open admissions and declining Scholastic Aptitude Test scores (verbal).
3. *Unabated efforts to refine theory into effective techniques and practices.* Although the mechanics intrinsic to good writing are timeless and universal, composition instructors have learned that merely focusing on the symptoms of poor writing accomplishes next to nothing by way of assuring that students' writing disabilities will be cured. They are constantly evolving new techniques out of newly emerging theories in an attempt to cure those ills.

It is important to recognize in the pattern outlined above that enduring efforts to solve the writing problem, however partial and incomplete they may prove, have been stimulated and carried forward as a result of pressure generated by society and its educational establishment.

If that is an accurate brief summation of the composition tradition, it is possible to examine the library instruction situation in a new light. In contrast with writing instructors, user instruction librarians have in no way felt cultural pressure, or even much pressure from the education establishment, to adopt and develop a teaching function. They have not even found it in significant measure when they went seeking a mandate. But, like teachers of writing, instruction librarians have realized that they own no subject content, and they have experienced much frustration in attempting to construe a body of theory beyond basic library search strategy to communicate to users, much less a methodology by which to teach it. So they have begun their work by basing it first on the direct evidence of user incompetence that bombards them daily. From that body of evidence they have perceived an implicit educational need, and they have tried to formulate and meet that need. By means reminiscent of grammarians—lo, those many years—they have, naturally enough, attempted to treat first the symptoms of library user disability.

In so doing, they have hoped that from their instructional efforts there would emerge a theoretical base that would attract enthusiastic support from their colleagues in education, and would win (almost incidentally) a tradition of broad cultural acceptance. Thus have they sought to work their way up the ladder of identity step by step into a useful tradition.

It has truly been a grass-roots effort, but it has not seized the popular imagination in education. Conversely, it has resulted in the need for instruction librarians to spend themselves endlessly re-creating their reason for being. Symbolizing that pattern is the situation of a faculty member who decides to participate in a library user instruction program for the first time, gives over a class period to the instruction librarian, does not view any dramatic and immediate results, and never comes back for more. An active tradition for library instruction would not accommodate such a facile rejection of thwarted purpose.

ESTABLISHING THE ELEMENTS OF
A USER INSTRUCTION TRADITION

What may be needed in order to establish the necessary three elements of a useful tradition of library user instruction is more vigorous approaches to the causes, rather than to the symptoms, of the user instruction problem.

Generating Philosophical Support for Educational Change. The heart of the user instruction matter is the belief that the ability to use libraries effectively ought to be viewed as one of the classic resources of the educated person, that it has hitherto been much neglected in formal education, and that a corrective is badly needed. These perceptions form the basis of a vision that must first be explored in our own minds and then communicated to others with merciless clarity. In so doing, it will be necessary to seek to change users' concepts of and attitudes toward libraries by demonstrating, for example: (1) that libraries are the dynamic memory of civilization—not static, unchanging repositories of an outworn past; (2) that this memory can be consulted as one consults one's own memory, albeit with difficulty—not easily; (3) that libraries demand active, inspired effort for their riches to be exploited fully—not passive, perfunctory applications of mere mechanical motion. These concepts must be communicated to students, faculty, and administrators, recognizing that faculty (directly) and administrators (indirectly) hold keys to the means of shaping students' concepts of library use. This vision should be espoused through any available forum; these, of course, vary from time to time and from one local situation to the next. But broad, as well as narrow, forums exist—for example, the literatures of the academic disciplines and of college administration.

Heretofore, instruction librarians have been shy to raise their rhetorical voices, for surely, it was felt, the actions and effectiveness of librarians speak eloquently for themselves. But one ought not to rely solely, or even principally, on *inductive* means to convince colleagues in education that the entire establishment has missed an important boat, or they will probably never reach that conclusion. Rather, another avenue of effecting change is through *deductive* means, and this implies the use of rhetorical skills in making a persuasive argument. So, an essential element in coining educational change out of fresh perceptions of the library is a thoughtfully shaped rhetoric, for myths (such as the one that libraries are easy to use) can be exploded only by a combination of evidence, logical argument, and rhetoric.

Of course, flourishes of rhetoric without substantive structure usually earn a deservedly swift death; yet rhetoric (nowadays unfairly used in the pejorative sense) assumes a necessary role in nearly any movement for change—witness the civil rights and women's liberation movements. For rhetoric to be effective in bringing about change, it requires a theoretical and logical base rooted not only in principles, but also in a vision of a need, possibilities for meeting that need, and the means of doing so. The rhetoric of instruction librarians, then, must not exist solely for the purpose of inducing others to share their vision, isolated from the content and method of their teaching;[4] rather, it should enhance everything that they communicate, and it is essential to establishing their identity. Whorfian theories of linguistics teach us that we create our language, and our language, in turn, creates us. Or, as Orwell points out, if our language corrupts our politics, our politics will surely corrupt us. In other words, instruction librarians can explore the correctness of their vision, the way they seek to implement it, and the nuts-and-bolts instructional activity by the means of improving their rhetoric; and, as the quality of the rhetoric improves, so will the quality of thinking about library user instruction.

Establishing User Instruction Theory and Methodology.   In order to discover the substance of the teaching, it is necessary to explore fully the individual perceptions that constitute the vision, and seek the logical extensions of those perceptions by which process the body of theory and methodology can become informed. In so doing, instruction librarians will discover the contribution to students' education that is distinctly theirs to make. The following are suggestions toward building a theory.

As instruction librarians, we need to establish teachable broad concepts of the library, for example: that it contains not just information (as in "information retrieval"), but also knowledge, data, ideas, opinions, stories, polemics, myths, wisdom, lies, facts, reports of research, memories, etc., and that all this immense variety is manifested in various genres of library materials, and in various formats. Furthermore, we need to lead students beyond the viewpoint of library research as simply the process of finding the right mechanical conduit, i.e., one question, leading to one source, yielding one answer.

We need to teach the concepts of research that often are given short shrift by our colleagues in the classroom, for example, concepts (but not the mechanical forms) of documentation; for another, the use of primary versus secondary resources in library research.

We need to teach students the process of selecting and shaping workable topics, if only because very many of our colleagues in the classroom default on this important aspect of research design. In adopting this teaching function we need to be sensitive to the boundaries of our expertise and the potential hazard of intruding on the course instructor's prerogative in the matter. Yet, our hesitation here maintains a vacuum in most students' educational experiences.

We need to teach the role of the library in the thinking process, for example, that sources of information in the library may be crucial to an examination of the major and minor premises that underlie logical analysis.

We need to teach students that all library resources are not created equal. In other words, students need to learn use of library resources for critical evaluation of sources—for example, use of book reviews, annotated bibliographies, review articles, biographical sources, citation indexes—and perhaps beyond those, students' own resources for exerting critical judgment.

We ought to learn to exert our own evaluation of students' work, for example, by examining with students their research progress, and then pointing out to them the level at which their bibliographic efforts reside in the range of possibilities for exploiting resources on the topic.

In order to communicate our theory, we need to inform our methodology; following are some suggested possibilities.

We need to find the best ways of stimulating students' thinking about library research, for example, by using the traditional methods of comparison and contrast—even metaphor. Specific example: can we explore the differences between flabby and shapeless research topics versus ones exhibiting sharp focus and built-in energy?

We might inquire into possibilities for teaching imaginative new uses of reference resources, in addition to the traditional uses. Examples: Can a quotations dictionary in any way be used as an index to the history of some ideas? Can the scope of an index such as the *Monthly Catalog of U.S. Government Publications* tell us anything about the priorities of our government?

We may want to look for effective ways of inspiring our students to stimulate, and then respond to, their hitherto unfelt information needs. We may do so by providing them with affective, as well as cognitive, learning experiences wherein they learn to take delight in recovering information—for example, by teaching them how half an hour spent with the last five annual cumulations of the *New York Times Index* can provide them with a surprising body of overview knowledge about developments on a specific topic—say, abortion—in recent years.

We ought to find ways of preparing students for dealing with the frustrations of library use, for example, by teaching the inadequacy of subject access to books through Library of Congress headings; or, for another, the prospect that certain indexes yield access to sources that will probably not be locatable in the college library a great percentage of the time.

We should develop ways of illuminating the qualitative differences between various resources pertaining to a topic, for example, a news article on multinational corporations versus: a scholarly article, testimony in Senate hearings, an article in *Reader's Digest*, a statistical source.

Refining Techniques and Practices of User Instruction.   The preceding discussions of philosophical principles and the theories and methodology of user instruction carry logical implications for activities in the classroom and at the reference desk. If instruction librarians adopt the principle stated earlier that it is necessary to attack the causes, not so much the symptoms, of library user ignorance, then classroom instruction should emphasize concepts of libraries, and of library use, such as those suggested above. They should avoid classroom presentations devoted mainly to mechanics, for example, the specific use of specific tools on a list. When the focus is on specifics, such as a transparency of a page from a source, they should be used to illustrate general principles, for example, how one uses an overview source as a springboard for a research paper topic. Or, a specific source could be used to suggest the range of information possibilities, for example, that one can find out how many people have indoor plumbing in one's home neighborhood. A list of the basic reference resources for research in the subject field probably should be provided to the student only at the end of the presentation, and the idea should be presented that instruction will continue at the reference desk (or in conference in library offices) as specific difficulties inevitably arise. If worksheets prove helpful for students, they should be used, but they should not constitute exercises unrelated to students' actual research projects.

In the follow-up tutorial work responses should be worked into the context of the previous instruction. Most tutorial work should involve systematically evaluating with students their research progress: topic selection and research design, use of overview sources, appropriateness of access sources to the purpose, evaluation of resources, etc. As instruction librarians perform these functions with students from courses in which they have made presentations, these students will increasingly come to seek the librarians' expertise in the context of other courses.

Furthermore, it is important to reduce the involvement with teaching mechanics of use of resources at the reference desk. Although the mechanics of library use will not automatically take care of themselves (as a result of their not having been taught), they should probably be dealt with primarily by mechanical measures. To perform this function reference librarians will need thoughtfully produced handouts (or point-of-use media packages), each detailing isolable library procedures, for example, finding government documents, using indexes and abstracts, and the like. Questions will still arise about their use, to be sure, but they will be specific ones requiring only specific responses, not the repeated elaborations some librarians now find so necessary in working with students individually.

All this ought not to imply that traditional information services should be forsaken, for reference librarians should, of course, continue to supply users with the costs per ton/mile for shipping by rail versus by truck, for example. Rather, what the preceding discussion pertains to is an expanded role for reference librarians, and the relationship between effective classroom instruction and tutorial reference desk activity.

This discussion is intended to suggest (certainly not to define comprehensively) a possible route to a very large goal. Not all of these ideas represent entirely new thinking, of course; they draw upon a large body of useful work that has been carried on and reported in the past. Nevertheless, these suggestions argue a new emphasis for, and an extension of, approaches to library user instruction that have proven most useful.

No one, of course, would consciously wish to be indicted for runaway idealism, and the suggested means to the goal espoused here—establishing a user instruction tradition in the small academic library—may seem to some librarians unconscionably grand, if not grandiose. Yet, the impasse to users' understanding of the library is worthy of our best efforts to dislodge it, and the myths about library use ought to be challenged repeatedly until they are driven off the land.

Whether or not the approaches to solving the library user instruction problem advanced here prove to be a useful guide, surely any major progress that is made in furthering the education of students for more effective library use will be measured both by the strength of instruction librarians' vision and by the imagination and energy exerted by them to establish a sound teaching tradition. Furthermore, the means must be improved for communicating that vision outside the profession, and for sharing within the profession newly emerging theories and techniques that prove effective. Finally, as a necessary catalyst to that instruction, librarians must seek to inspire all of their constituencies—students, faculty, college administrators, indeed, all of society—to know, and better understand, "How index-learning turns no student pale/Yet holds the eel of Science by the tail"—Pope, *Dunciad*, I, 279.

NOTES

1. William A. Katz, *Introduction to Reference Work, Volume II: Reference Services and Reference Processes*, 2nd ed. (New York: McGraw-Hill, 1974), p. 63.
2. Indeed, responsible voices within the library profession espouse the view that our professionalism inheres in just that sort of mechanical expertise—plugging users into the appropriate information sources. Katz, for example, compares librarians with mechanics and doctors. Ibid., p. 62.
3. *New York Times*, February 7, 1977, p. 1.
4. Corollary to this view is the notion that librarians should not merely seek to instruct students, but to inspire them as well to make better use of libraries.

APPENDIX: RESULTS AND ANAYLSIS OF QUESTIONNAIRE SURVEY ON USER INSTRUCTION

Regarding the design of the questionnaire, this researcher was early on pricked with the desire to investigate not only some of the facts about current practices in library user education, but also opinions of instruction librarians and their perceptions of their own effectiveness, problems, needs, and the like. The result was a questionnaire that was intentionally "soft" in methodology. As such, it is amenable to the kinds of criticisms that can be made of any impressionistic survey leading to speculative interpretation.

The questionnaire was sent out mid-January, 1978, to 220 academic libraries at institutions self-identified as liberal arts, with enrollments ranging from about 500 to 3,000 students. By April, 160 responses had been received, for a total return of 72.7%. Considering the glut of questionnaires that commonly bombard the desks of librarians, and considering the amount of respondent time demanded by the length and design of this particular instrument, one can only conclude that a nearly 73% response betokens almost raging current interest of librarians in the matter of educating the users of college libraries.

A total of 136 (85%) of the small college libraries surveyed perceive themselves as having an "ongoing program of user instruction" (not including incidental instruction in the course of consultations at the reference desk). Of these, 135 (99.3%) provide library *orientation* to both individuals and groups, 121 (89%) are involved with *instruction* to individuals, and 135 (99.3%) involve themselves with group *instruction*. Despite the much-heralded media revolution, limited use of nonprint media was reported by user instruction librarians: 41 (30.4%) programs doing orientation (n = 135) use some form of nonprint media for that purpose; and 31 (25.6%) programs instructing individuals (n =121) use a form of nonprint media for this purpose. Regarding use of nonprint media other than overhead transparencies with group instruction, the following pattern of use was indicated (n =135):

usually: 9 (6.7%)
sometimes: 29 (21.5%)
seldom: 10 (7.4%)
almost never: 80 (59.3%)
[no response: 7 (5.2%)]

Regarding frequency of use of overhead transparencies in that setting:

usually: 25 (18.5%)
sometimes: 16 (11.9%)
seldom: 8 (5.9%)
almost never: 79 (58.5%)
[no response: 7 (5.2%)]

By contrast, the library tour format is used by 118 (87.4%) respondents (n =135) for orientation, and even by 90 (66.7%; n =135) respondents for group instruction ("in-depth" tour).

As might be expected, the most commonly used format for group instruction is the single-session classroom presentation, according to the results of the survey, for it is used by 112 (83%) responding libraries doing group instruction. Considerably fewer librarians responding (46—34.1%) reported taking the opportunity to develop their presentations over a period of time in multiple sessions with a given group.

Regarding the perennial issue of credit courses versus integrated instruction (the backbone of which, presumably, is the classroom-style presentation mentioned above), not only are the credit courses far less common, as one might expect, but the credit courses are most often general in nature, as opposed to being tailored to a particular subject. These and other details are illuminated in the accompanying table.

Orientation of individuals and/or groups: 135 (99.3%)
   specified means: tours: 118 (87.4%)
                 printed handouts: 109 (80.7%)
                 audiocassette: 10 (7.4%)
                 filmstrip or slides: 12 (15.6%)
                 slide/tape: 21 (15.6%)
                 videotape: 10 (7.4%)
                 other media: 6 (4.4%)
                 lectures/discussions: 13 (9.6%)
Instruction to individuals: 121 (89%)
   specified means: printed handouts: 100 (82.6%)
                 programmed instruction (printed):   11 (9.1%)
                 audiocassette: 7 (5.8%)
                 filmstrip or slides: 8 (6.6%)
                 slide/tape: 18 (14.9%)
                 videotape: 5 (4.1%)
                 computer-assisted: 1 (0.8%)
                 "tutorial" instruction: 62 (51.2%)

Instruction to Groups: 135 (99.3%)

Type of Instruction	*General*	*Subject-tailored*
"In-depth" tours (beyond orientation)	57 (42.2%)	76 (56.3%)
Single-session classroom presentation	51 (37.8%)	108 (86.4%)
Multisession classroom presentations	16 (11.9%)	37 (27.4%)
Noncredit mini-courses, clinics, etc.	20 (14.8%)	20 (14.8%)
Credit courses taught by librarian(s)	31 (23.0%)	13 (9.6%)

Instruction librarians commonly conceive that handouts tailor made to the presentation in class will enable users to refer to material presented, as the frequency of their use indicates:
   usually: 74 (54.8%)
   sometimes: 41 (30.4%)
   seldom: 12 (8.9%)
   almost never: 7 (5.2%)
   [no response: 1 (0.7%)]
Use of worksheets, exercises, and the like, in accompaniment with group instruction, is less commonly practiced:
   usually: 31 (23%)
   sometimes: 38 (28.1%)
   seldom: 18 (13.3%)

almost never: 41 (30.4%)
[no response: 7 (5.2%)]

The questionnaire asked if there are forms of instruction with which respondents have become "disenchanted," and 51 (37.8%) expressed misgivings about one or more forms of instruction. Specified responses divide neatly into two categories: 20 (39.2%) of the disenchanted faulted one kind of media or another, while 36 (70.6%) pilloried some form of group instruction. (Several respondents mentioned forms of instruction falling into both categories.) Within those broad categories, slide/tape incurred the most disfavor in the former; whereas, in the latter, general group instruction unrelated to a specific purpose (especially "new student" tours) aroused the most enmity.

The questionnaire attempted to analyze the nature of instruction librarians' involvement with faculty generally, and in various academic divisions and departments. Incidentally, at 100 (73.5%) of the 136 reporting libraries, professional librarians enjoy either faculty rank or status (or both), while at 26 (19.1%) they do not. [Other: head librarian only—7 (5.1%); some professional staff only—1 (0.7%); no response—2 (1.5%).]

Asked to estimate the percentage of their *total* user instruction effort that is integrated with course work in the regular curriculum, respondents perceived widely varying degrees of integration of their instruction.

Estimated percentage of instruction that is integrated:

   0-24% integrated: 20 (14.7%)
   25-49% integrated: 18 (13.2%)
   50-74% integrated: 26 (19.1%)
   75-99% integrated: 38 (28%)
   100% integrated: 12 (8.8%)
   [no response: 22 (16.2%)]

In attempting to discern in another way the degree of integration of instruction with course content, the questionnaire asked respondents to estimate the percentage of departments (or interdisciplinary programs) on campus making conscious use of instruction programs. The range of responses shows that departmental breadth of user instruction integrated with regular course offerings is quite varied among the libraries surveyed.

Estimated percentage of departments involved with user instruction:

   0-24% of departments: 37 (27.2%)
   25-49% of departments: 37 (27.2%)
   50-74% of departments: 19 (14%)
   75-99% of departments: 8 (5.9%)
   100% of departments: 2 (1.5%)
   [no response: 33 (24.3%)]

One respondent questioned whether breadth of involvement with academic departments is a necessarily desirable pattern—surely a valid philosophical question. An individual library's response to that question would dictate certain strategies for involvement with faculty on a given campus, for example, whether instructional efforts should be keyed to a few select departments.

Respondents were asked to list the three departments/programs on their campuses that were most receptive to integrated bibliographic instruction, and the results produced the following list of departments receiving ten or more mentions (number of times mentioned and percentage of respondents in parentheses):

English (81: 59.6%)
History (41: 30.1%)
Education (35: 25.7%)
Political Science (31: 22.8%)
Sociology (31: 22.8%)
Biology (29: 21.3%)
Psychology (18: 13.2%)
Religion (14: 10.3%)
Economics and business (13: 9.6%)
[no response: 10 (7.4%)]

Being asked, then, to list the three departments/programs that would seem to profit most (for example, because they require a large quantity of student research; or because access to their literature is complex, or diverse, etc.) from user instruction, but that have not shown an interest to date, respondents generated in varying order exactly the same list of departments (plus an additional two at the bottom) mentioned ten or more times:

Psychology (33: 24.3%)
History (31: 22.8%)
Education (25: 18.4%)
English (23: 16.9%)
Economics and business (23: 16.9%)
Sociology (21: 15.4%)
Biology (15: 11%)
Political Science (15: 11%)
Religion (14: 10.3%)
Chemistry (11: 8.1%)
Art (10: 7.4%)
[no response: 27 (19.9%)]

Repetition of department names from the "most responsive" list to the "least responsive" list would seem to indicate: (a) certain departments not on either list (for example, philosophy) are commonly perceived not to be especially fertile soil for sowing the seeds of user instruction; (b) there is still considerable headway to be gained in advancing user instruction on many campuses, namely, those where departments on the former list would occur on the latter list; and (c) though vagaries of local situations will likely exist, instruction librarians may most profitably focus their efforts on the nine departments making both lists.

In light of Ralph Perkins's 1965 study of prospective teachers' library skills—especially his perception that the training of primary and secondary school teachers may represent an approach to breaking the cycle of generally widespread ignorance of principles of effective library use[1]—this researcher was interested in an investigation of the current pattern of involvement of education departments with user instruction in small colleges. Indeed, 126 (92.7%) of the libraries surveyed serve an education department. Those respondents were asked to rate, on scales of one to four, (a) the extent to which their education departments require library research, and (b) the extent to which their education students are instructed in the use of the library. Following are the responses.

Estimated extent of research required of education students (n = 126):

1 (great extent):   11 (8.7%)
2   39 (31%)
3   35 (27.8%)
4 (little extent): 35 (27.8%)
[no response: 6 (4.8%)]

Estimated extent of instruction to education students:

1 (great extent):   13 (10.3%)
2   28 (22.2%)
3   35 (27.8%)
4 (little extent): 38 (30.2%)
[no response: 12 (9.5%)]

A matrix of the responses to the two questions (not shown) indicates that even when responses tend toward an indication of "great extent" of research required of education students ("1" or "2" checked on the scale), the instruction afforded these students tends toward "great extent" in only 25 libraries (19.8%) of the sample. These results inspire little confidence that current crops of teachers will be capable of transmitting a fresh vision of library use to future generations of primary and secondary school students, let alone be able to identify and satisfy their own professional (and personal) information needs.

Another section of the questionnaire attempted to assess the planning and administration of user instruction programs. Respondents (n = 136) were queried as to the degree of overall administrative support for their programs, both within and outside the library.

Estimated commitment to and support for program by *library* administration:

1 (high):   105 (77.2%)
2   20 (14.7%)
3   3 (2.2%)
4 (low):   2 (1.5%)
[no response: 6 (4.4%)]

Estimated commitment to and support for program by *college* administration:

1 (high):   29 (21.3%)
2   40 (29.4%)
3   33 (24.3%)
4 (low):   23 (16.9%)
[no response: 11 (8.1%)]

The perceived level of support by library administrators may suggest that the user instruction "movement" is thought to be riding a crest within the profession, whereas the level of support indicated on behalf of college administrators surely indicates that much remains to be done to convince them that this instructional vacuum exists (has always existed) in education generally.

In order to establish some measure of the extent to which user education programs have become "institutionalized" in their local settings, the questionnaire asked respondents whether user instruction is specifically represented in their libraries' budgets: 15 (11%) responded yes and 116 (85.3%) responded no [no response—5 (3.7%)]. Asking if the program is institutionalized in another way yielded a response of 67 (49.3%) yes and 59 (43.4%) no [no response—10 (7.4%)]. Of those responding yes to the question (n = 67), 51 (76.1%) checked annual reports as a vehicle for institutionalizing their program and 24 (35.8%) checked the category "special reports." Clearly, many libraries with instruction programs have yet to develop the potentially long-range asset of existing on paper, for the effective institutionalizing of user instruction can help to assure continuity of support, can gain desirable visibility for the program, and can tend to fuel continuation of the program within the library—in the face of internal staff changes or shifting priorities, for examples.

Do libraries responding to the survey have concrete plans for the future development of their instruction? Response: 102 (75%) do, and 32 (23.6%) do not [no response—2 (1.5%)]; and somewhat more of those who have such plans (n = 102) tend to perceive a greater need for quantitative growth (need to reach more students) than for qualitative growth (improvement of what they are now doing)— 32 (31.4%) to 15 (14.7%). However, most librarians with concrete plans—53 (52%)— see about equal need for quantitative and qualitative growth of their programs.

In terms of respondent perceptions of their library's own stage of development of a user instruction program, the following data tend to support the conclusion that many instruction programs remain far from maturity.

Estimate of individual libraries' state of program development:
about full blown: 3 (2.2%)
well along: 27 (19.9%)
modestly developed: 59 (43.4%)
just begun: 34 (25%)
[no response: 13 (9.6%)]

In the past, a commonly perceived hallmark of a solidly established program of library user instruction has been the development and use of performance objectives by which to locate the basis for instruction and measure its results. Probably the best-known performance objectives for instruction in library use are those developed by the ACRL Bibliographic Instruction Task Force in 1975.[2] However, performance objectives are used by only 50 (36.8%) of the respondents, including those who use them only in credit courses. Even at that, extent of use of performance objectives is not generally high.

Estimated extent of use of performance objectives (n = 50):
1 (great extent):   10 (20%)
2   13 (26%)
3   16 (32%)
4 (little extent):   9 (18%)
[no response: 2 (4%)]

That performance objectives have yet to find widespread use by instruction librarians arouses the suspicion that steady evaluation of programs, based on firm factual foundations, remains very much in its infancy in college libraries, perhaps because of the time and effort involved in establishing them and evaluating the degree to which they are being achieved.

Exactly half the respondents (68) have attempted some assessment of the outcome of their instruction. Those who have *not* evaluated align themselves in

almost classic distribution when asked to gauge impressionistically the overall
effectiveness of their programs.

Impressionistic assessment of outcome of instruction (n = 68):

    1 (highly effective):   6 (8.8%)
    2   21 (30.9%)
    3   26 (38.2%)
    4 (slightly effective):   7 (10.3%)
    [no response: 8 (11.8%)]

Thus, librarians who have no quantified measure of their teaching effectiveness
can scarcely be characterized as overwhelmingly confident that they are achieving
the desired results.

Those who have evaluated their instruction, on the other hand, have tended to
find more positive results.

Estimate of overall results of evaluation (n = 68):

    1 (very positive):   15 (22.1%)
    2   28 (41.2%)
    3   19 (27.9%)
    4   4 (5.9%)
    5   1 (1.5%)
    6 (negative):   0
    [no response: 1 (1.5%)]

For this question six options, rather than the usual four, were provided in order
to enable finer distinctions, but the difference in question design may vitiate
comparison with the results reported earlier from responses made by librarians
who had evaluated only impressionistically.

Nevertheless, those librarians who have evaluated their instruction have tended
to employ "soft" measures (for example, surveys of attitudes) in so doing.

Means used by those who have evaluated their instruction (n = 68):

    testing user performance: 29 (42.6%)
    measuring performance in another way: 17 (25%)
    surveying faculty attitudes: 41 (60.3%)
    surveying student attitudes: 50 (73.5%)

Some respondents checked more than one means of evaluation. Regarding their
purposes in evaluating, respondents created the following ranking (multiple
responses possible—n = 68):

    improvement of instruction program: 61 (89.7%)
    justify program to self: 29 (42.6%)
    justify program to faculty: 27 (39.7%)
    justify program to college administration: 21 (30.9%)
    justify program to library administration: 12 (17.6%)

For all that, evaluation was perceived to tend only slightly toward being helpful
in improving programs of instruction.

Estimate of evaluation helpfulness toward improving a program (n = 68):

    1 (great extent):   13 (19.1%)
    2   25 (36.8%)
    3   14 (20.6%)
    4 (small extent):   11 (16.2%)
    [no response: 5 (7.4%)]

In recent years we have seen instruction librarians pushing on several fronts for the inclusion of courses in the curricula of the graduate library schools to prepare librarians for their teaching function. Predictably few responding libraries have staff members who have already taken such a course for graduate credit: 12 out of 136 (8.8% versus 89% who have not) [no response—3 (2.2%)]. Of those who have not taken such a course (n = 121), 38 (31.4%) were aware that courses do exist; 78 (64.5%) were not [no response—5 (4.1%)]. Asked whether graduate credit courses in theory, methods, and materials of educating library users ought to be offered, 108 (79.4%) responded yes; 9 (6.6%) responded no; and 12 (8.8%) were undecided [no response—7 (5.1%)]. Only one person who had taken a course felt that such courses should not form a part of the library school curriculum; another was undecided.

Respondents were asked if their instruction programs had consciously borrowed ideas and/or materials from other librarians and their programs. Most, of course, had borrowed: yes—120 (88.2%); no—12 (8.8%) [no response—4 (2.9%)]. Following is a list of sources of borrowing, ranked in order of popularity with respondents who have borrowed (n = 120):

    informal discussions with outside librarians: 103 (85.9%)
    literature of librarianship: 99 (82.5%)
    conferences and workshops: 83 (69.2%)
    staff meetings and discussions "in house":   72 (60%)
    clearinghouses, for example, Project LOEX: 61 (50.8%)
    contacts made through directories: 21 (17.5%)
    [no response: 4 (3.3%)]

Regarding the overall usefulness of conferences and workshops to those who have borrowed from them in developing a user instruction program (n = 94):

    1 (highly useful):   20 (21.3%)
    2   32 (34%)
    3   35 (37.2%)
    4 (of little use):   7 (7.4%)

Regarding the overall usefulness of the literature of librarianship to those who have kept up with it in developing a user instruction program (n = 125):

    1 (highly useful):   13 (10.4%)
    2   52 (41.6%)
    3   43 (34.4%)
    4 (of little use):   17 (13.6%)

The last two sections of the questionnaire asked the individual respondents to express some personal views about user instruction trends. First was their rating of the total library profession's commitment to, and support for, library user instruction (six choices again permitted a more precise response than the customary four; n = 136):

    excessive: 3 (2.2%)
    about what it should be: 19 (14%)
    approaching a proper balance: 38 (27.9%)
    not what it should be: 49 (36%)
    quite inadequate: 15 (11%)
    pitifully meager: 3 (2.2%)
    [no response: 9 (6.6%)]

A nearly bell-shaped curve emerges, with just a slight tendency toward the negative spectrum. Respondents were then asked to estimate how far librarians have come:

(a) in terms of *identifying* the proper approaches to user instruction
    responses: 1 (very far):   12 (8.8%)
                 2   40 (29.4%)
                 3   51 (37.5%)
                 4 (just begun):   27 (19.9%)

(b) in terms of *developing* the specific techniques of effective instruction
    responses: 1 (very far):   3 (2.2%)
                 2   33 (24.3%)
                 3   64 (47.1%)
                 4 (just begun):   30 (22.1%)

(c) in terms of *implementing* those techniques on a widespread basis
    responses: 1 (very far):   3 (2.2%)
                 2   14 (10.3%)
                 3   59 (43.4%)
                 4 (just begun):   54 (39.7%)

[no response to all three of the above series of questions: 6 (4.4%)]

The overall pattern indicates that many user instruction librarians feel that large-scale accomplishments remain ahead of us in the field.

Second, personal responses were solicited to some "open-ended" questions in the last section of the survey, and these results are difficult to quantify; 80 (58.8%) of the respondents answered one or more of the questions.

In identifying the most "distinctive, unusual, or exciting aspect" of their instructional programs, many persons forwarded general responses (for example, "Just getting started is exciting"), but some mentioned specific developments, for example, creation of a new slide show. Most responses pertained either to some aspect of arousing enthusiasms of faculty, students, and other staff members for user instruction, or to the achievement of some new measure of integration of user instruction with students' regular course work.

Asked if there were new ideas about user instruction that they would like to begin exploring and developing, most respondents sounded the familiar themes: integration of instruction with course work, development of self-paced instruction for individuals, audiovisual developments, and stimulation of faculty involvement with user instruction.

In expressing their greatest support needs, most respondents mentioned time, staff, and money; faculty involvement and support for their program; and support from the college administration generally.

Asking what the user instruction "movement" most needs at this time elicited the familiar yearnings for faculty and college administration involvement in user instruction, and also for development of increased support within the library profession. Other commonly mentioned needs were for the development of ways of presenting instruction (expressed, for example, as "methodological foundations"); proponents for further research on, and evaluation of, user instruction were abundantly in evidence. Also posited as a need by some respondents was something variously referred to as "intellectual goals," "a body of theory," and "historical, philosophical, and theoretical research" for the advancement of library user education.

APPENDIX NOTES

1. Ralph Perkins, *The Prospective Teacher's Knowledge of Library Fundamentals* (New York: Scarecrow, 1965), p. 195.
2. American Library Association, Association of College and Research Libraries Bibliographic Instruction Task Force, "Toward Guidelines for Bibliographic Instruction in Academic Libraries," *College & Research Libraries News*, no. 5 (May 1975), pp. 137–139, 169–171.

LIBRARY INSTRUCTION IN UNIVERSITY UNDERGRADUATE LIBRARIES

Allan J. Dyson

Head, Moffitt Undergraduate Library, University of California, Berkeley

Perhaps the most difficult library instruction task is the one faced by the staffs of university undergraduate libraries. A recent report indicated a 1976–1977 average of 5,416 undergraduate students per undergraduate librarian in these libraries,[1] more students than are found in the entire undergraduate population at most colleges. And many of the librarians are busy selecting books, running technical services units, or managing these libraries, in addition to any public service programs they hope to provide.

It is not surprising, therefore, that Passarelli and Abell painted a relatively bleak picture in their excellent essay on university undergraduate libraries some five years ago.[2] Despite the fact that one of the purposes of an undergraduate library is to serve as a base for instruction in library use,[3] they found a disturbing lack of such activity. As they put it, "considering . . . that the goal of active programs has been legitimized repeatedly in the literature, it is alarming to find so few in this group [of undergraduate libraries] actually responding to the challenge, or even considering a response in the immediate future."[4]

Other studies confirm the lack of the library instruction activities in undergraduate libraries. Billy R. Wilkinson, in his 1971 article "A Screaming Success as Study Halls," found the libraries serving a useful "social-center" function, providing a good basic browsing collection and reserve book service, and supplying a convenient and comfortable location for students to study their own materials, but seriously lacking in reference and instructional services.[5] Dyson, in the 1973–1974 research for his Council on Library Resources fellowship study of administrative patterns in university library instruction programs, found only a limited amount of activity based in undergraduate libraries. In addition, he found that the most extensive programs tended to be at medium-sized universities such as Eastern Michigan and Southern Illinois–Edwardsville, schools without separate undergraduate libraries.[6] Thus, research in the period 1970–1973 indicated a clear failure on the part of university undergraduate libraries to establish themselves as centers for educating library users.

One could easily assume that little happened in the intervening five years to change that fact. "Steady-state" or declining budgets have generally been the rule; these presumably would have hurt undergraduate library services the same as those elsewhere on campus. Several small undergraduate reading room collections have been disbanded or integrated into main libraries, which one author, in a poorly reasoned article, interpreted as signaling the beginning of the end of the separate undergraduate library.[7] It is not clear to the public that university libraries, let alone undergraduate libraries, should provide library instruction at all—a 1978 article in *Publishers Weekly* stated offhandedly that teaching students how to use the library is "a responsibility which, if assumed at all in universities, is taken over by faculty members."[8]

CURRENT LIBRARY INSTRUCTION TRENDS

In order to see if previous studies of library instruction in university undergraduate libraries remain accurate, a survey was conducted in early 1978 of the 25 largest such libraries in the United States and Canada. Almost all the libraries have been in operation for some time; only one (SUNY–Buffalo) opened after the Passarelli and Abell study was completed. The libraries surveyed had professional staffs of three FTE or more, and contained both a collection of open-shelf materials that could be charged out for one to four weeks, depending on the library, and materials on reserve for undergraduate classes.[9] Most undergraduate libraries meeting these criteria are housed in buildings separate from the main (or research) library, and in fact some authors define "undergraduate library" in this way.[10] This criterion was not used, however, and undergraduate libraries differently housed—for example, in a separate wing of the main building—that otherwise met the criteria were included in the survey.

All libraries replied; however, the questionnaire from one Canadian library was received too late for inclusion. The high response rate plus the extensive comments included in cover letters and on the questionnaires is indicative of the great interest in the topic on the part of undergraduate librarians.

The first and most important finding of the survey is that there has been a substantial increase in the amount of time spent on library orientation and bibliographic instruction over the past five years.[11] Despite budget crises and other problems, not a single library reported having cut back on its library instruction program. Only three libraries, in fact, were running their programs at the same level over the five-year period, a surprising 21 of the 24 reporting increased activity. Several librarians included comments describing the change; the questionnaire remarks below are typical:

> Over the last five years, library instruction has evolved from nothing to a fully developed course. Need and demand, as well as the stated mission of the undergraduate library, along with energetic librarians dedicated to library instruction, helped foster the atmosphere to provide a program.

The existence of "energetic librarians dedicated to library instruction" is no accident. Twenty-two of the 24 libraries include "ability to participate in bibliographic instruction program" as part of their hiring criteria for librarians, and for half of the 22 this criterion has been added within the past five years. As one librarian put it:

> We now have instructional activities written into all undergraduate librarian job descriptions, and we look for past teaching experience or related instructional experience in a candidate.

The greater commitment to library instruction is coming not only from the public service staff, but also from the administration in the undergraduate library. Several replies noted that it was the appointment of a new head librarian that give impetus to an expanded program. Others reported that additional money or staffing was found to help the program along. Once started, the programs often begin to generate their own momentum if genuine educational needs are met. As one librarian commented, "Faculty expectations grow as needs are met." This in turn feeds back to the hiring process; another commented, "We are making the emphasis on library instruction stronger each time we hire a new librarian."

Why has there been such an expansion of library instruction activities? The questionnaire replies point to several reasons. First, many librarians feel strongly that it is a professional responsibility to teach users how to make the best use of library resources, and, specifically, that the undergraduate library should be in the forefront in educating its particular clientele. As one librarian put it,

> The Undergraduate Library must be active in educating the library's users and is not offering full bibliographic services unless it is a leader on campus in such activity.

Another commented that while the undergraduate library will not stand or fall on whether it has a bibliographic instruction program, without one "it will stand in mediocrity."

Second, library instruction is seen as a way of dealing with a seemingly endless number of clients. One librarian summed up this view as follows:

> With limited resources, libraries cannot afford to spend unlimited time on a one-to-one basis dealing with the same basic problems and questions.

It seems possible, however, that the result of these programs might not be a reduction of the work load at reference desks, but rather a substitution of a smaller number of more sophisticated (and time-consuming) questions for larger numbers of repetitive and boring ones.

Third, some librarians mentioned the need for a more visible professional identity, in part because of the move toward at least titular faculty status. Librarians must often prove themselves to be "real faculty," in fact as well as title.

The final reason was a sense of self-preservation. Often faced with decreasing enrollments and budgets reduced by inflation, campuses are taking a hard look at all activities, and to be visible and identified with the teaching/learning process is to survive. As one librarian put it,

> Unless faculty and academic departments . . . utilize the library as an integral aspect of the educational process as opposed to apart from it, the real potential of the undergraduate library will never be realized (except as a place for getting reserve materials)— and for many this will spell their demise.

This may well suggest the reason for the abandonment of a number of small (and often poorly staffed) undergraduate reading rooms within the past few years. Where the collections simply duplicated main library resources, they seemed a frill—especially when a new, often open-stack, research library was built. But where a full range of undergraduate services is offered—including handy access to a "core collection," user-oriented high quality reference service, and extensive library instruction programs—the undergraduate library is thriving.

NEW ADMINISTRATIVE PATTERNS

As one might expect, the trend toward substantially increased library instruction programs for undergraduates has brought with it the need to affix the responsibility for such activities more clearly, both within the library system and within the undergraduate library. In most library systems with undergraduate libraries, that responsibility now belongs to the undergraduate library staff. Of the 24 libraries responding, 19 indicated they had such responsibility. In four other instances the responsibility was held by, or shared with the undergraduate library by, the head of the main library reference department or the head of an instructional services unit library-wide. In only one instance was no responsibility taken for undergraduate library instruction within the library system.

While it is hardly startling to learn that most undergraduate libraries have assumed responsibility for teaching their primary clientele how to use the library, the pattern of responsibility within the undergraduate library is more interesting (see Table 1). Almost half of the programs (11 of 24) are now coordinated by a specifically designated library instruction coordinator. This is a recent administrative pattern; 10 of the 11 coordinators have been assigned their responsibilities within the last five years. The typical coordinator spends one-quarter to one-half time on library instruction, and reports directly to the head of the undergraduate library. It should be emphasized that the coordinator is not responsible for giving all the instruction; almost all responses noted that most or all of the librarians took part in the activity. This particular approach probably bodes well for undergraduate library instruction programs. Dyson, in his Council on Library Resources research mentioned above, concluded that the most effective

Table 1. **Coordination of Library Instruction within Undergraduate Libraries (N = 24)**

Position	No.	%
Director of undergraduate library	3	13
Assistant director	1	4
Head of undergraduate library public services or reference	5	21
Reference librarian in undergraduate library	3	13
Coordinator of library instruction within undergraduate library	11	46
Program not coordinated within undergraduate library	1	4

method of organizing programs was to appoint a coordinator who is responsible for administering the program, but who involves others in the actual instruction.[12]

Several other libraries, while not appointing coordinators, have provided more time to reference librarians for library instruction activities and research, and have included such activities in the job descriptions of the librarians for the first time. It is clear that instruction has now been incorporated into the regular functions of most undergraduate libraries. No longer is it done only after all other demands on the undergraduate library have been met.

TYPES OF LIBRARY ORIENTATION
AND BIBLIOGRAPHIC INSTRUCTION PROGRAMS

All the undergraduate libraries surveyed offer some type of orientation *tour* of the library. The most common format is the staff-led tour (the approach used in 21 of the 24 libraries), usually given at the beginning of fall quarter, but often available at the beginning of other quarters, at regular times during the year, or upon request. The staff-led tours are given most often to campus students, but nine libraries regularly or occasionally give tours to outside groups such as high school classes. Other approaches to the tour are also gaining acceptance. Printed, self-guided tours are available in 15 of the libraries, and 8 make available hand-held audiocassette self-guided tours. One library uses a "self-guided trail"— students follow "footprints" affixed to the floor that direct them to a series of stations where signs identify library facilities and services.

Table 2 indicates the *level of staff* giving tours. Two points should be noted. First, almost all the libraries with staff-led tours have professional staff giving at least some of the tours. In view of the fact that countless writers over the years have excoriated staff-guided library tours as often worse than worthless, it certainly is surprising that so much expensive staff time is being spent on guiding students about the library. Mary Jo Lynch has made one of the best statements regarding what value can be made of such tours:

> Too often librarians have acted as if users could learn all about a library in a brief tour. . . . Once those great expectations are abandoned, however, and the tour is seen as a means of introducing people to a complex physical structure with a collection of

Table 2. Staff Involvement in Orientation Tours
(N = 24)

Level of Staff	No.	%*
Librarians	20	83
Career support staff	5	21
Library school students employed in library	3	13
Undergraduates employed in library	2	8
No staff-led tours given	3	13

*Several libraries use more than one level of staff for tours.

material organized for their use and a staff ready and willing to offer many services, the tour can be assessed realistically as a valuable part of the user-education program.[13]

Obviously, librarians in undergraduate libraries have recognized that self-guided tours can be effective (hence the large number of printed and audiocassette tours that have been developed), but so far at least they are unwilling to give up the more traditional approach.

The second point worth noting is the converse of the first—that four of the libraries do *not* have librarians giving tours. In fact, three of these libraries (at the universities of Maryland, Tennessee, and Texas) rely solely on self-guided tours of one form or another. Since these are three of the largest undergraduate libraries in the United States, with good-sized library instruction programs, it is clear that some undergraduate library staffs have concluded that professional time can be put to better use when it comes to educating library users.

Twenty-three of the 24 libraries surveyed provide *bibliographic instruction* for their users. As might be expected, the most widespread activity is the preparation of orientation leaflets and printed guides to the use of particular reference tools. A large variety of other techniques are also used, however; they are summarized in Table 3.

While 19 of the 24 libraries give bibliographic *lectures to classes*, there is a very wide variation in the number of classes reached. Using as a yardstick how many classes were reached in the 1977 fall quarter, the libraries fall into three distinct groups. Five libraries reached fewer than six classes, eight libraries reached 12 to 35 classes, and six reached 70 or more classes. Clearly some libraries must be advertising the availability of staff to give class-related lectures, while others wait to respond to faculty requests.

Table 3. Types of Bibliographic Instruction Programs
      (N = 24)

Program	No.	%*
1. Point-of-use materials or printed handouts	22	92
2. Bibliographic lectures to classes	19	79
3. Course for credit	9	38
(a) Sponsored by library	(3)	
(b) Sponsored by department outside the library	(6)	
4. Self-guided workbook	5	21
(a) Credit	(2)	
(b) Noncredit	(3)	
5. Noncredit course or minicourse (one-day clinics, etc.)	3	13
6. No involvement	1	4

*Most libraries use several types of programs.

The number of sections of *credit courses* taught by undergraduate librarians is small, averaging two sections per library where this approach is used.

In five libraries additional sections are taught by other librarians on campus, but on four campuses the only librarians teaching such a course are in the undergraduate library. Since these courses usually include only 20 to 25 students per section, this approach cannot be said to be reaching a large number of undergraduates on most campuses.

Six of the nine courses are sponsored by departments outside the library. This is perhaps one indication that the move toward faculty status has not gone so far as to allow many library systems to sponsor their own credit courses. Most often the courses are sponsored through academic departments, but two schools on the West Coast, the University of California campuses at Berkeley and Los Angeles, give undergraduate credit courses in bibliography through their library schools. The course at Berkeley should be noted as the most extensive use of the credit-course approach—some 14 sections (totaling several hundred students) taught each quarter. Only two instructors for the course, however, come from the undergraduate library; most of the others are hired by the library school specifically to teach the course.

Five libraries used self-guided workbooks as part of their library instruction program, reaching anywhere from a little over one hundred to over one thousand students in the 1977 fall quarter. While this approach has not gained wide acceptance, it shows the clear potential of reaching many more students than most other forms of instruction. It is interesting to note that there was no correlation between the number of students doing the workbook and whether or not it was for credit, although the sample was too small to generalize from the experience of these libraries. A variation on the *self-paced instruction* approach, used at the University of Texas–Austin, is described in a separate section.

Audiovisual materials have been incorporated in a variety of ways into the library instruction programs of all 24 libraries surveyed. Audiocassettes are used primarily for self-guided orientation tours, while slide/tape programs and videotapes are employed to introduce students to the campus library system, basic search strategy, and indexes and abstracts. Transparencies of index pages, catalog cards, and the like are shown on overhead projectors during class visits. (See Table 4.)

**Table 4. Use of Audiovisual Equipment
in Library Instruction (N = 24)**

Type of Equipment	*No.*	*%**
Audiocassettes	9	38
Overhead projectors	3	13
Slide/tapes	17	71
Slides without sound	1	4
Videotapes	6	24

*Many libraries use several types of equipment.

In addition to the use already made of audiovisual materials, several libraries are in the midst of preparing new material on a variety of topics. This expansion is in part because of audiovisuals' versatility—the same slide/tape, for example, can be used both by individual patrons in the library and as part of a class presentation. In any case, undergraduates will be seeing more slides and videotapes in the future. Fully one-third of the libraries indicate they will be putting more effort into producing audiovisual materials over the next few years.

THE UNIVERSITY OF TEXAS AT AUSTIN: A CASE STUDY

The library that seems most successful in reaching almost its total population of undergraduate users is the undergraduate library of the University of Texas at Austin. Because it uses a unique combination of self-paced and course-related instruction, and because it could well prove a model for other instruction programs, it is described here in depth.[14]

The genesis of the program was the library's commitment in 1975 to the development and implementation of bibliographic instruction as a primary goal. Surveys of faculty opinion the same year indicated that the majority of instructors at the university gave assignments requiring library research, but over 80 percent of the instructors rated student library skills as fair to poor. A corresponding library skills test administered to a sample of students in English classes confirmed student ignorance of basic reference sources—for example, a majority thought *Readers' Guide* to be an index either of all magazines and journals in the United States or of all those received on the campus.

Working together, the staff of the undergraduate library and those responsible for freshman English instruction developed a program for incorporating library skills into a two-semester course sequence. Basic to the program was the conscious decision to reach as many students as possible, at least at a minimal level, rather than giving intensive instruction to a few. The result is a program that reaches an enormous number of students—close to 150 sections of freshman English in fall 1977 alone. (The entire library instruction program of the undergraduate library, of which this is the major component, now extends to some 8,000 freshmen each year with a total professional staff of six.) Rather than meeting with every English class, the librarian's contribution consists of preparing printed guides and other materials for distribution in class, orienting English instructors to the library instruction program through participation in a course for new teaching assistants, conducting evaluations of the program, and, of course, working closely with the students in the reference area.

In the first semester, students initially take a self-guided tour of the library and a short exercise (corrected by their English instructors) designed to reinforce the material on the tour. This is followed by instruction in basic library skills and search strategy through a term-paper assignment. Students select their term-paper topic from a list of 90 topics that have been thoroughly researched by the library staff to ensure that the students have a successful "first-search" experience. Where necessary, additional materials have been purchased to handle the intensive demand for materials on the topics.

Students begin their term-paper assignment by preparing bibliographies using research-paper worksheets and more than a dozen study guides prepared by the library staff. The guides cover subject encyclopedias, periodical indexes, and the card catalog, as well as more specialized topics such as biographical sources, literary criticism, and statistical information. When the course is completed, some of the bibliographies and term papers are returned to the undergraduate library so the staff can review the effectiveness of their guides.

In the second semester, students are required to use the study guides to write themes or research papers on a topic of their choice. The course work reinforces the basic skills introduced in the first semester.

Several points should be noted about the program. First, while the study guides and worksheets are generalized—that is, they could be used by anyone needing guidance on what the guide covers—they are put into a strongly motivating context by tying their use to the freshman English class. Second, the library staff seems to have recognized early the impossibility of personally reaching all under- ✕ graduates with a professional staff of six. Rather than giving up, they worked on selling the program to a much larger corps of "helpers"—the instructional staff of the freshman English program. Third, the library staff seems to have been careful in deciding what they did and did not have time to do. They did not spread themselves too thin (for example, by accepting responsibility for correcting the exercise that follows the self-guided tour) and therefore were able to concentrate their energies on design, guidance, and evaluation. These three points—placement of the instruction in a motivating context, extensive cooperation with faculty, and a realistic assessment of staff capabilities—may well be the keys to organizing successful large-scale programs elsewhere.

THE FUTURE OF LIBRARY INSTRUCTION
IN UNDERGRADUATE LIBRARIES

There has been an almost radical (and some would say gratifying) expansion of library instruction programs in undergraduate libraries during the last five years. Several elements have contributed to the expansion—a sense of professional duty, a need to cope with an enormous user population, a move toward a more visible teaching role, and a sense of self-preservation. Within this period library instruction has become part of the normal activity of the libraries; coordinators have been designated, reference librarians have been given time to work on the programs, and new librarians are being hired in part because of their ability to take part in the programs.

Nevertheless, library instruction is in addition to, rather than in lieu of, traditional undergradate library activities. Perhaps the greatest professional time-consumer, staffing the reference desk, is still given high priority; indeed, high quality, user-oriented reference service is considered to be the complement of a program of library instruction. Most libraries appear unwilling to give up professional involvement in orientation tours, but a few, especially those with extensive bibliographic instruction programs, are experimenting with other approaches to library orientation. It seems inevitable that other libraries will also cut back such involvement as more time is committed to bibliographic instruction.

One means of coping with the need to find more time for user education has been the increased use of audiovisual equipment in both library orientation and bibliographic instruction. This use will expand considerably over the next few years.

Yet it must be recognized that no amount of audiovisual equipment or improved coordination or staff enthusiasm will make up for the fact that, compared with the total of professional staff at these research-oriented universities, "the amount of FTE actually in bibliographic instruction . . . is infinitesimal," as noted by one librarian. Attempting to handle all bibliographic instruction for as many as 30,000 or more undergraduates with undergraduate library staffs of six or seven librarians will lead to a great deal of burnout and frustration. It is significant that two of the largest, although completely different, bibliographic instruction programs in the United States—the credit course at Berkeley and the course-integrated program at Austin—have relied heavily on instructors outside the undergraduate library. Perhaps the role undergraduate librarians will play increasingly in the future will be more that of organizing, guiding, and evaluating bibliographic instruction than teaching.

This author has said before (and will probably say again) that a basic objective of academic librarianship *must* be that every student, by the time he or she completes an undergraduate education, should be able to make effective use of library resources. It is beginning to appear that even on campuses with the most collections-oriented administration or with the largest number of undergraduates, this just might be possible.

NOTES

1. "Summary and Analysis of Selected Undergraduate Library Statistics," *UGLI Newsletter*, no. 12 (January 1978), p. 6.
2. Anne B. Passarelli and Millicent D. Abell, "Programs of Undergraduate Libraries and Problems in Educating Library Users," in John Lubans, Jr., *Educating the Library User* (New York: R. R. Bowker, 1974), pp. 115-131.
3. See, for example, Irene Braden, *The Undergraduate Library* (Chicago: American Library Association, 1970), p. 2.
4. Passarelli and Abell, "Programs of Undergraduate Libraries," pp. 117-118.
5. Billy R. Wilkinson, "A Screaming Success As Study Halls," *Library Journal* 96 (May 1, 1971): 1567-1571.
6. Questionnaires and other data in the files of the author.
7. Henry W. Wingate, "The Undergraduate Library: Is It Obsolete?" *College and Research Libraries* 39 (January 1978): 29-33.
8. Pyke Johnson, Jr., "A Day with a College Librarian," *Publishers Weekly* 213 (January 9, 1978): 41.
9. Selected on the basis of statistics in the December 1976 *UGLI Newsletter* were Cornell, Harvard, Indiana, McGill, Michigan State, Ohio State, Southern Illinois-Carbondale, Stanford, and SUNY-Buffalo, and the universities of Alberta, California-Berkeley, California-Los Angeles, California-San Diego, Illinois, Miami, Michigan, North Carolina-Chapel Hill, Tennessee-Knoxville, Texas-Austin, Toronto, Washington, and Wisconsin. Added to these

were three that had not submitted statistics to the *Newsletter* but that were known by the author to fit the criteria: the universities of British Columbia, Hawaii, and Maryland.

10. See, for example, Wilkinson, "A Screaming Success," p. 1567.
11. On the questionnaire, "library orientation" was defined as "teaching students the layout of the building, how to check out a book, etc." The term "bibliographic instruction" was used for "teaching the use of reference tools, how to do a literature search by subject, etc." In this article, "library instruction" is used to cover both activites.
12. Allan J. Dyson, "Organizing Undergraduate Library Instruction: The English and American Experience," *Journal of Academic Librarianship* 1 (March 1975): 13.
13. Mary Jo Lynch, "Library Tours: The First Step," in John Lubans, Jr., *Educating the Library User* (New York: R. R. Bowker, 1974), p. 255.
14. The author is most grateful to Jay Martin Poole, Head Librarian of the University of Texas Undergraduate Library, for his extensive description of the program. Much of what follows draws heavily on Mr. Poole's description.

EDUCATING LARGE NUMBERS OF USERS IN UNIVERSITY LIBRARIES: AN ANALYSIS AND A CASE STUDY

BETTY L. HACKER
Assistant Reference Librarian, Colorado State University

JOEL S. RUTSTEIN
Social Sciences Librarian, Colorado State University

The education of university library patrons is both challenging and exasperating. The rapid expansion of higher education in the 1960s has been replaced with the more sobering retrenchment of the 1970s. Library instruction in the last decade grew and expanded with the growth in higher education. Optimism and confidence abounded. In an eclectic sense, as the Great Society expressed eternal faith in solving the riddle of poverty, so librarians believed the opportunity was at hand to make all students effective users of library resources. This principle has not diminished. Few librarians, even with the retrenchment in higher education, think in terms of curtailment. Indeed, one librarian recently commented: "A basic objective of academic librarianship must be that every student . . . should be able to make effective use of library resources."[1]

These Benthamite objectives notwithstanding, librarians concerned with instructional programs must face the reality of staff shortages, budget reductions, limited goals, and the more prevalent phenomenon of temporary personnel appointments made as a cost-saving contrivance. A valid argument for the continuing emphasis on reaching as many users as possible is the abundance of information resources and their occasionally baffling complexities. There exist few gauges to measure the success or failure of library instruction programs. The enigma persists in the identification of those who need aid, the provisions available to render aid, and at what time and to what extent aid is given. Without standardized tests, librarians rely for the most part on attitudinal responses, an inefficient means of measurement. Small wonder librarians use a shotgun approach in their educational programs.

TRENDS IN THE 1970S

Until the 1960s, attitudes about educating the university library user were often sympathetic with the impression that the reluctant user can never be reached, that all resources should be mobilized for those who are "true readers," providing them with whatever help is necessary.[2] Studies in the 1960s concluded that an unsettled atmosphere permeated views on library instruction. An effort was initiated toward more media-related presentations, including programmed learning and self-paced instructional methods. Media were contemplated as a possible panacea in reaching large numbers of users. After all, if young people were attending college in ever greater numbers, then the elitist view of library instruction needed alteration. Melum's survey corroborated the commitment to instruction, and also confirmed the rise of audiovisual technology. She concluded that library instruction was "meaningful only when motivated by need," but consensus was and is still lacking concerning the proper methods for mass library instruction.[3]

The mid-1970s have witnessed a continued growth in the communication of ideas and methods concerning academic library instruction and orientation. Duplication of effort has been and still is a fundamental issue in this field. Endeavors have been promulgated on the national scene to help resolve this expensive dilemma. Attention appears to be focusing on individual institutions such as Eastern Michigan University, which hosts the annual (and successful) library orientation conferences. The communication and exchange of ideas has also centered at Eastern Michigan through the medium of Library Orientation—Instruction Exchange (LOEX), and is updated by the LOEX newsletter. A new periodical, the *Journal of Academic Librarianship*, includes a regular column for exchanging ideas and opinions on library instruction. More regional clearinghouses for information exchange are supported in several states, for example, New York and Wisconsin. On the national level, both the American Library Association (ALA) and the Association of College and Research Libraries (ACRL) have units on library instruction and have galvanized efforts to standardize and set guidelines for educating the library user. Supporting these activites is the practice of the Council on Library Resources and the National Endowment for the Humanities to fund various library instruction programs through the College Library Program, which has already funded 24 institutions at a cost exceeding one million dollars.[4]

Another answer to the duplication of effort question would seem to lie with commercial, standard instructional packages. Although such packages exist, few are considered acceptable in terms of quality or adaptability. An obvious reason for their lack of popularity is the very nature of university libraries. Internally, classification systems may vary, and the unique physical layout of individual libraries tends to diffuse instructional methods and objectives. Externally, university libraries are not entities unto themselves, since their mission relates directly to the objectives of the academic community they serve, with all its variables.

Recently, there has been a small but detectable shift toward teaching concepts and values in library instruction, although this does not imply a return to the library-college model. Technological tools are an aspect of this new emphasis, but librarians should be intellectually committed to new concepts and methods accommodating the trends in higher education.[5] It remains to be seen whether this evocative response to accepted norms of library instruction will find followers.

OVERVIEW OF INSTRUCTION/ORIENTATION PROGRAMS

No large university libraries are fully integrated into the resident instruction program of the institution. An ideal situation might include the following tenets: (1) librarians have academic (not general) faculty status; (2) they serve on important faculty committees (such as curriculum committees); (3) there exists an ongoing systematic program of library instruction at all levels, in close cooperation with faculty instructors; (4) evaluation analysis includes behavioral methods; and (5) the staff structure is organized so that library instruction is a primary mission.

Mass instruction programs developed specifically to serve large numbers of users are usually designed for lower-division undergraduates. There are arguments pro and con such programs' being relevant to subject course work, or being part of required English composition classes. It has been recommended that library instruction be delayed until there is some involvement with direct assignments. Any instruction previous to this would be merely introductory; students would be oriented to the physical structure and perhaps shown a few basic sources. At the same time students would be reminded that more "sophisticated" learning will occur later in their educational career.[6]

Some librarians are at pains to differentiate the term *orientation* from library instruction, or even bibliographical instruction. Orientation implies direction, while *instruction* connotes a learning process. Library orientation is often considered synonymous with mass instruction, though this is by no means entirely valid. Orientations are generally restricted to providing an awareness of physical location, staff, and services, but they can also serve small numbers of people with specific information needs. An example might be a group orientation to the Educational Resources Information Center (ERIC) collection for educational psychology students. Such an orientation may be guilty of letting a little learning slip through. If nothing else, orientations are considered of value because the audience is actually confronted with a librarian, something that cannot be said of self-instructional programs.[7] Although perhaps no longer in vogue, orientations are very much alive in university libraries.

The literature is filled with examples of the types and levels of instruction offered. Types of instruction are generally broken down into these categories: (1) formal courses with or without credit, (2) course-related instruction, which is part of a regular class activity, (3) self-instruction, or individualized self-paced instruction, (4) intensive—a broad term that incorporates tutorials, seminars, and special individualized instruction, and (5) library orientation. Mass instruction programs generally fall into categories two, three, and five.

The makeup of an instructional program depends on the library user education policies, the objectives of the program, the composition and attitudes of the faculty, the student body, library administrative support, the physical size of the

Table 1. Collection Development and Instructional Levels

	Collection Development Levels	Library Instruction Levels
Basic	Not sufficiently intensive to support courses, but works of a reference nature—dictionnaries, encyclopedias, handbooks, etc.	Elementary instruction in basic tools and their location; audiovisual systems, point-of-use methods, reference interviews
Instructional	General undergraduate teaching and learning; complete range of reference materials, fundamental subject indexes.	Devising simple search strategies; printed guides, self-paced instruction
Beginning research	Support research in teaching through master's level; fundamental works of scholarship and selected source material	Sophisticated search strategies; documented research papers, government documents, state of the art, specialized bibliographies, course-related, formal courses, programmed learning
Intensive	Scholarly collections to support doctoral and applied research programs	Understanding networking and computer retrieval systems; research method courses, special minisessions in refined tools of research; frequent subject librarian contact

library, and the available resources.[8] In distinguishing levels of instruction, a rational system could be one of tying collection development policies in with instructional objectives. Table 1 is a model format for this approach.[9]

INDIVIDUALIZED INSTRUCTION
AND THE EMPHASIS ON MEDIA

As described above, the trend toward the use of media in the 1960s is now an accepted element of mass library instruction programs. A survey published by Hardesty in 1976 reveals that at least 85 percent of academic libraries have some form of media presentations.[10] The reasons are clear for the increased popularity of packaged audiovisual programs: (1) they are available at all times to deal with specific student needs; (2) if carefully prepared, they could replace the guided library tour, with all its alleged drawbacks; and (3) they may be cost-effective in the long run since much staff time is saved and released for more advanced instructional levels.[11] In reply to the query, "Do you support the opinion . . . [that] . . .

the use of audio-visual presentation [is] indispensable to a successful orientation/ instruction program?" one respondent stated: "In a time of economic hardship for academic libraries, anything which thus allows general instruction to reach more users while allowing librarians to concentrate on the difficult questions . . . is certainly worth encouraging."[12]

Media programs employ various kinds of equipment. These include audiotapes, computer-assisted instruction, films, programmed learning devices, slides, slide/tapes, teaching machines, and videotapes.[13] Slide/tape devices are still the most popular form due to their relatively low cost, easy handling and revision, and durability.[14]

The commercial availability of media programs is meager. Hardesty reported that barely a dozen of the 150 institutions surveyed had packages for sale (although several stated that their packages were adaptable to other systems).[15] As discussed earlier, the great obstacle is determining adaptability to local needs, a statement that can be applied to the whole problem of uniformity in library instruction.

Self-instructional units are among the more popular types of learning methods. These comprise workbooks or a combination of printed material and audiovisual devices. They are usually designed for the lower-division student and available on a required or voluntary basis, although many specialized programs of this type have been designed for upper-division students. Examples of successful programs utilizing the workbook method are at the universities of Arizona, Michigan, California at Los Angeles, and Texas.

Besides some of the general advantages a "canned" presentation has over a "live" presentation, self-instructional units have these benefits: (1) they allow for alternative learning methods; (2) they provide flexibility in time scheduling; (3) students may have the instruction repeated as often as necessary.[16] Individualized instruction is considered by some to be more effective than other instructional techniques since it forces the student to become directly involved in the learning process. For mass instruction this is important because it lessens production-line attitudes and offers the student a sense of identity and self-worth.[17]

Computer-assisted instruction (CAI) is still only of peripheral interest in library instruction programs. It has little application for educating large numbers of users since the terminals and software are extremely expensive. Perhaps as libraries become more automated and the cost of equipment drops, CAI may eventually find a place in programs of educating library users.

IMPLEMENTING THE PROGRAM

A survey conducted several years ago revealed that faculty apathy was one of the greatest handicaps faced in implementing library instruction projects. Student indifference and insufficient funds followed far behind.[18] Since there may be a certain percentage of students, faculty, and administrators who view librarians as little more than clerical support staff, communication and action are vital to bridge the gap between librarians and faculty. On the other hand, the academic institution must produce and sustain an environment encouraging easy access to library instruction programs.

No mass instruction program can be successful without a strong and effective commitment from the library administration. Staff time, space, materials, clerical support, and enthusiastic library instructors are the essential ingredients in successful programs.[19] Library administrators can rearrange assignments, provide staff-release time, aid committees, and integrate instructional goals with the overall library mission. They also act as liaisons (and buffers) with university officials in clearing bureaucratic channels. Above all, no program can succeed without a budget, and usually only administrators can make this feasible.[20]

Few would argue that close faculty-librarian relationships are the key to a successful instruction program. Yet, as pointed out above, the greatest difficulty in implementation is overcoming faculty apathy. In planning the program, firm guidelines are necessary in approaching faculty, for example: (1) demonstrating that students are unskilled in library use and how this affects curriculum assignments, (2) convincing faculty of the importance of librarians in the learning process, (3) furthering the cause of making effective use of library resources, (4) emphasizing values in library education, (5) requesting from faculty their aid and advice in reaching large numbers of students, and (6) working through faculty committees for adjustments benefiting mass instruction programs.[21]

Various studies have confirmed the need for close working relationships between faculty and librarians. Academic departments have few internal bibliographic instruction courses, yet excuses from faculty for not utilizing library aid range from the course content is already too full so library instruction cannot be fit into the syllabus to the disclaimer that students *are* referred to the reference desk, should that not be enough?[22]

Since library instruction for large numbers of users emphasizes the lower-division courses with large enrollments and many sections, teaching assistants or graduate teaching assistants (GTA's) are a major factor in a program's success or failure. As with regular faculty, GTAs can be ill-informed and unconcerned about library instruction. The problem may be compounded with them because many are transient and are apt to be less committed to academic teaching on the whole. After all, with their heavy commitment to finishing their own coursework, let alone dissertations, there is plenty for them to be concerned about outside the provision of library skills.[23] Through hard experience librarians have learned to work with individual faculty and *not* through department heads, because of the independence and frequent autonomy within academic departments. Library instructors in mass education programs must go one step further and keep in touch with the GTAs, since their attitude and cooperation can make or break the program. The need for a good relationship between librarians and faculty was echoed by Patricia Knapp, who, in discussing the Monteith College Library experiment, believed the most important component was an awareness among the university community of the theoretical context for library outreach—that without this, there could be no successful library instruction program.[24]

Implementing a program of instruction in basic library skills is a particular dilemma for large university libraries in these days of shrinking budgets and personnel. While some large universities attempt to meet the challenge through the "workbook" method, others have opted for a manageable program on a more limited scale. Institutions vary widely in the resources available to them. The existence of a library school with graduate students attached to the university, or an active instructional media department with outreach staff, or a large cadre of instructional librarians, or an adequate budget within the library for instructional purposes will often determine the type of instructional program offered.

The following case study is an example of an ongoing program within a structure of limited resources.

CASE STUDY: COLORADO STATE UNIVERSITY LIBRARIES

Colorado State University (CSU) is a land-grant institution with a student body of 17,500. The enrollment is divided among nine colleges, the largest of which is the College of Arts, Humanities, and Social Sciences; however, the university is best known for its research-oriented programs in engineering, forestry, and veterinary medicine.

The CSU libraries' million-volume collections, facilities, and staff are housed in the William E. Morgan Library, centrally located on the main campus. (A small collection is in the Engineering Sciences Branch Library on the research campus several miles away.)

Responsibility for library use instruction is shared between the reference department and nine subject specialist librarians. One member of the reference department, designated as a part-time library instruction librarian, coordinates instruction in basic library skills for undergraduates. Other reference librarians assist in general-information tours and lectures. Subject librarians serve as collection development bibliographers, but provide specialized reference services in addition to instructing classes in the use of subject-related reference materials. These classes consist largely of upperclassmen or graduate students.

As background to a discussion of the present library instructional programs at CSU, we should note that well into the late 1960s, the only basic library instruction offered to large numbers of students was a videotape shown to freshman English classes. Use of the videotape was discontinued in 1968, due to a change in the freshman English course structure. For several years there existed no mode for large-scale library use instruction.

The need for such instruction became urgent at precisely this same time, as CSU enrollments increased sharply in accord with the national trend for land-grant institutions. The student population in 1960 was 6,100; in 1970, 17,000.

A grant from the CSU Office of Instructional Development in 1971 led to a fresh opportunity to instruct students in basic library skills. Relying on the demonstrated success of point-of-use instruction developed at Massachusetts Institute of Technology[25] and elsewhere, the CSU libraries' staff used the grant to produce self-instructional programs explaining the use of the card catalog, periodical indexes and abstracts, and U.S. government documents. The programs were of two kinds, sound/slide and audiotape, and were housed in prototype cabinets designed by the CSU Office of Educational Media. The use and evaluation of these programs (called Auto-Instructional Media for Library Orientation [AIMLO]) has been described.[26] They have continued to be revised and expanded into other subject areas.

In 1973, instructors in an Education Department course offered to students needing help with study skills approached the libraries' staff with a request for a library use instructional tool. *Using the CSU Libraries—A Tour and Exercise* was the result of this request. The authors of this chapter developed the *Exercise* (see Appendix to this chapter), experimenting first with a group of about 200 students. To each *Exercise* was attached a student reaction sheet. Reaction from both students and instructors was highly favorable. The introduction to the five-page *Exercise* stressed use of the AIMLO programs as a preparation for completing the assignment. Thus, slide/tape media and a printed instructional tool were combined.

An agreement with the Department of English, based on success with the education classes, led to a widely expanded use of the *Exercise*, beginning in 1975. Each semester approximately 1,500 students in the basic English composition course complete the library use assignment. The assignments are graded by GTAs using answer keys supplied by the libraries' staff (see Appendix). The student reaction sheets are returned to the library, and are compiled and analyzed at the end of each semester. Results continue to show a very positive response from students (see Appendix).

During the past year a new development has occurred that seems to indicate an additional dimension to the *Exercise* as a learning tool. In response to invitations from the libraries' instructional staff, the GTAs in charge of administering the *Exercise* are bringing large numbers of students to the library for a one-hour lecture/tour immediately preceeding the assignment. Since the *Exercises* are distributed to classes at the rate of 150 per week over a semester-long period, the lecture/tour sessions (for classes of about 25 students each) are also held throughout the semester. In 1977, more than half of the students completing the *Exercise* also had the benefit of the lecture/tour, which is specifically designed to assist students with this assignment.

What is the *Exercise*? As the introduction (see Appendix) tells the student, the three purposes are "first, to conduct you on a self-guided tour of several areas of the Morgan Library; second, to show you the proper procedures for starting the search for information on a subject; and third, to acquaint you with some of the important library tools for general undergraduate use." The assignment requires use of the three sections of the divided card catalog, two periodical indexes, the serials record, and the microform area.

Behind the purposes of the *Exercise* as outlined to the student lie other reasons for using this method of introduction to library use. Some are purely pragmatic:

1. Introductory composition courses provide a captive audience of lower classmen composed of students from all majors and all colleges of the university, in an identifiable group.
2. The English department's GTAs form a corps of available help in grading the *Exercise* and making sure it is completed; the libraries' staff is responsible only for designing and revising the instrument and compiling evaluation statistics.
3. The *Exercise* itself is short enough to be reproduced in mass quantity at low cost.
4. The basic form of the *Exercise* allows easy adaptation to a wide variety of subject fields, thus dispersing students to many parts of the library building and

to many reference tools; several hundred students may be completing the assignment simultaneously without great impact on the library environment.

These reasons for continued use of the *Exercise* are primarily economic, in terms of both staff and materials.

Other factors, however, contribute to a conviction that this method of providing basic library use instruction to large numbers of students is valid. While intuitive and philosophical in nature, these are:

1. The *Exercise* is designed to be a nonthreatening, relatively simple, welcoming introduction to the library, leading to a successful library experience.
2. Initial instruction of this kind builds confidence and provides a basis for later subject-oriented instruction on a more sophisticated level, conducted by subject librarians.
3. The ongoing evaluation procedure has produced data showing a high degree of acceptance by students.
4. Given present constraints of budget and staff, there is a certain euphoric quality to the realization that even rudimentary instruction is being provided to over 3,000 students each academic year.

The future will certainly hold opportunities for more intensive evaluation of the effectiveness of the *Exercise*. Now that it is firmly established as part of the routine of basic English composition classes, more attention will be devoted to determining how to expand its usefulness. In the 1970s, CSU has subscribed to the theory of a multifaceted approach to library use instruction, and the *Exercise* is part of the total program.

CONCLUSION

This chapter has touched on some of the trends in mass instructional programs as they are reflected in the literature, and has documented the system in use at Colorado State University.

The missionary zeal of instruction librarians in the 1960s can be compared with trying to achieve the quixotic goal of a well-informed electorate in a democratic state. In the cold practicality of the 1970s, academic librarians in large institutions have, in many situations, adapted their sights to the possible.

Declining public support and budget constraints may have some positive implications.[27] In certain cases, lower enrollments lead to smaller classes, whose instructors may find more opportunity to utilize library instruction. Continuing and adult education programs have found footholds on many large university campuses, and the implications for instruction are strong. As the swing away from the massive acquisitions programs of the 1960s continues, more emphasis can be placed on the efficient use of existing collections, and instruction should be a basic factor in this effort.

Uppermost in the minds of many instructional librarians seeking mass teaching methods might be the thoughts of Rice and Richards:

> The most important thing is establishing a basic set of library skills early on in the student's college career. . . . Many freshmen are afraid. . . . If we can give them some chance to be familiar with how the library works, we're helping them, through a re-

duction of barriers. In part, it's not only library instruction, but public relations as well.[28]

NOTES

1. Allan J. Dyson, "Organizing Undergraduate Library Instruction: The English and American Experience," *Journal of Academic Librarianship* 1 (March 1975): 13.
2. Stanley E. Gwynn, "Library Service to Undergraduates: College Library at the University of Chicago," *College and Research Libraries* 14 (July 1953): 7-8.
3. See Verna Melum, " A Survey to Aid Your Fall Planning: Library Orientation in the College and University," *Wilson Library Bulletin*, September 1971, pp. 59-66, and "1971 Survey of Library Orientation and Instruction Programs," *Drexel Library Quarterly* 7 (July–October 1971): 225-253.
4. Michael Brittain and Ann Irving, *Trends in the Education of Users of Libraries and Information Services in the USA: A Report Submitted to the British Library Research and Development Department* (Loughborough, England: Loughborough University, April 1976), p. 7.
5. See Robert Vuturo, "Beyond the Library Tour: Those Who *Can*, Must Teach," *Wilson Library Bulletin*, May 1977, pp. 736-740; response: June Biermann, *Wilson Library Bulletin*, September 1977, p. 26. See also Topsy N. Smalley, "Bibliographic Instruction in Academic Libraries: Questioning Some Assumptions," *Journal of Academic Librarianship* 3 (November 1977): 280-283.
6. Verna M. Beardsley, "Library Instruction in Colleges and Universities in the Seventies: A Viewpoint," in John Lubans, Jr., *Educating the Library User* (New York: R. R. Bowker, 1974), pp. 111-112.
7. Jay M. Poole et al., *Preliminary Paper toward a Comprehensive Program of Library Orientation/Instruction for the Libraries of the State University of New York at Buffalo* (Buffalo, 1974), p. 12. ERIC document ED092 137.
8. Thomas Kirk et al., "Bibliographic Instruction in Academic Libraries" (Edited transcript of a panel discussion, Association of College and Research Libraries, New England Chapter, 1974), p. 15. ERIC document ED112 946.
9. Cf. *Second Annual Report to the Council on Library Resources and the National Endowment for the Humanities, for the Year July 1, 1975–June 30, 1976* (Lexington: College Library Program, University of Kentucky, 1976), p. 3 (ERIC document ED126 900); also Poole, *Preliminary Paper*, p. 14; Mary B. Cassata, *Library Instruction Program Proposal* (Buffalo: State University of New York, 1973), p. 5 (ERIC document ED077 541); and Elizabeth Frick, "Information Structure and Bibliographic Instruction," *Journal of Academic Librarianship* 1 (September 1975): 12-14.
10. Larry Hardesty, *Survey of the Use of Slide/Tape Presentations for Orientation and Instruction Purposes in Academic Libraries* (Greencastle, Ind.: DePauw University, 1976), p. 9. ERIC document ED116 711. Conclusions published as "Use of Slide-Tape Presentations in Academic Libraries: A State-of-the-Art Survey," *Journal of Academic Librarianship* 3 (July 1977): 137-140.

11. Roger C. Palmer, *Project Report: Audiovisual Orientation for Freshmen, Summer Program* (Buffalo: State University of New York, 1973), p. 11. ERIC document ED081 455. See also Kirk, "Bibliographic Instruction," p. 17, and Peter P. Olevnik, *A Media-Assisted Library Instruction Orientation Program Report* (Brockport: State University of New York, 1976). ERIC document ED134 138.
12. Katherine G. Cipolla in "Library Instruction: A Column of Opinion," ed. by Carolyn Kirkendall, *Journal of Academic Librarianship* 3 (March 1977): 34–35.
13. Philip John Schwarz, comp., *The New Media in Academic Library Orientation, 1956–1972: An Annotated Bibliography* (Stout: Media Retrieval Services, University of Wisconsin, 1973), p. 2. ERIC document ED071 682.
14. Hardesty, *Survey of the Use of Slide/Tape Presentations*, pp. 1–2.
15. Ibid., p. 2.
16. Thomas Kirk, *Academic Library Bibliographic Instruction: Status Report, 1972* (Chicago: Association of College and Research Libraries, 1973), p. 34. ERIC document ED072 823. See also *Proceedings of the Seminar on User Education Activities, the State of the Art in Texas* (Papers delivered at a conference of the Texas Library Association, Houston, April 1976. Published in 1977). ERIC document ED138 247.
17. D. H. Revill, "Teaching Methods in the Library: A Survey From the Educational Viewpoint," *Library World* 71 (February 1970): 247.
18. Arthur P. Young et al., "Survey of User Education in New York State Academic Libraries" (Paper presented at the New York Library Association annual conference, New York City, October 6, 1971), p. 7. ERIC document ED055 621.
19. A. P. Marshall, "Library Orientation—What's That?" (Paper presented at the fifth annual conference on Library Orientation for Academic Libraries, Ypsilanti, Mich., May 16, 1975), p. 5. ERIC document ED108 710.
20. Kirk, "Bibliographic Instruction," p. 11
21. John Lubans, Jr., "Program to Improve and Increase Student and Faculty Involvement in Library Use. First Annual Progress Report to the Council on Library Resources and the National Endowment for the Humanities for the Year Sept. 1, 1973–Aug. 31, 1974" (Boulder: University of Colorado Libraries, 1974), p. 3. ERIC document ED097 864.
22. John Lubans, Jr., "Program to Improve and Increase Student and Faculty Involvement in Library Use. Second Annual Report to the Council on Library Resources and the National Endowment for the Humanities for the Year Sept. 1, 1974–Aug. 31, 1975" (Boulder: University of Colorado Libraries, 1975), p. 13. ERIC document ED114 097. See also Poole, *Preliminary Paper*, p. 10.
23. *Second Annual Report to the Council on Library Resources* (University of Kentucky), p. 11.
24. See Patricia B. Knapp, *The Monteith College Library Experiment* (Metuchen, N.J.: Scarecrow Press, 1966).
25. See Charles H. Stevens and J. J. Gardner, "Point of Use Library Instruction," in *Educating the Library User*, ed. by John Lubans, Jr. (New York: R. R. Bowker, 1974), pp. 269–278.

26. See Betty L. Hacker and Richard C. Stevens, "Evaluating the AIMLO Project," in *Evaluating Library Use Instruction*, ed. by Richard J. Beeler (Ann Arbor, Mich.: Pierian Press, 1975), pp. 51-65; Richard C. Stevens, Betty L. Hacker, and Karen W. Fachan, "AIMLO: Auto-Instructional Media for Library Orientation. Final Report," mimeographed (Ft. Collins: Colorado State University Libraries, 1974). ERIC document ED105 882.
27. Richard H. Werking, *The Library and the College: Some Programs of Library Instruction* (n.p., 1976), p. 23. ERIC document ED127 917.
28. Sheila Rice and Tim Richards in "Library Instruction: A Column of Opinion," ed. by Carolyn Kirkendall, *Journal of Academic Librarianship* 3 (July 1977): 154-155.

APPENDIX: USING THE CSU LIBRARIES—
A TOUR AND EXERCISE
Topic: History of Motion Pictures*

This exercise has three purposes: first, to conduct you on a self-guided tour of several areas of the Morgan Library; second, to show you the proper procedures for starting the search for information on a subject; and third, to acquaint you with some of the important library tools for general undergraduate use.

The exercise is designed to assist you in locating information from two sources: books and periodicals. This is done in two steps: using the card catalog and periodical indexes, and then finding the item on the shelves. While this exercise is an example of methods used to begin gathering information on one specific topic, the same general approach can be adapted to cover other subject areas in a wide range of interest fields.

No matter how experienced you are in using libraries, it is highly recommended that before you begin this exercise, you inform yourself of the specific arrangement of library materials and services at CSU. Auto-tutorial machines located near the stairway have short slide/tape programs, one on using the card catalog, another on periodical indexes, and a third program on U.S. documents. A series of printed *Guides to the Libraries* is available on a table near the Loan Desk. Guide No. 8 is a Directory and Floor Plan. Use of these various instructional aids will make your exercise easier.

I. LOCATING INFORMATION IN BOOKS

A. The Card Catalog

The major tool for locating information in books is the card catalog. The catalog is divided into three sections: author, title, and subject. Go to the subject section, and look up the heading (Motion pictures—History). Look at one of the first three cards under this heading and write the name of the author. (1) _____
_____. What is the title of the book? (2) _____
_____. Who is the publisher? (3) _____. Where was it published? (4) _____. When was it published? (5) _____. What is the call number? (6) _____. Look at the bottom of the card. You will see listed there, by Arabic number (1, 2, etc.), all the subject headings under which your book

*Words and phrases in parentheses are applicable only to *this Exercise*. Ten "topics" are chosen for use each semester, and each of the ten is tailored to one specific topic. Indexes used vary according to the subject matter. The basic form of the *Exercise* remains the same for each topic.

will be listed in the subject section of the catalog. Are there any additional headings besides (Motion pictures—History) for your book? (7) _____. If so, what are they? (8) _____. This means that there are other subject headings you might consult in the subject catalog, for additional books relating to your topic. Look at the sub-headings under (Motion pictures). If you were looking for (a history of movies in Russia), what would your heading and subheading be? (9) _____.

(Robert Sklar) has written a book on the (social history of American movies). If you did not know the title, and were unsure of the subject heading, to what part of the card catalog would you go to get the rest of the information about this book? (10) _____. What is the title of this book? (11) _____ _____. What is its call number? (12) _____.

The title of a book on the history of motion pictures is *(Behind the Screen)*. You do not know the author, and are unsure of the subject heading. To what part of the card catalog would you go to find the author? (13) _____. Who is the author? (14) _____. What is the call number? (15) _____.

B. Searching for Books

Most books in the library are classified and shelved according to the Library of Congress classification scheme. The call numbers begin with letters, and are further delineated with numbers (for example, DA448/M54). There are some books still left in the Dewey Decimal system, but these are gradually being reclassified into the Library of Congress system. The call numbers in Dewey are arranged principally by number, with no letters preceding the numbers on the top line (for example, 398.48/F68r).

You should have written three separate call numbers on this exercise . . . [items 6, 12, and 15]. Take one of these numbers and see if it can be located on the shelves. To find its specific location, use a *library locator*, available at the Reference Desk and the Loan Desk. There is also a large call number locator on the wall just south of the Loan Desk. The *first letter on the top line* of your call number is the key to its location. The library locator will indicate on which floor and wing you will find your book.

Go the the area where your book is shelved. At the end of each range of shelves (also called "book stacks"), are rectangular, white slip inserts giving the call number sequence for the books housed there. What is the call number sequence for the range in which your book is shelved? (16) _____.

If this were an actual search and not an exercise, you would see if the book were on the shelf, examine it, and if it contained the information you wanted, go to the Loan Desk to check it out. If the book you seek is not on the shelf, several things may explain its absence: (1) someone else may have checked it out, (2) it may have been misshelved (check the shelves nearby), (3) someone may be using it within the building, (4) it may be lost. The Loan Desk has a computer print-out of books and periodicals currently checked out, on reserve, at the bindery, lost, etc. The print-out is arranged by call number. When you cannot find the item you want on the shelf, this is the place to go. If the item you want is not listed on the print-out, ask someone at the Loan Desk for help. For the purposes of this exercise, however, please do not remove the book from the shelf unless you actually plan to use it.

II. LOCATING INFORMATION IN PERIODICALS

A. Periodical Indexes

The best way to find articles in periodicals, on any subject, is through a period-ical index. Some of the frequently used indexes are on tables in the South Foyer, just west of the Reference Desk.

A popular periodical index is the *Readers' Guide to Periodical Literature*, be-cause it indexes articles on a wide range of subjects taken from well-known maga-zines. The *Readers' Guide* is divided into many volumes. Each volume covers articles from periodicals published within a certain time period. A full list of those periodicals indexed by *Readers' Guide*, and their abbreviations, will be found in the beginning of each volume.

Go to (volume 26) of the *Readers' Guide,* located on the index table at the west end of the South Foyer. What are the dates encompassed by the volume? (17) ____ _____. Look up the subject heading (Moving pictures—History). Who wrote the article ("You can't release Dante's Inferno . . .")? (18) _____. What is the *full name* of the periodical in which the article was published? (19) _____. Is there a volume number of the peri-odical in which this article appears? (20) _____. On what pages can you find the article? (21) _____. What is the date of the issue in which the article appears? (22) _____. (Most periodical indexes, including *Readers' Guide,* have an explanation of how to read and use the citations, near the front of each volume.)

The *Readers' Guide* is only one of many periodical indexes. Remember, the *Readers' Guide* primarily indexes periodicals that are of a general, not scholarly, interest. As you progress in your college career, you should depend less on the *Readers' Guide* and more on specialized indexes.

There are many specialized indexes that concentrate on one particular subject field. Anyone doing a literature search on the history of motion pictures should consult the *(Art Index),* where such a topic would receive broad coverage. This index covers periodicals concerned primarily with the field of art and related subject fields, including films, and is located on an index table at the East end of the South Foyer.

Go to (volume 23) of the *(Art Index).* Look up the subject heading (Moving pictures—History). The article entitled ("Evolution of the film star") is found in the periodical (23) _____ (full title), volume number (24) _____, pages (25) _____. The date of the issue of the periodical is (26) _____.

B. Searching for Periodicals

You are now ready to begin the search. To find the call numbers and library holdings for your periodicals, use the Serials Record, a card catalog that contains a listing of all the library's periodicals. The Serials Record is located in the South Foyer, just west of the Reference Desk. The cards in the Serials Record give the holdings for all the bound volumes, or in some cases, microfilm. Current, un-bound issues are not recorded in the Serials Record.

[*Please read carefully the following "Important Tips about Finding Periodicals in the Library" before attempting to complete the exercise.*]

EXAMPLE OF SERIALS RECORD CARD

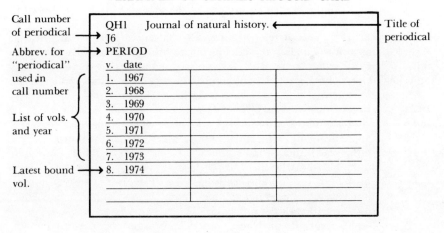

Call number of periodical ——→

Abbrev. for "periodical" used ,in call number

List of vols. and year

Latest bound vol. ——→

QH1
J6

Journal of natural history. ←————— Title of periodical

PERIOD
v. date
1. 1967
2. 1968
3. 1969
4. 1970
5. 1971
6. 1972
7. 1973
8. 1974

IMPORTANT TIPS ABOUT FINDING PERIODICALS IN THE LIBRARY
Much Confusion Can Be Avoided If You Read These Carefully

1. Each periodical is assigned a call number. Always be sure to write down the call number of your particular periodical.
2. All *bound volumes* of periodicals are shelved in the stacks (book shelves), by call number, with the books.
3. Many unbound, current periodicals are shelved on the "current display shelves." These are slanted, hinged shelves, located at the beginning of the wing running north, on the basement, first, and second floors. Here current periodicals are arranged by title, not by call number. The slanted display shelves can be lifted to reveal other, current issues. A list of the periodicals shelved on current display shelves is available for use on the tables adjoining the Serials Record.
4. There are also many current, unbound magazines that are shelved in the stacks, with the bound volumes (they are in pamphlet boxes), because there is not enough room to display all the library's periodicals on the current display shelves. Since they are in the stacks, with the books, these periodicals are arranged by call number.
5. Many back runs of periodicals are received as microform* (see explanation of microform in starred paragraph . . . [below] of this exercise). *If a periodical is on microform, this will be indicated in the Serials Record.* Most micromaterials are housed in the Microtext Room, just west of the Loan Desk.
6. Call numbers marked with the word "Folio" mean that the publication (book or periodical) is oversize, and is shelved in a separate location, with other oversize materials.

You should have references to two different periodicals you found listed in two different indexes. Go the the Serials Record to find the call number of each one.

What is the call number of the *periodical* you found listed in the *Readers' Guide?*
(27) _____. What is the call number of the *periodical* you found listed in
the *(Art Index)*? (28) _____.

The two articles you have references to are found in older, back issues of each
respective magazine. The library does one of two things with back issues of periodicals. They are either bound when the volume for a particular year is complete,
and shelved in the book stacks by call number; or, they are received on microform,
whenever the microform becomes available for each completed volume, and
placed in the Microtext Room. *The Serials Record indicates which periodicals
are on microform, usually by means of a note typed in red at the top of the card.*

    (29) The periodical you found listed in the *Readers' Guide* is located
        A. In the stacks, in a bound volume   (circle one letter)
        B. In the Microtext Room
    (30) The periodical you found listed in the *(Art Index)* is located
        A. In the stacks, in a bound volume   (circle one letter)
        B. In the Microtext Room

*Go to the Microtext Room where your periodical on microform is located.
Is the microform in this room arranged by title, or by call number? (31) _____
_____. There are three kinds of microform; microfilm (35mm negative reels),
microfiche (translucent negative cards), and microcard (opaque positive cards).
Which form is yours? (32) _____.

If this were an actual search, rather than an exercise, you would then place the
microform on one of the viewing machines (called readers) and proceed to read
your article. If you have never used microform, a library staff member from the
Loan Desk or in the Microtext Room will be happy to show you how to use the
equipment.

Except for those periodicals that have ceased publication, most periodicals
listed in the Serials Record are received currently, on a regular basis. Current,
unbound issues of magazines are either placed on the current display shelves (as
described in No. 3 of "Important Tips about Finding Periodicals"), or they are
shelved in the book stacks, in pamphlet boxes, along with the books and bound
volumes of periodicals.

    (33) Current, unbound periodicals on the display shelves are arranged by
        A. Title   (circle one letter)
        B. Call number
    (34) Current periodicals shelved in the stacks are arranged by
        A. Title   (circle one letter)
        B. Call number

This brief exercise has introduced you to a few of the library's resources, and
methods of locating materials. If you need assistance in your library research,
please consult a Reference Librarian. The General Reference Desk, on the first
floor, and the Science Reference Desk, on the second floor, are staffed during
most of the hours the building is open.

*[Your opinions and advice are valued.
Please complete the student reaction sheet.]*

Student Reaction Sheet

Your answers to the following questions will help in the evaluation of this type of exercise and its effectiveness in assisting your use of library resources. Please put the appropriate numbers in the boxes at right of page.

A. Do you think this test will help you in using the Library?
   1. Yes   2. No   3. Not sure

B. Did you find the test
   1. Too long   2. Too short   3. About right

C. How long did it take you to do the test? Please give the number of minutes.

D. Were you confused by any part or parts of the test?
   1. Yes   2. No

E. If the answer to "D" is yes, please write the number for that area which confused you most in the box at right.
   1. Identification and Location of Periodicals
   2. Periodical Indexes
   3. Microtext Materials
   4. Use of the Card Catalog
   5. Other _____

F. Do you think this type of self-guided exercise is more helpful than a guided tour of the Library, or a lecture on using the Library?
   1. Yes   2. No   3. About the same   4. Not sure

G. Is there anything in the test you would like to see added, deleted, or changed? Please write out your answer below.

Answer Key: History of Motion Pictures

1.-6. Rhode, Eric
   A history of the cinema. N.Y., Hill and Wang, 1976.
   PN1993.5/A1R46

   Wenden, David John
   The birth of the movies. N.Y., Dutton, 1975.
   PN1993.5/A1W4

   Armes, Roy
   Film and reality. Harmondsworth, Penguin, 1974.
   PN1993.5/A1A74

7.-8. No

9. Motion pictures—Russia—History
10. Author
11. Movie-made America
12. PN1993.5/U6S53
13. Title
14. Macgowan, Kenneth
15. PN1993.5/A1M28
16. PN1031   PN1996
    A85   to   P55
    1967

17. March 1966–February 1967
18. S. N. Behrman
19. New York Times Magazine
20. No
21. 6-7+
22. July 17, 1966
23. Films in Review
24. 25
25. 591-4
26. December 1974
27. AN1/N4/NEWSP
28. PN1993/F6473
29. B
30. A
31. Call number
32. Microfilm
33. A
34. B

NOTE TO Col02 INSTRUCTORS:

During the course of the semester, new books on this subject may be acquired, and additional cards filed under this subject heading, making the answer key outdated. We will try to inform you of any changes.

Please caution students against marking or otherwise defacing the pages of the periodical index volumes they are asked to use. This is a serious problem we'd like to avoid.

Please see that the student evaluation sheets are returned to Morgan Library (room 116) so that we may continue to evaluate and improve this exercise. Thank you.

Student Reactions

Results from 1092 completed reaction sheet forms, 1977-78 semesters

Your answers to the following questions will help in the evaluation of this type of exercise and its effectiveness in assisting your use of library resources. Please put the appropriate numbers in the boxes at right of page.

A. Do you think this test will help you in using the Library?

   1. Yes 915   2. No 82   3. Not sure 91   No response 4
          84%   7%   8%   .3%

B. Did you find the test

   1. Too long 268   2. Too short 14   3. About right 800   No response 10
              25%   1%   73%   1%

C. How long did it take you to do the test? Please give the number of minutes.

      Mean   Mode   Median   Range
      55 min.   60 min.   56 min.   10-150 min.

D. Were you confused by any part or parts of the test?

   1. Yes 433   2. No 648   No response 11
         40%   60%   1%

E. If the answer to "D" is yes, please write the number for that area which confused you most in the box at right.

   1. Identification and Location of Periodicals 103—7%
   2. Periodical Indexes 89—8%
   3. Microtext Materials 157—13%
   4. Use of the Card Catalog 25—3%
   5. Other 76—7%
     No response 624—60%

F. Do you think this type of self-guided exercise is more helpful than a guided tour of the Library, or a lecture on using the Library?

   1. Yes 642   2. No 129   3. About the same 195   4. Not sure 113
        60%   12%   17%   9%

   No response 12—1%

G. Is there anything in the test you would like to see added, deleted, or changed? Please write out your answer below.

PUBLIC LIBRARIES: TEACHING THE USER?

SHERYL ANSPAUGH
*Director of Learning Resources, Houston
Community College; Formerly Administrative Assistant, Tulsa City-County Library*

Library use instruction has become a vital issue of concern to nearly all librarians except those associated with public libraries. School libraries, college and university libraries, even special libraries, are realizing the need to educate people to effective library use. Public librarians have not yet realized that this is a need of their users.

A review of the literature on library use instruction relating to public libraries can be accomplished very quickly. There are no listings for public libraries under the heading "Library Use Instruction." Using the index *Library Literature*, 1974 to the present, one finds citation after citation on the subject as it regards schools and colleges and universities. In 1976, one citation appears for an article in *Sovetskaia Bibliografiia* on adults and library use instructions. In 1974–1975, three citations appear under adults: one is to a chapter in John Lubans's book *Educating the Library User* (R. R. Bowker, 1974); a second relates to engineers and library use instruction; and the third is in *Technicheskaia Informatsiia*. If public libraries are working with library use instruction, it is being kept a secret.

In 1977 there was one public librarian at the American Library Association (ALA) conference program on instruction in the use of libraries. College, university, and school librarians were the members most in attendance. Teaching people to effectively and efficiently use libraries and to be knowledgeable of their many resources has not yet come of age in the public library. For now, library use instruction lies sleeping and is only gently nudged by the libraries' public relations efforts.

In an attempt to gain a sense of developments in library use instruction in public libraries, a brief questionnaire was sent out. Public libraries of varying sizes across the nation were asked to respond to 14 questions. Of the 130 surveys mailed, 75 responses were received, answering questions on concepts and attitudes toward library use instruction and programs developed for instruction, plus a question on public relations.

FORMAL AND INFORMAL METHODS
OF LIBRARY USE INSTRUCTION

The few library use instruction programs that were substantiated by the survey are generally of two styles. One is the formal "class" presentation in which a public library offers a program on library use and education to a group of people at a particular time. It is usually a class in how to utilize the library, its services and resources. This trend is encouraging since most participants, upon evaluation, state that they have found the course valuable and interesting. Unfortunately, in a year's time a public library may reach only 20–30 people, helping them to become enlightened library users.

One such successful program with implications for most city libraries is aimed primarily at secretaries. People in business frequently need information—a telephone number or address, the names of corporate stockholders, assets held, competitors in other countries. Often secretaries are expected to locate this information. Libraries, especially central public libraries in the downtown business district, can become valuable resources to the business person via the secretary, and sending a secretary to a "how to use" class can be a real benefit to the employer or company.

Along this same line of formal library instruction is the opportunity for public librarians to address the General Education Development Test (GED), literacy or adult basic education classes. These and similar programs either may be offered by the public library or library space may be provided for classes given by the high school or other community groups. Students in these classes, realizing the limitations of their education or language skills, seek knowledge aggressively. One question on the survey asked if Adult Basic Education literacy-program students were taught the role of the library and its use. Half of the respondents said that they taught library use not at all or only sometimes. Of the half who said they did offer library instruction, some programs may consist of only a tour or a handout.

There seems to be a high correlation between those people who do not ask for help and those who do not get what they want from the library.[1] Unsuccessful use can easily become nonuse when people who have poor library skills do not ask for help, thus never giving the librarian an opportunity to teach the most basic skills in a one-to-one encounter. This "informal" method of library use instruction is the assistance and instruction given by the reference librarian when approached by the user. This is the oldest, most traditional, and incidentally probably one of the best methods of library use instruction. However, for it to be an effective method, several things must occur. First the user must be bold enough to seek assistance. All reference librarians hear: "I hate to ask a stupid question, but. . . ?" People assume the arrangement of knowledge is simple, and are ashamed or uncomfortable at not being able to locate the needed information. Second, the librarian must explain and instruct the user in the design and use of the system as it specifically relates to the information sought. If this is done the user becomes a learner and more adept at self-help on a return visit with a similar question. Two drawbacks to this method are the limited knowledge and narrow scope of library use that can be imparted in a single question/interview and the assumption that the librarian *is* a teacher and has taken the time and effort, beyond pointing to the card catalog, to teach usable skills.

Yet library use instruction is considered important by public librarians. According to the 75 librarians responding to the survey, 69 indicated that instruction in the use of libraries was important or necessary. But over half of those indicating its importance had no program of library use instruction or only the informal instruction received by the individual seeking assistance from the reference librarian. And of this group, 66 percent had had no previous programs of library use instruction while 33 percent had discontinued such a program. The main reason given for discontinuing a program was a lack of either public interest or staff time. A certain subjective passiveness to the entire idea of library use instruction in public libraries prevails in the survey responses.

Perhaps many public librarians have not yet firmly established in their minds the necessity of formal library use instruction programs. This may be an area they feel is better suited to the academic environment. Certainly the concept and philosophy of library use instruction is fairly new, but it has caught on rapidly in the world of education—probably because of courses requiring term papers and reports, hence library use. Or perhaps, since little or nothing was offered on this topic during librarians' training, an awareness of such instruction's possible incorporation into public library activities is still dormant. A major reason for the lack of interest and achievement with regard to library use instruction could be the idea that public libraries may be doing it—but calling it public relations instead. A good public relations program may be the first step toward a library use instruction program, but it is not the rest of the dance.

At the 1975 ALA Conference in San Francisco, Dr. Marcia J. Bates addressed the Instruction in the Use of Libraries Committee program. Dr. Bates mentions that the role of librarians and their view of themselves should be one of "an increasingly important and central profession, educating the public about the importance of information skills, and manifesting those skills ourselves in an increasingly visible and essential way in our society." The question will no longer be instruction versus finding it for them, but doing both. "If we educate the public to what is there, teach them how to find information for themselves, and help them find the more difficult stuff . . . we can have a real effect. . . ."[2]

This attitude should be especially important to public librarians. Stating the obvious (which is often overlooked), public librarians are supported *by* the public *for* the public. Revenue for operation comes from the public tax dollar appropriated by politicians. Salaries, book budgets, building and maintenance budgets, depend on the public and the politician. The public library needs to educate and serve its public. That is the source of its political support and revenue. Each library user served is a voter or potential voter. Librarians should campaign every day for their libraries, and that means service, instruction, and confident, competent users. If citizens are educated throughout their lives to library use then perhaps they would provide the strong, solid base of support public libraries need. The 75 percent of our society that has seemed willing to subsidize the 1.8 percent that uses the libraries is now looking critically at tax-supported services.[3] The culmination of efforts to get that support is the National White House Conference on Libraries and Information Services, where nonlibrarians will be the largest number in attendance—a recognition that the support must come from the people.

As the importance of information-finding and information-gathering skills becomes more evident, public librarians are developing a political awareness. This was corroborated in the survey. Eighty percent of the responding librarians indicated that their library use instruction programs have "just begun" or are "modestly developed." A well-developed program was indicated by only 4 percent, while 13.6 percent indicated no programs. Seventy percent of the responding librarians indicated some staff interest in library use instruction. High staff interest existed at 25 percent of the responding libraries, while 5 percent said library use instruction had never been discussed.

Two types of programs of library use instruction have been mentioned. These are the formal class presentation and the informal one-to-one reference tutorial. Other public library programs less "library-use oriented" and more "services oriented" are those with junior and senior high school classes, adult independent learners, and information center users.

Unfortunately the public librarian rarely seems to have the opportunity to plan with teachers an effective presentation on using the library. More often than not, a Sunday afternoon produces students requesting books on alcoholism or child abuse. The librarian patiently searches all the available books, indices, and magazines, and after the seventh request on the identical topic realizes that it is term paper time. But if librarians find it frustrating, it is not too difficult to empathize with the students whose papers are due on Tuesday. It is maddening to tell user after user and sometimes parent after parent that all the material has been checked out.

In an attempt to ameliorate this frustration, some public libraries have developed preprinted forms explaining to the classroom teacher that materials on a particular topic are exhausted. Also, some librarians will suggest alternative topics for term paper reports.

Public librarians reported through the survey that high school students have only minimal library skills. These skills improve to satisfactory on the college level, but only a few respondents indicated adequate skills on either the high school or college level.

In a second question regarding library use instruction, 38 percent of the responding librarians indicated that they conducted programs of user education with the high schools in the area. This could mean anything from a tour of facilities to a basic lesson on use of the public library to having every student sign up for a library card. But it does indicate an effort, weak as it may be, to lessen the frustration of the "Sunday panic."

Extending the concept of the GED in the public library is the recently emphasized service to adult independent learners. This is an in-depth service to individual self-motivated learners. The service has the potential of providing opportunity for an excellent program of library use instruction on a one-to-one level as a continuous working relationship is developed between user and librarian. However, there is still a failure to instruct many learners in the independent use of the library.

Another effort by public libraries to reach users is through "information services." Detroit has TIP (Total Information Place), Tulsa has Citizen Information, San Francisco has BARC (Bay Area Reference Center), and there are others. Truly "information" centers in the broadest sense, they will supply verification of lottery number winners, provide assistance on whom to contact for welfare or the name of an ombudsperson to help with "city hall." As Bates says, "public libraries are moving in . . . with information and referral services. But this should not just be viewed as a public library function or as a frill or extra in any library's activities. In a society of growing complexity such as this one, information is becoming central to life success. You need information to negotiate the system and you need the system to stay alive and thrive."[4]

Information centers offer a much needed service and generally result in a good public image of the library. However, they do not promote or encourage library use instruction. People recognize that the public library does indeed have information for them, but it is a giant step from receiving information to learning how to use the library. As public libraries become more concerned with nonusers and as they develop instruments to measure use an interest in library use instruction will undoubtedly develop in public libraries. But for now little if any thought has been given to tying libraries and library use skill together.

PUBLIC RELATIONS IS NOT LIBRARY USE INSTRUCTION

In recent years public libraries have become aware of public relations and the need to project a positive, progressive image. A good public relations program is vitally important to the public library but it must not be mistaken for library use instruction—it is merely the first step. Developing a community awareness of the library is important; getting people interested through travel programs, dog shows, "meet the (politicians) candidates," and book talks make a community conscious of libraries. Story hours, summer reading programs, space for meetings of all types, special displays, amnesty days for overdue books—all entice the people but stop short of developing them as users.

Public relations programs have been developed by 83 percent of the responding public librarians. The two most popular efforts are with newspapers and radio. Television rates third. Thus, efforts *are* being made to get the public in. But when librarians were asked what they offer to those seeking library use instruction, two-thirds responded that they give a tour of the facility and resources. A tour orients users to the physical facility. They now know where the reference and/or circulation librarian sits, where the water fountain is, perhaps the location of the *Readers' Guide* and very likely the card catalog. But they still do not know where to go first for the information they need or what to do when they get there. And orientation tours tend to lose people—if not physically, at least mentally.

Printed handouts, if well done, with colors, big type, pictures, and white space, can provide basic information that will be read. But it should be limited to the basics, or people will not read it. Fifty-two percent of the public libraries surveyed use printed handouts as a library instruction tool.

Visual and auditory media produce stronger impressions and impart more information, so media programs have been developed to provide orientation and instruction. Media presentations are used in 25 percent of the responding libraries. Good media programs, like clever handouts, require hours of planning, developing, and implementing. Knowledge and talented assistance are needed if the final product is to look professional. It takes time and money and even then the results are sometimes disappointing.

A class presentation in the use of resources is offered by 35 of the 75 public libraries responding. However, the questionnaire did not provide for further specification of what is meant by a "class" in library use instruction. It could be an in-depth program for secretaries, or a one-time presentation to junior and senior high school classes preparing papers, or a community service multiple-session program such as Denver's, given for anyone who wants to sign up. The extent and depth of the program depend on the librarian and the user.

Library instruction appears to be limited at this time, closely associated with public relations and general library orientation. Tours of the public library facility seem to be the most popular service. Printed handouts, class instruction, and media presentations are listed second, third, and fourth respectively as orientation programs. Evaluations of any kind are conducted by only one-third of the libraries, thus making it difficult to determine effectiveness.

Efforts at public relations and interesting the citizenry in public libraries have not stopped with handouts and story hours. Public librarians know that public relations are vital. Interesting all parts of the community in library services is a true challenge, especially in competition with television. So some libraries lend tools to go with the do-it-yourself books; others lend toys and have programs for parents in how best to utilize toys with their children for educational benefit. Other libraries lend records, sculpture, graphics, and art reproductions, all of which are a delight to the borrower. All citizens are offered the niceties of our culture usually limited to the affluent. The public library philosophy has been to provide the opportunity for education, growth, success in achievement, to everyone. With free secondary education and a university education attainable by more and more people, the public library seeks a new role in democratizing society.

Libraries offer to all the music, art, and toys the individual cannot always afford to buy. However, the ones who should be availing themselves of these riches are probably still standing outside the huge glass and stone structure of the library looking in at the large sign reading "Bibliographic Information Center." If they cannot say it, they will probably not ask about it and would never think of using it. A simple sign saying "Information" or "Ask for Help Here" with a friendly person to guide the user, would serve better.

Edward Montana offers the following advice on library signs. "Signs using library jargon do not serve their purpose and can even reinforce the patron's feeling that he would rather be somewhere else. They also waste the staff's time, making them give information that should have been on signs in the first place. 'Kardex,' 'Xerox,' 'Vertical File,' 'Subject Entry,' even 'Reference' and 'Interlibrary Loan!' The librarian might as well be talking Greek."[5]

The reluctant person who stops at the information desk to seek help while apologizing for being so dumb was mentioned earlier. What about all those who never muster enough courage to even approach the desk? Librarians' getting up and making the first contact with the user probably does more for public relations than any one single public relations piece. This idea is substantiated by Montana when he says, "As far as the staff's attitude is concerned no more needs to be said than that they should know when to help and when to leave the patron alone and that a smile and a willing manner can do more to improve a library's image than almost anything else."[6]

Public relations and library use instruction complement each other. Citizen awareness of libraries increases with public relation efforts and citizen use and appreciation of the library increase with understanding and instruction in the resources.

COOPERATION AMONG TYPES OF LIBRARIES

Public librarians have not yet realized their own importance in the world of information gathering and information exchange. Until they do and can convince others of their importance, library use instruction will be only a frill, not a necessity. An aggressively cooperative attitude between librarians and educators requires continued development. The ineptitude of most instructors when it comes to libraries is amazing. A start should be made in the educational program of teachers to learn about library services and resources. Public and school librarians, educational administrators at all levels, and teachers all need to work together.

For example, Houston Community College students are being given further opportunities to use the public library while having the support of their campus librarian. In an experimental program begun in the summer of 1978, the Houston Public Library catalog on microfilm is available at Houston Community College campuses. Students are encouraged to use the public library catalog, learn the Dewey decimal system, and make requests for public library materials. Students in the occupational skills classes have had their librarian take them to the Houston Public Library to introduce them to public library facilities and staff members. These people will soon be graduates of the college, and the public library will become their resource for remaining knowledgeable in their careers. The students thus have the opportunity to develop a comfortable feeling with public libraries while still holding on to their community college library apron string.

Through computer access and miniaturized catalogs more material and information are becoming available; catalog duplication and exchange is feasible and exists. Knowing how to get around one library is a start but having a working ability and understanding to get around libra*ries* is becoming increasingly important. All libraries are in the business of education. Surely there is a mutual responsibility during this phase of development.

It is important to lobby legislators on matters of concern to libraries, and request library schools to provide course work in effectively implementing library use instruction programs.

It is up to librarians to make the library a viable, vital part of the community. No one else is going to do it. If people do not use the library, do not know of its riches, they will not continue paying for it. Library use instruction, on all levels, is absolutely essential to libraries' existence and, if Bates is correct, it is essential to the public's existence.

NOTES

1. Suzanne Boles, Tulsa Public Library Community Services Coordinator, Telephone Conversation, May 11, 1978.
2. Marcia J. Bates, "Educating Librarians and Users for a New Model of Library Service" Keynote Address, Instruction in the Use of Libraries Committee Program, American Library Association, San Francisco, July 1, 1975 (cassette tape) Los Angeles: *Development Digest*, 1976.
3. C. M. Tiebout and R. J. Willis, "The Public Nature of Libraries," in *The Public Library and the City*, ed. by Ralph W. Conant (Cambridge, Mass.: MIT Press, 1965), pp. 97-98.
4. Bates, "Educating Librarians."
5. Edward J. Montana, Jr., "Public Relations for the Metropolitan Library," in *Public Relations for Libraries*, ed. by Allan Angoff (Westpark, Conn.: Williamhouse-Regency, Inc., 1973), pp. 15-47.
6. Montana, "Public Relations," pp. 15-47.

BIBLIOGRAPHY

Allen, M. "TV Technique Is Fighting T.V." *Library Association Record* 78: (Spring '76): 427.

Angoff, Allan, ed., *Public Relations for Libraries*. Williamhouse-Regency, Inc., 1973.

Bates, Marcia J., "Educating Librarians and Users for a New Model of Library Service." Keynote Address, Instruction in the Use of Libraries Committee Program, American Library Association, San Francisco, July 1, 1975 (cassette tape), Los Angeles: *Development Digest*, 1976.

Boles, Suzanne, Tulsa Public Library Community Services Coordinator, Tulsa Oklahoma. Interview, May 11, 1978.

Fitzgerald, S. "Effective Approach to Library Instruction in Departmental Training Courses." *State Librarian* 25 (July 1977): 25.

Galloway, S. "Nobody Is Teaching the Teachers." *Booklegger Magazine* 3 (January-February 1976): 29-31.

_____. "Helping Users Find Their Way." *Wisconsin Library Bulletin* 73 (July 1977): 145-166.

Kirk, T. G. "Past, Present and Future of Library Instruction." Bibliography. *South East Librarian* 27 (Spring 1977): 15-18.

McGowan, O. T. P. "Library Instruction Needed." *Catholic Library World* 48 (November 1976): 185.

_____. "One Third of the Nation Has Never Used a Library." *New York Library Association Bulletin* 24 (Fall 1976): 6.

Poyer, R. K. "Improved Library Services through User Education." *Medical Library Association Bulletin* 65 (April 1977): 276-277.

INNOVATION IN LIBRARY INSTRUCTION APPLIED TO AN ADULT EDUCATION COURSE

Christopher Compton
Library Consultant, Denver, Colorado

In the spring of 1977, I decided to test some personal ideas about library education that had grown out of my experience over a period of years. This is a personal account of the background of these ideas, the ways in which they were actualized, and the responses on the part of the people involved.

Having served in both high school and college libraries, I had observed fully the variety of postures toward libraries by a majority of students: ineptitude, indifference, fear, frustration, and, to be sure, hostility. I was never content to accept these postures as being static; perhaps because of a deep affection for libraries long before becoming a librarian, I was incapable of accepting such attitudes. Then, too, there had been those nourishing experiences in which such postures were fractured, when some student somewhere yielded to the lure of the riches I proffered via the library. In such conversion experiences, I have wondered whether it is the student or the librarian who has the greater reward. In one sense, surely, each is the other's reward.

Dissatisfaction with negative and ignorant student attitudes sent me more than once to the literature of library education. Somehow, whatever good or applicable ideas I took from the literature dead-ended in the institutions to which they were brought. There was never enough time, or enough staff, or enough money, or enough interest. (Or all of the above.) I continued, nevertheless, to search for new ways of dealing with old problems.

A NEW DIRECTION

During the early part of 1974, the Department of English of the college at which I was a reference librarian scheduled library orientation tours for all its freshman classes. The first day of the tours was awful; with individual exceptions, apathy and boredom were preponderant in every group. At day's end, I was determined to prevent such an experience from being repeated.

The following day, I began the first tour by taking the group aside and asking what some of their personal interests were. There was no response. A new freshman class, the students were self-conscious among themselves and they were hesitant to trust a faculty member whom they didn't know with such personal information. I treated their silence lightly and invited them to speak out as we went along. I told them that most of my time was spent helping students find information—not only for their courses but also for their personal pursuits.

We began with specifics at the periodical index tables where I had earlier selected entries on certain topics that I knew interested most students. Moving from one index to another, I would turn to a preselected entry, read it aloud, and mention related sources of information on the same topic. In each case, I would ask for any questions about the topic of the entry. Slowly, the questions began to come. Usually, at the close of each topic discussed, I would point out that that particular index would be a great help to anyone in a particular course.

The methodology employed at the index tables was adapted, whenever possible, to orient the students to every resource and every service of the library. By the conclusion of the tours, we had discussed sources of information in various forms on music (rock, folk, guitar, performers), drugs, motorcycles, vans, cars, sports, and a number of other subjects, including information about various careers. At the end of every tour, the students were told to return as soon as possible and learn how to use the tools that could lead them to information they wanted on any subject, that they had to know how to use these tools for their courses anyway, and so the sooner they took care of the matter, the better it would be for them. The point of learning to use information resources was treated casually—a person either was sharp, well-informed, knew the score, kept on top of things, knew that information was *power* to shape things for the self, or else a person walked around in a fog, forfeited the power of self-determination, and thereby let the world decide for him or her. With a parting assurance that any help needed would be available if only they would *ask*, each tour was concluded.

Within the two weeks following, a small number of students did return and ask questions related to the tours. How many students returned on their own, without a word to me, cannot be known. The crucial distinction is, of course, the contrast between the tours of the first day and those of the second day. On both days, the students were shown the same resources and informed of the same services. On the first day, students were given a rather perfunctory tour in which the educational resources of the library available to support their courses were indicated to them. Response was virtually nil. On the second day, students were given a very personalized introduction to library resources in which generalities were replaced with specific appeals to their interests. The increase in response and attention was dramatic and, wonderously, some students began to express thanks at the end of the tours.

The insinuative strategy of inducing students to learn library skills by appeal to their interests and appetites appears to offer great promise for those ignorant of libraries and lacking the self-motivation and self-discipline to undertake the task—i.e., the majority of students. Academic matters are neither omitted nor ignored, but rather subsumed under the more arresting and penetrating appeal of personal interests.

Four years have passed since the tours and I have used the strategy many times on an individual basis with numerous people of various ages. In the beginning, I thought a profound breakthrough had been achieved and, in the area of my own personal performance, that was true. In retrospect, however, I would have to say that there is nothing profound involved. What is involved is, very simply, *good teaching*. Good teaching has many attributes; the two that seem crucial in the area under discussion are creativeness and enthusiasm invested as energy in the subject.

AN EXPERIMENT

In time I decided that the methodology employed in the orientation tours should be tested within the structure of a course. In 1975, such a course was designed and was supported by the library director of another college where I served as a reference librarian. Due to a series of circumstances in which the college moved to a new campus and my contract ended, the course was never offered in the college. Because I have not worked in an academic library since that time, the course was set aside but not forgotten.

In 1977, the idea came to me to offer the course in the area of adult education. Denver Free University (DFU), the facility chosen for the course, is not a school with a campus and a library. It simply provides administrative services in which teachers as independent contractors are brought together with interested students who choose to receive instruction from those teachers.

My course was easily changed to accommodate adult education. What could not be changed was the fact that the course could not be offered without a library.

In keeping with the guiding principle of appeal to personal interests, the course was entitled, "How to Find Out about Everything." In the DFU catalog, it was described essentially as an introduction to the tools and techniques of retrieving information on any and all subjects. Mindful of the negative images that the word *library* brings to so many unenlightened minds, that word was avoided in the course listing and description except for necessary use in listing the course text, *Guide to the Use of Books and Libraries* by Jean Key Gates (McGraw-Hill, 1974). The course lasted for eight weeks, met every Monday from 6:00 P.M. to 7:30 P.M., and received the maximum set enrollment of twelve students.

The first meeting was in a junior high school classroom. The students were told that the course had something for everyone, that for whatever reason they were there—help in some studies, job advancement, upgrading a routine existence—by the time the course was over they would not be disappointed if they had done their part in the learning process. "How to Find Out about Everything," they were told, was based on the premise that if they learned the basic tools and techniques of finding information, and later progressed on their own to more advanced methods, they should be able to find out about everything that is knowable.

Everyone was given paper on which to write name, occupation, occupation preferred if present occupation was undesirable, personal interests and hobbies, and choice of subjects for emphasis in the course. (This information was useful to me in getting to know the students and in being able to appeal to their interests.)

With all questions discussed, goals and guidelines set, and texts distributed, the meeting was adjourned.

The solution to the problem of providing a library for the course resulted in an innovation that might never have evolved had the problem not existed. For the next seven weeks, the class met in different libraries in downtown Denver. A tour was given by a staff member of each library and in the process the class not only saw nonpublic areas and operations but also learned of (and saw) resources they might otherwise never have discovered. By the end of the course, the class had toured the following libraries: Department of Documentary Resources, State Historical Society of Colorado; Denver Public Library (main facility); The Western History Library; The Conservation Library; Colorado State Library; Auraria Higher Education Complex Library; Environmental Protection Agency Library; and the Learning Resources Center, Community College of Denver (Auraria Campus).

It was a fine mixture of the general and the special, and of municipal, state, and federal facilities. Clearly, the tours were a significant library educational experience.

Following each tour, the class met in a prearranged space within the library toured. At these meetings, selected chapters from the course text were surveyed and supplemental information in the form of pamphlets or duplicated material was sometimes distributed. Usually, written questions covering the material assigned were distributed. The questions involved finding information in and by means of the sources discussed. A student could later take the quiz to almost any library to find the answers.

The students were told that since they were involved in adult education they were being treated as adults. The chapters assigned and the quizzes distributed were for their learning and advancement and it was assumed that everything was being read and understood. There wasn't enough time, they were told, to have the tours and full class discussions. If the reading contained something they did not comprehend, or if there were questions to which they failed to find the answers, I offered to meet with them before or after class—or they could telephone me at home.

The class membership was varied, with seven females and five males, ranging in age from near 20 to past 60. There was one counter-culturalist, one part-time college student, a retired engineer, a housewife, a writer's research assistant, a high school counselor, a community resource coordinator, two registered nurses, and three mechanics. The educational levels of these people are not known (such questions are not asked), but nobody had difficulty with comprehension in the course.

The counter-culturalist dropped out about two-thirds of the way through the course. The high school counselor missed most of the course due to illness, but at the end was given a special two-hour class to cover some of what she had missed. All other students completed the course and most attended every class.

At the last class meeting, an evaluation form was given to the students. All were very definite that the course had "fulfilled their expectations." Some said their expectations were exceeded and some even asked for a follow-up course. Most indicated that the course needed more time. Under "comments and suggestions," the enthusiasm of the teacher was cited as a major factor in the course.

In the fall, the course was offered once again at DFU. Each class was extended to two hours. The same libraries were visited except for the federal library segment. The class was taken this time to the Federal Building (downtown Denver) where there were staff discussions at a U.S. Government Printing Office bookstore, a Federal Information Center, and a Department of Labor library. A class meeting in a small Health, Education and Welfare library concluded the meeting.

The single, large difference between the first and second offerings of the course was the enrollment and the number of students completing the course. On the second offering, only eight enrolled and only four finished. The problem was that the course met from 4:00 P.M. to 6:00 P.M.; DFU is primarily a night school operation. Evaluation forms from the students who completed the second course duplicated the response of the first class: very positive.

Next term, two sections (more if required) of the course with twenty students each will be offered through "Learning for Living," an adult education arm of Metropolitan State College in Denver. The classes will again meet for two hours, but the course has been shortened (by the school) to six weeks. There are so far no changes contemplated in content or methodology, and the same positive response is expected.

CONCLUSION

In terms of approach, the only difference between the orientation tours in 1974 and the courses in 1977 has been one of scope and degree. The operating principle behind both was the appeal to the personal interests of the students. On the orientation tours, students were exposed to one library for less than one hour. In the courses, students were guided through eight libraries—and one-half of a library handbook—in 16 hours. The very popular library tours in the courses were simply another appeal to their interests. No real learning took place, beyond discovery of existence and location of materials. For the learning, the students must return, on their own, and must do for themselves. It is at once, an invitation and a challenge.

For a librarian, the approach described herein is hard work. Gone are facile discussions of the abstract, and the endless piling up of generalities so deadly to attention and any initial interest. There must be a constant sentience toward the students, a creative readiness to respond with substance and ingenuity, and an enthusiasm that creates interest (or even excitement) without overwhelming. For the librarian or teacher who is vitally interested in library education (the lukewarm need not apply), it will come as no surprise that I recommend the methods described.

I had a parting message for each class:

If I were any one of you and I had found this course valuable, this is what I would do. I would set aside some weekly time that suited me, take my text, and in some library I would start the course over again. When I got to the point where this course stopped, I would continue to the end of the book. In doing this, I would expect all the things we covered so quickly to "sink in" and thus become my own.

In all librarianship, I believe, there can be no greater calling than to take people from any and all walks of life and open up their minds and show them new horizons, helping them to see that they are far more than they seem to themselves to be. It is both an adventure and a fulfillment—for the librarian and the people.

THE LIBRARY SCHOOL: ITS ROLE IN TEACHING THE USE OF THE LIBRARY

VIDA STANTON

Assistant Professor, School of Library Science, University of Wisconsin-Milwaukee

A question frequently asked of library educators deals with the desirability of incorporating library skills instruction into the educational program for library students. Presently it seems to be receiving affirmative responses and follow-up action for a variety of reasons. Guidelines presented by professional groups and disseminated through the literature have emphasized this need. New guidelines developed by the American Library Association's (ALA) Reference and Adult Services Division specify that "a specific plan for the instruction of individuals in the use of information aids is to be developed and coordinated among all types of libraries, information centers or units of library activity."[1] The Standards for College Libraries approved by the Association of College and Research Libraries (ACRL) in 1975 state, "Proper service shall include: the provision of continuing instruction to patrons in the effective exploitation of libraries. . . ."[2] The Bibliographic Instruction Task Force of ACRL (now the ACRL Bibliographic Instruction Section) developed "Guidelines for Bibliographic Instruction in Academic Libraries," which were approved as policy by the ACRL Board of Directors on January 31, 1977, "in order to assist college and university libraries in planning and evaluation of effective programs to instruct members of the academic community in the identification and use of information resources."[3] *Media Programs: District and School*, published by the ALA and the Association for Educational Communications and Technology in 1975, points out that "the school media program recognizes the need for helping learners acquire and maintain skills in researching, choosing, and using all forms of media" and the same source identifies one of the ongoing activities within the school library media program as "planning and providing instruction in the use of the media center and its resources."[4] More and more descriptions of public service positions include references to the need for competency in instructional duties. The phrases identifying the need for this qualification may be disguised in a variety of terms; examples cited recently include "interest in library user programs," "actively promote the use of the library," "instruction in the use of scientific literature," and "involves bibliographic instruction, library tours, and some reference service." One recent advertisement in *Library Journal* is quoted here in part because it brings together aspects of this specialization with which library educators should be concerned:

> INSTRUCTIONAL SERVICES Librarian. The successful applicant for this new position will have the freedom to develop programs that maximize student and faculty utilization of the library's resources, and support the academic goals of the university. The librarian will teach sections of Bibliography I, an all-university course requirement, will plan and implement innovations in modes of instruction and format for these lower division classes, will, in cooperation with upper division faculty, design and present course related instructional modules that focus on the literature and research strategy of a specific discipline, and will develop appropriate bibliographic and library user guides. Minimum qualifications include an M.L.S. from an A.L.A. accredited school, a broad general education background, superior communication skills and the ability to provide the imaginative and dynamic leadership needed to give direction to and further develop the teaching function of the library. . . .[5]

One might say this advertisement was written by an exceptionally forward-looking library administrator. If the decision makers in library education were equally forward-looking, curriculum committees could give this specialty a high priority in their deliberations, admissions counselors could be identifying some of the competencies desired that may come from curricula outside the library school, and program advisers and placement specialists could be aware of the increasing number of opportunities for this type of specialty. In addition to prospective employers, other groups that show a growing interest (even expectation) in formal instruction of new librarians for educating users are the ALA Committee on Instruction in the Use of Libraries, the ACRL Bibliographic Instruction Section, and the recently formed ALA Library Instruction Round Table (LIRT). All three of these groups have discussed and promoted the acceptance of this responsibility by graduate library schools over the past few years.

THE NEED FOR TEACHING LIBRARY INSTRUCTION IN LIBRARY SCHOOLS

A library instruction course integrated into the regular library school curriculum should prepare students for planning and implementing instructional programs before graduation rather than their being put into frequently stressful "planning from panic" situations on the job. It might also improve a recent graduate's chances of being considered for professional positions requiring this type of special skill or knowledge. Certainly the case for the library schools' offering a course with this content is related to the goals of most library education programs, which usually state in some way that the school intends to prepare students for *professional* service in libraries, information systems, and media centers. The preceding paragraphs should dispel any doubt that library instruction is considered a part of professional service by the practitioner; therefore its proponents in the field believe that if library education programs do indeed prepare students for professional service, then courses offering training in library instruction should be much more evident in the curricula of library schools.

Library schools often insist that the topic of instruction is covered within "type of library" or reference courses. "Cover" may be the key word—added to the existing overload of those courses, library instruction usually does not receive the emphasis it deserves and is covered in various degrees and with a variety of approaches, if at all. If one accepts the concept of library instruction as a major process and activity whereby the user is taught to exploit information sources efficiently, neither of the two courses suggested can sufficiently instruct the library school student or serve to emphasize the importance of this concept. My own reaction to seeing position descriptions requiring specific library instruction responsibilities is that the topic has not been taught in the past in a way that meets the needs of employers; otherwise they would not be stating their need so directly.

A major aspect of library instruction is the *teaching* function. Unfortunately, the basic educational foundations that require knowledge of learning theories and experience with teaching methodologies are not included in the content of library school courses. A competency in instructional program design, an awareness of the most effective uses of instructional media, and an understanding of the basic principles of human learning need to be the basis of any well-designed library instruction program. Because these concepts are not covered in other library school offerings, they need to be incorporated in a course on teaching the use of the library. The appropriate time for students to take this course is after they have gained a general knowledge of reference sources and services, an understanding of technical services, and an overall awareness of general procedures and administrative structure in a library. This background could then be drawn upon to design a total instructional program and plan its implementation as the major exercise of the course.

A survey taken by Galloway in 1975 of 100 instruction librarians found that "librarians with *previous* teaching experience were most actively engaged in library instruction . . . [and] that librarians with no teaching experience were much less likely to take the initiative in setting up instructional programs. . . . Fifty percent of those without previous teaching experience were still in the planning stages for an instructional program, while only 27% of the experienced group were. She concludes that "the possession of previous teacher training and experience is decisive."[6] My classroom experience with students taking a course in teaching the use of the library concurs with Galloway's findings and the response of the students also parallels the results of her survey. The school librarians in this course, who had to meet the requirement of a valid teaching certificate before being certified as school librarians, were much more able to identify long-range goals, short-term objectives, enabling objectives, performance objectives, and behavioral objectives; they were not deterred by the terminology of instructional design. The students who had not had that experience first needed to familiarize themselves with the terminology and to achieve some proficiency in educational planning so that the essential elements for evaluation and revision could be incorporated from the start. Several of these students who lacked a teaching orientation were just completing the library school master's program, but others were librarians with impressive records of experience. All gained a greater understanding of the principles of instructional design and also developed greater competencies in applying these principles to practical situations. Pedagogically it should be kept in mind that these principles of instructional design are not limited in a library situation to just the library instruction program, but can also be used in conducting programs of staff development, training paraprofessionals, and establishing goals and objectives for a library.

PLANNING FOR THE COURSE OFFERED
AT THE UNIVERSITY OF WISCONSIN-MILWAUKEE

It should be noted that the Committee on Education in Library Use of the Wisconsin Association of Academic Librarians (WAAL) was instrumental in providing background information on the need for a course such as this one offered by the School of Library Science at the University of Wisconsin-Milwaukee (UWM). The 1976 committee, of which I was a member, had as one of its objectives "to promote the development of a regularly offered course or courses in library instruction at one of the graduate library schools in the state." Discussion topics for the committee in dealing with this objective centered around the approach that should be taken in contacting library schools and suggestions for the content of the course.

After some deliberation, a draft of a proposal was distributed to directors of library education programs and directors of academic libraries within the state. We requested from them responses as to whether bibliographic instruction was indeed a valid offering for a library school curriculum and whether their attitude was favorable toward the committee's viewpoint. The responses were generally positive on both counts, although some of the responses could have been interpreted as more positive than others. The coordinator of public services in one academic library replied, "I support your appeal for exposure to 'Instruction in Library Use' in library schools. I've discovered through a quick check with our newest staff members that they, at least, did not receive this; they also felt that it should have been offered. I would hate to see such courses come out as 'just another audio-visual' however. I believe that librarians are teachers and that a base of learning theory should precede an introduction to techniques." The director of an academic library responded, ". . . while trying to recruit professional staff, we have encountered a serious problem. It has been virtually impossible to recruit new graduates with even a minimal knowledge of bibliographic instruction methods and procedures. I do hope library schools will make a serious attempt to remedy that situation." Another director supported the idea that "instruction is a vital and necessary public service for all types of libraries and for university and research libraries in particular." His further remarks, however, were disappointing: "It is my understanding that instruction in library use is already a conceptual unit in most of the types of library courses" and perhaps contain a clue to his own priorities for the subject: "Hopefully your proposal will be an impetus to the library schools in Wisconsin in moving toward courses specifically on library instruction *as soon as funding permits*" (italics added).

The input from the WAAL committee was quite valuable when, as a faculty member, I prepared an outline and syllabus to present to the UWM School of Library Science curriculum committee and faculty. The course was suggested as an offering under the "catchall/experimental" course title *Special Topics in Li-*

brarianship with the subtitle for this particular course *Teaching the Use of the Library*. Although the course was approved without any difficulty, comments from individual faculty revealed that there was not complete agreement on and support for the concept as a whole and for this course in particular. Background specialization of the individual and the professional perspective from which the functions of instruction and service were viewed seemed to influence their responses.

Jan Kennedy, at that time Director of Libraries, Alverno College, assisted in planning and teaching the course. Essentially the purpose of the course was to present the concept of library instruction as the process whereby the user or patron learns to exploit information resources efficiently, whatever the setting, and to prepare librarians with the skills necessary to develop such library instruction programs. The 15 students registered were almost evenly divided between students interested in postsecondary and academic libraries and those interested in school library media centers. Little interest was expressed from the public library sector. A few inquiries for information came in, but no registrations. We could not determine if the reason for public librarians' lack of representation was that the class schedule did not fit into public library work/vacation commitments or that the content of the course was not considered appropriate. The following were the overall competencies students were expected to achieve.

The student will be able to: (1) identify the ingredients necessary for establishment of an excellent instruction program, (2) explain the components in instructional program design, (3) explain basic principles of human learning, (4) discriminate among the three strata of library instruction, (5) describe various techniques of instruction possible at each of the three strata, (6) locate and become familiar with examples of instructional programs in different types of libraries, and (7) use the principles of instructional design and human learning together with the concepts of library instruction to design a total instruction program for a selected library and plan its implementation.

Specific objectives were identified for each week's sessions.

First week. The student will be able to (1) explain the concept of library instruction as the process whereby the user is able to independently and efficiently identify and use information resources and (2) identify the ingredients necessary for establishment for an excellent program of library instruction.

Second week. The student will be able to (1) explain the components of instructional program design, (2) explain basic learning theories, and (3) utilize principles of human learning in the design of a bibliographic instruction program.

Third week. The student will be able to (1) discriminate the three strata of library instruction—library orientation, simple search strategy with instruction in the use of the reference tools at each point of strategy, and advanced discipline-oriented search strategy with instruction in the use of reference sources related to the discipline; (2) explain the various techniques of instruction possible at the first level (orientation); and (3) become familiar with an example of an instruction program in a library (field trip to University of Wisconsin–Parkside at Kenosha).

Fourth week. The student will be able to (1) explain the search strategy and various instruction techniques possible at level two of library instruction and (2) become familiar with an instruction program in a library (field trip to Alverno College).

Fifth week.   The student will be able to (1) explain the various techniques for instruction at level three of library instruction, (2) identify, for an academic situation, the role of faculty in successful achievement of an instructional program, particularly level three, and (3) identify the contribution to the library instruction program of public service librarians in their daily interactions with library users.

Sixth week.   The sessions on this final meeting would be devoted to student demonstrations of competence. The student, using the principles of good instructional design, would outline a total instruction program for a selected library, explaining one technique of instruction to be used along with the instructional aids or materials developed to enhance the learning situation, or would give a detailed description of the development of such instructional aids or materials. The plan was assessed for effectiveness according to the following criteria: clear identification of program participant needs, a statement of short- and long-range educational objectives to be attained by program participants, practicality of program implementation, and inclusion of evaluation techniques for measuring participant level of achievement and for effectiveness of program.

The UWM course met one day per week for six weeks. Because an 8:30–11:30 A.M. and 1:00–4:00 P.M. schedule presented challenges to attention spans and physical stamina, the activities within the day were varied. I am convinced that the time spread of six weeks was preferable to compressing the content into, for example, three successive weeks for several reasons. This schedule allowed somewhat more time for assimilating information, reflecting on concepts, and reading independently. Some working librarians could be away from jobs one day a week, while two days away would not have been practical, and scheduling the class on Wednesdays did not interfere with long weekends "up north," which have a high summer priority for Wisconsinites! Other time combinations could be successful, and in offering the course again, it would be desirable to be able to schedule field trips to school library media centers where exemplary library instruction programs are in existence.

COURSES OFFERED ELSEWHERE

Although there has not been a proliferation of courses that focus on teaching librarians how to teach the use of the library, there is evidence that more library schools are getting involved, even if only on a trial basis. The spring semester course *Special Topics: Bibliographic Instruction* at the University of Michigan School of Library Science is probably the one offered most regularly. Attendance at the annual Eastern Michigan conference on library instruction is included directly in the schedule of activities for the course. The University of Wisconsin–Madison offered a four-week course for graduate credit during the summer of 1976 under the title *Topics in Reader Services: Instruction in the Use of the Library.*

Programs emphasizing course work for school library media specialists incorporate into specific course annotations some of the concepts for preparing students for the responsibility of library instruction. The State University of New York–Buffalo lists *Curriculum Role of the Media Specialist* and C. W. Post Center of Long Island University offers *Teaching Methods in School Media Centers*, both three-credit electives, and the University of Denver includes a two-quarter hour course *The Media Center: User Guidance.*

Even as a library educator, I was confused with the terminology (library-ese) of one course title and description. *Librarian as Learning Consultant* was described thus: "Systematic exploration of the persuasive and interactive patterns upon which the specialist in media, library, and information service can model his behavior as a human change agent. Emphasis is on methods and techniques that activate the behavioral cycle in effective communication."[7] If this course is involved with preparing students to plan library instruction programs, we may see new job descriptions coming out with phrases such as "must be qualified to activate the behavioral cycle in effective communication." Perhaps such terminology plays a part in the absence of library instruction courses.

In reality, the reasons for not offering such a course on a regular basis probably vary from one school to another. There may also be present some of the inherent problems of academe, so that an individual school or department may be inhibited from playing a leadership role or responding to needs expressed by practitioners about library instruction. Whatever the reasons, many people involved in the day-to-day education of library users are discouraged not to see it treated in the library school curriculum.

Presently, the need for training in library instruction seems to be being met primarily in practitioner-sponsored conferences and workshops. This may prove to be a short-term solution that does not effectively deal with the actual needs of librarians. The content of a course to prepare librarians for developing instructional programs cannot be compressed into weekend sessions or an all-day workshop. Although these meetings, in many cases focused on a narrowly defined concern, may be beneficial and may indeed fulfill specific needs, it is too often the background people bring to the workshop situation that is the real key to the effectiveness of the experience. If this background has not included a basis for instructional design, the workshop or conference experience cannot be equated to the learning gained from a planned course meeting over a longer period of time. Individual workshops might be compared to fitting pieces into a jigsaw puzzle that can never really be completed without the piece marked "competency in instructional design."

Finally, there is a need for more constructive input by individual practitioners, committees, and interest groups to the curriculum committees of library schools. Every request may not get prompt affirmative action, but, unless the school I am associated with is an exception, the communication is given serious consideration and may assist the library school in long-range planning as well as in attempting to respond to immediate needs.

NOTES

1. American Library Association, Reference and Adult Services Division, Standards Committee, "A Commitment to Information Services: Developmental Guidelines," adopted January 1976. *RQ* 15 (Summer 1976): 328

2. "Standards for College Libraries," mimeographed (Chicago: Association of College and Research Libraries, 1975), p. 13.
3. "Guidelines for Bibliographic Instruction in Academic Libraries," *College and Research Libraries News* 38 (April 1977): 92.
4. American Library Association and Association for Educational Communications and Technology, *Media Programs: District and School* (Chicago and Washington, D.C.: The Associations, 1975), pp. 8, 15.
5. *Library Journal*, November 15, 1977, p. 2373.
6. Sue Galloway, "Nobody Is Teaching the Teachers," *Booklegger Magazine* 3 (January/February 1976): 30.
7. University of Pittsburgh Bulletin, The Graduate School of Library and Information Sciences 1975–1977, p. 25.

PROGRESS AND RECENT DEVELOPMENTS IN BRITISH LIBRARIES

CHARLES CROSSLEY
University of Bradford Library, Bradford, England

In considering progress and development in the field of user education in Britain, it is pleasing to be able to report advances in many aspects. There has been a continuation of existing work in almost all institutions, despite the fact that the mid-1970s have been the most difficult years in recent history in the nation as a whole and in the realm of library service as an inevitable consequence. This has been a period of consolidation but also a time during which there has been an expansion of interest and activity in user education in general. There have been many instances of experimentation. Coordination and support at a national level have become apparent and from this national effort there have arisen review, reappraisal, and research. In addition some attention has been paid to such desirable activities as integration and evaluation. It is hoped that the optimism implicit in this brief recital of factors will be justified by the following overview.

This chapter will not attempt to list and describe many instruction programs, but will draw attention to a few as typical of the good-quality work in each area.

Several reviews of the state of the art have been published and the reader's attention is directed to these for further detail. Stevenson[1] has surveyed the field thoroughly. His 1977 paper draws on the material included in his review for the British Library Research and Development Department (BLRDD)[2] of work in colleges and universities, and enlarges the scope to include an examination of some of the problems inherent in user education. In this way he gives some account of practices and programs in schools and of courses and orientation provided for schools by institutions of higher education. Other reviews that list descriptive accounts of instructional activities will be mentioned later.

REVIEW AND RESEARCH

In 1974 there was set up in Britain a Review Committee on Education for Information Use. To understand the reason for this and to see the Review Committee's terms of reference in context, it is necessary to look back to September 1973, when the Office for Scientific and Technical Information (OSTI)—the predecessor of the BLRDD—sponsored a workshop at the University of Bath on "The Education of Users of Scientific and Technical Information." This workshop established a general principle that has been of great and continuing importance: There should be emphasis on the development of skills in handling information "as an integral part of the educational process" rather than on user education, which was seen to be a remedial and short-term aim. At all levels of education a student's knowledge of a subject should be advanced by planned utilization of sources of information. Thus instruction in the appropriate skills should begin in childhood and continue throughout the years of formal education and beyond into adulthood, where individuals were engaged in any form of continuing education. Because there was a substantial number of students at the higher education level who had received no systematic instruction before proceeding to college or university, and who were receiving none or little during their present studies, in spite of well-developed activities in a number of institutions throughout Britain, it was felt to be essential to promote the appropriate instruction of these individuals as a top priority but, at the same time, to take steps to tackle the long-term aim: the introduction of such instruction at all levels of education. In such circumstances the Review Committee on Education for Information Use began its work with terms of reference that required: (1) a review of research on user education and the education of those who provided such instruction, (2) the commissioning of reviews in particular areas of activity, (3) the identification of gaps in the research record, (4) a search for ways of ensuring action and the implementation of research, and (5) recommendation of objectives and projects for further research.

The committee completed its work within two years and published its final report in 1977.[3] Although reference to this report will provide a fuller account of the work performed by various bodies and persons on behalf of the Review Committee, a brief mention of certain projects here will serve to present a state-of-the-art survey of recent research in Britain.

Stevenson[4] fills a gap in the library literature in relation to descriptive accounts of experience and expertise in British universities and colleges. By visits and by questionnaire he collected information regarding the principles and practices of user education at seventy institutions. His report covered aims and objectives, orientation, course content, teaching facilities, and the qualities of the librarian-educators. The programs of nine universities and polytechnics were outlined in some detail and the report ended with a discussion of some particular problems and a glance at the future.

Because many librarians presently teaching information-handling skills lacked formal training in teaching and learning methods, Hills[5] was commissioned by the Review Committee to investigate the needs of librarians in this area. His report is discussed later in this chapter.

The Review Committee felt that the use of educational technology was particularly important and commissioned a literature review in this subject area. From their survey of the literature, Crossley and Clews[6] drew several conclusions that were accepted by the Review Committee, notably that future research in Britain should be directed toward (1) evaluation of advanced-level instruction, with a view to identifying those methods best suited to particular elements of courses; (2) the study of variables such as student personality, learning conditions, and long-term retention of learning; and (3) comparisons of the relative efficiency of self-directed learning, group study, and formal instruction. The committee further suggested a study of particular teaching aids—how they were used and what guidance was necessary in their use.

The most effective means of utilizing on-line bibliographic searching systems was investigated through the provision of such services in selected institutions for limited periods in return for feedback from users. The use of intermediaries was thereby confirmed and the need was at once recognized for the proper training of these intermediaries. The schools of librarianship and information science had a clear role in this and several were given grants by the British Library to investigate the implications for the education of librarians and information scientists.

A report by Wood[7] is an example of the work under this scheme. The committee recommended further experimental user education projects and favored the "travelling workshop" approach described later. The committee also noted with approval seminars and courses in on-line techniques run in Britain by Aslib and the EURONET organization.

The committee drew attention to the implications for user education of the results of user studies and surveys of information needs, in the belief that the findings could shed light on the problems of defining the objectives of information-handling instruction and of designing the necessary courses or self-guided learning packages. It issued a call to the Center for Research on User Studies, set up at the University of Sheffield in 1975 under the sponsorship of the British Library, urging the center to organize its research and study projects in such a way that the results would be "of maximum use to persons concerned with user education."

Although the Review Committee owed its origins to a workshop concerned with the education of users of scientific and technical information, it recognized that workers in humanities had problems in meeting their information needs and that, although their information handling was a very different activity because of the supreme importance of documents as sources, appropriate and effective instruction was possible and should be examined. Smith[8] reported on the findings of a meeting to discuss the matter.

The Review Committee laid stress on the need for adequate, continuing, and coordinated activity in user education and, noting the existence of the Information Services Group set up by the Standing Committee of National and University Libraries (SCONUL), sought to ensure that the work of this group would receive support in the demanding task of collecting and disseminating information in the subject field by urging the BLRDD to appoint an Information Officer for User Education. This was done in 1976, and the work of this officer is described later in this chapter.

In considering user education in British schools, the Review Committee noted a lack of published work and found no evidence that there was significant worthwhile activity. The committee drew strength from various statements and recommendations of the Bullock Report,[9] which appeared during the time it was at work. This report, with its theme the preeminence of reading as an educational activity, was recognized by all concerned with schools and libraries as a document of great and lasting national importance if its recommendations are acted upon. The Review Committee therefore recommended that the British Library encourage user education work in schools but pointed, at the same time, to the real opportunities for cooperation in this effort between schools and local college and public libraries. As a result of a further recommendation, a meeting of parties interested in this work in schools was held in June 1976 and, in consequence, investigations into the problems began, funded by a grant from the BLRDD, with a survey of existing practice and methods of instructing pupils in the effective use of information resources. This survey was based at Liverpool Polytechnic, and the final report on the project is due to be submitted shortly. Discussion of the findings will be presented in this chapter in the section concerned with user education in schools. In addition to this support for exploratory work, the British Library has sponsored a project that reflects two interests and neatly draws them together: user education and community information. The work is directed at identifying in a school the information sources available that are relevant to everyday problems of life; seeks to isolate the methods of organizing the information; and examines the possible techniques for teaching use of the information to senior pupils. This work will also be described further in the section on schools.

The Review Committee made several other recommendations and asserted its opinion on many aspects of user education, but this account has drawn attention only to certain cases where some activity or research has taken place in consequence of such recommendations. The reader should note, however, that its final report constitutes guidelines for concerted and effective action in Britain on a scale not previously considered or attempted.

USER EDUCATION IN SCHOOLS

As part of the wider program of research into user education activities and needs in schools initiated by BLRDD, Fay Winkworth has surveyed existing literature from mainly British and American sources and has produced a review and bibliography.[10] From this examination she has derived theoretical and practical factors of relevance in the planning and design of information-handling instruction and in the establishing of appropriate standards of provision and has also drawn conclusions and made recommendations on research needed and gaps to be filled.

Her synthesis should form the basis for the future development of user education in schools. She emphasizes that integration with all subject teaching is not only possible but essential and that it fits perfectly into current thinking on the value of self-directed learning and independent study and into the trend away from teaching directed exclusively at externally set examinations. The importance of a problem-centered approach in the instruction given is also stressed, and her review includes an analysis of the learning skills needed by the pupil as distinct from library skills.

It is not possible here to quote in detail from Winkworth's report but, in a chapter on what progress has been made in user education in Britain, it is relevant to point out that much of her exposition derives from accounts of existing British practice and thinking (even though her debt to American writers is explicitly stated).

As regards the future, she sees clearly the need for exploring the possibilities of cooperative production of teaching materials in the United Kingdom and recommends their provision in several different media. Teachers will need to receive instruction in teaching library use as part of their own training syllabus and they must be involved in this work in their schools along with the librarian. Effective and constructive methods of evaluation must be devised and implemented so that efforts to integrate library instruction into subject teaching and project work are not obstructed.

Reference has already been made above to another BLRDD project that set out to establish a register of methods for the education of library users in schools. The researcher, Ann Irving, carried out her work in the context of increasing library consciousness, occasioned by the slow but steady increase in the number of posts in schools for professional librarians. The number overall is quite small (perhaps 500–600 in England and Wales) and the provision is distinctly patchy on a geographical basis—certain authorities appoint librarians as policy but this is nowhere nearly uniform. The project therefore concentrated on two English county education areas, Cheshire and Nottinghamshire, where there were qualified librarians in about half of all secondary comprehensive schools. (The age range of pupils was mainly 11–18.)

Librarians or teachers with library responsibilities were interviewed to discover what they taught about the library, how and when this was done, if the work was integrated into the curriculum and if it was evaluated in any way; and their opinion was sought on various matters connected with libraries and user education in schools.

Using the data obtained from the interviews, illuminated by observation of practice, the report of the project[11] presents an informative picture of the state of information-handling instruction in the survey schools, revealing what is going on and demonstrating clearly the potential for development. The report draws attention to the need for extension of the survey into other regions of Britain and for relating the work much more closely with library instruction at other levels, and emphasizes that a greater measure of agreement on the content of such instruction is desirable, along with training in teaching for school librarians.

The Inner London Education Authority (ILEA) has been much more progressive in its outlook on library provision in schools and in its policy of appointing school librarians. The authority also attempts to give some assistance and guidance to these librarians by centrally based advisers. As a result, many schools in the ILEA area can point to active programs in which children at various ages are shown how to incorporate the library resource center into their information-seeking activities. Instruction in use of catalogs, indexes, reference works, periodicals, etc., is supported by printed and duplicated handout materials, often of high standard and employing a variety of methods to put across their message or teaching point, using "topic webs" (diagrams displaying the relationship between a subject and its various aspects and subdivisions), algorithms, or whatever proves effective.

John Lindsay[12] has given a detailed account of the work of a librarian in a large (1,000 students) mixed-ability comprehensive school in East London, describing the systematic training in information handling given to children over six school years. The problems tackled (arising from diversity of needs, variety of aptitudes and academic attainments, multiplicity of media, and scattered resources) and the constraints endured (inadequate funds, shortage of time, and limits on availability) are starkly outlined, but the writer's enthusiasm and faith show through in the account he presents of the content and methods of the courses given.

He stresses that information techniques cannot be taught and that the librarian's task is to manage a learning program so that individuals acquire the skills.

Barbara Smith[13] has described ways of introducing new entrants to a secondary school into the library and the simple routines of using it. She notes the popularity of audiovisual presentations and discusses problems associated with videotape and slide/tape.

Work outside the London area is reported by Léonie Poole,[14] outlining her "Library Skills Program" for first-year entrants to a comprehensive school in Cheadle Hulme, Cheshire. Examples of the practical work given to the children uphold the writer's firm intention to avoid any attempts to train "little librarians." (She is right to draw attention to this danger, which is apparent in some instruction programs noted.) These instances of work in schools are representative of much more that is going on unsung and unrecorded.

Reference was made earlier to a British Library research grant concerned with user education in schools and access to community information. The project, entitled "The Need to Know," is headed by John Lindsay, and is centered on the South Hackney School in an area of London that presents all the problems of contemporary urban life at an unfortunately high level: bad housing, many single-parent families, low household incomes, many children admitted to care, and much unemployment. Over a one-year period, the project will be concerned with collecting and organizing the information available to the pupils in the catchment area of the school and will attempt to evaluate methods used for teaching the retrieval of such information in daily problem solving. The important question it will seek to answer is: What information-handling skills should children acquire before leaving school?—but it would be unjust to fail to point out that the project has other aims that are of direct and permanent value to the children in preparing them for life after school. In the words of Research Officer Terence Brake (from whom further details are available): "The aim is not simply to provide an information service in the school but to offer the pupils a chance to exercise skills in self-determination."[15]

HELP FROM UNIVERSITIES

The need for cooperation among various types of libraries in relation to user education work has been mentioned several times. One example of the way a university library might help the pupils of local schools can be quoted. Carolyn Rowlinson of the University of Stirling in Scotland has described a school program project in her library instigated by Robin Davis whereby sixth form students (aged 16–18 years) are introduced to the university library and given assignments that require consultation of several major reference works.[16]

As these students are steered in their final school year toward university-level studies they discover two needs. One is for much more private study time and the second is for access to a greater range of information materials than can be found in their school libraries on which to base research effort in pursuit of a project topic. It is obvious that this deficiency can only be made good by some other library in the area and a good college or university library can provide what is needed. In the case of Stirling, because of its position in a lightly populated region, a tradition of involvement with the locality had already grown up and the library has merely built on the liaison work with schools that had already been actively conducted for some time past.

The library has determined its objectives clearly, acknowledging a debt to Patricia Knapp: to ensure that students learn to look upon the library as a source of information and the librarians as friendly guides; to ensure that the students acquire the ability to find and handle information for both work and leisure purposes; to ensure that the student learn the nature and function of various reference works; to ensure that the students learn the basic steps in a literature search as part of the process of problem solving; to ensure that the students learn how to locate, select, and evaluate various kinds of library materials.

The library staff have experimented with methods designed to meet these objectives and are convinced that, apart from the necessary orientation, the students gained most from working on their own set topics (on which they must produce a modest dissertation), aided and guided by the subject specialist staff of the library. Library assignments have therefore been abandoned as artificial and as barriers to meaningful learning of library skills.

Adequate staffing is the largest problem. Time is needed for preparatory work as well as for direct assistance to the students. The library staff suggest that, in a time of employment difficulties for newly trained teachers and librarians, unemployed members of both professions should be enabled to participate in this work, supported financially, perhaps, by government funds.

This project has been described in some detail because it is a lone example in the United Kingdom of an institution of higher education tackling the information handling and library use aspects of the problems of easing the transition for students from school to university.[17] This work should be undertaken in other British universities and colleges if the aim of providing continuous development of information-handling skills from childhood to adult life is to be achieved.

HELP FROM PUBLIC LIBRARIES

If the universities are not at present making any substantial contributions to the preparation of school students for the information-handling problems they will later meet, it might be thought that the public library has a role to play. After all, "library lessons" have been going on for generations, wherein children are brought from school to the local library to read, to be given elementary instruction in finding information, and so on. One major city public library system is doing very much more than this. In Sheffield there has been a school instruction officer for the past 30 years and Andrew Foster, the present holder of the post, is carrying on a long tradition in the service he provides for the younger pupils of almost 40 of the city's comprehensive schools. Of 272 classes that visited the Central Library in 1976–1977, comprising some 6,000 students, 226 were at second-year level. They each received a brief introduction to the city's library services, were given practical exercises involving using reference works and finding books via the catalog, and finished with a tour of the library building and its numerous departments. But in addition to this work, which is not in itself particularly note-worthy except in terms of the sheer scale of operations, the school instruction staff (of two) handled visits from 46 other classes of special groups such as immigrant or physically handicapped children and, significantly, sixth-form students from a dozen schools in the city. Their requirements were seen to be to have an introduction to the services and resources of the specialist departments of the Central Library and to receive instruction in the function and use of abstracting and other bibliographical works. Only one teacher has so far seen the virtue of integrating this activity with his own teaching program, thus ensuring that the learning and information-seeking habits of his students were interrelated, but "tall oaks from little acorns grow."

USER EDUCATION IN UNIVERSITIES
AND COLLEGES

Most university and college libraries in Britain continue to attempt to welcome and orient the new student, although all acknowledge the difficulty of the task and become increasingly concerned about the problem as student numbers grow. There is no common method of providing this orientation and examples may still be found of the traditional introductory talk by the librarian and the equally traditional tour. Slide/tape presentations, videotape, and conventional film guides are also in use. Several librarians have, of course, abandoned this attempt and have arranged to postpone the provision of information about the library until induction programs, arranged on a departmental basis, are given in the early weeks of an undergraduate course. The students are then much more recep-tive, the guidance is better tailored to their needs, the groups are smaller, and there is a good chance of integrating the instruction with some part of the course work. In certain libraries (e.g., Bradford University) the students still get a tour, but it is on a self-guided basis and the legwork involved is made more meaningful by obliging the student to do something (such as find particular works or spe-cific pieces of information) through the medium of a worksheet. This is part of the "move away from audiovisual aids" that Stevenson[18] noted. (It should be acknowledged at this point that student numbers, as well as the size of library buildings and collections and the staff complement, are all on a much lower scale than in the United States.)

A greater number of universities and many of the polytechnics have introduced systematic instruction during the students' first term and have found that this is most meaningful because the students have, by the time they receive this guid-ance, realized the need for it. At this stage close collaboration with lecturing staff can be particularly profitable and the librarian can fully integrate the program into the subject teaching or ensure that it fits into a course of communication skills or the like. The practical work so many students claim to like (no doubt as a welcome alternative to an excess of talk) then really finds favor, loses artifici-ality ("librarians' exercises"), and acquires real purpose.

Many of the courses of bibliographic instruction now being offered, at both undergraduate and postgraduate levels, are the result of experimental designs of the early 1970s and are now being consolidated in tried and tested programs. These are not infrequently constructed on a modular basis, especially in the polytechnics, whereby instruction is spread over the several years of an undergraduate course in a somewhat rigorous design that perhaps reveals the influence of librarians who have lectured in library schools at an earlier stage of their careers.

It is well worth noting, also, that the importance attached to user education in polytechnics arises not solely from the enthusiasm of the librarians, but also owes much to the fact that the degree courses have to be approved by the Council for National Academic Awards whose subject expert panels frequently insist that a certain number of hours of bibliographic instruction be incorporated in the course.

The expansion in the number of subject specialist librarians employed in British academic libraries and the impact of their activities have ensured that information-handling instruction programs have been slanted toward the needs of users in their own subject areas. It is apparent to students of these courses that the librarian has an expert's awareness and understanding of the literature of their subject but, much more importantly, the students are thus encouraged to make individual contact later and can benefit from the close attention then given to their particular needs. Some subject specialists (or librarians with subject liaison responsibilities) in several universities concentrate almost exclusively on this mode of guidance and give tutorials to individual students, helping them choose or refine a topic for a dissertation and offering guidance in the search process that follows. Examples at Bradford and Durham spring to mind. The demand on librarians' time necessitated by this, the ultimate in labor-intensive methods, is a price that few are willing or able to pay.

Some librarian-teachers in universities and colleges have sought to achieve the integration of their user education programs into undergraduate and postgraduate courses of study in the belief that such integration would bring rewards in the shape of increased cooperation with academic colleagues, higher motivation of students, greater use of library resources, and enhanced status for their courses of instruction. Their expectations have normally been justified. Other librarians have held the view that a course of study was incomplete without an element of bibliographic instruction, the objectives for which must be set only in strict conformity with those formulated for the course itself. Where these librarians have been able to take part in course design, they have used the opportunity to secure a proper and pertinent place for bibliographic instruction. The benefits listed above would still accrue. Integration is thus seen to be desirable, whether it is sought merely to give more relevance and purpose to an existing library instruction program or to add a dimension to a newly formulated subject syllabus, and it is fast becoming a shibboleth whereby librarians' teaching activities are judged by their fellows.

Despite differences and doubts about definition, there is no question that librarians in Britain have increasingly given a subject slant to their courses and that many have proceeded further and now offer instruction tailor-made to the needs of students at a particular juncture of their studies when the use of the library and its resources is inescapable. Clearly this cannot be achieved without the closest collaboration with lecturer colleagues. In certain cases this has been accomplished *ad hoc* as part of a general development of library instruction for established courses, but sometimes, as in degree courses approved for the polytechnics by the Council for National Academic Awards, the library training component has been explicitly written into the course design. Library involvement in new course planning has been rare outside the polytechnics; only two known examples in universities can be quoted: Bradford and Lancaster. It may be only a coincidence that librarians in both these institutions succeeded in having an explicit requirement for bibliographical instruction written into undergraduate course regulations many years ago, an example followed by several of the polytechnics.

One important consequence of the collaboration with academics brought by integration is that it is they who provide the practical work in the library that is an indispensable feature of effective learning by the student. Stevenson[19] cites examples in universities at Nottingham and Southampton and in the polytechnic at Hatfield. These, and the practical work given to students at Bradford, are all cases where the project is not only set and assessed by course tutors but is an integral part of the subject teaching.

An example of this type of project may be described. First-year chemical engineering students take a course designed to demonstrate to them their future role in society as engineers who will be involved somewhere along the line with exploiting raw material—a mineral or other chemical element or compound. They may extract it, process it, convert it to some other commodity, or use it in a manufacturing industry. They will bring about problems of energy use, waste creation, environmental damage, depletion of resources, and conservation measures, as well as contribute to technological advances, higher living standards, and so on. Each of them is allotted a particular element or compound, and must research it from the various points of view listed above, writing up the results in extended essays that contain supporting data and statistics of production, consumption, trade, estimates of reserves, etc. The librarian teaches them information-handling skills by a case study approach, illustrating the steps in the search for relevant information by choosing an element from the list provided by the tutor and demonstrating the results of a systematic literature search. Supported by a handout listing the relevant bibliographical and statistical source materials, the students then conduct their own searches, consulting the librarian if they find difficulties. The written work is assessed by the course tutor.

Another means of introducing library use into subject studies with complete integration has been investigated at Bath University.[20] Here Phillip Cooke has secured the cooperation of teaching staff in four science, engineering, and pharmacy schools of study whereby self-learning packages have been devised that make it obligatory for a student to proceed through a carefully planned sequence of information-handling operations in order to complete a course. Cooke has termed this "subject related instruction in the handling of information," although his academic collaborators might prefer to think of it as "library-oriented learning." (The parallels with the American library-college concept are obvious and not overlooked by Cooke.)

Each of the self-instructional packages has the same format. It shows clearly the pathway to be followed by the student to achieve a particular goal defined by the subject teacher. Step-by-step tasks ensure that the student requires access to discrete pieces of information and, as each need is revealed, appropriate instruction is given. Only when the required information has been found—and thereby mastery of the search techniques involved demonstrated—may it be used to complete a set task and proceed to the next step.

EVALUATION

Librarians in Britain were acknowledging the need for systematic evaluation of their instructional programs at the beginning of the 1970s and some were experimenting with methods of achieving it. Stevenson[21] noted that subjective assessment of courses was being practiced by means of questionnaires completed by course participants in the universities of Southampton, Surrey, and Bradford and in Plymouth Polytechnic. (Stevenson's illustration of the questions asked at Plymouth points to a greater willingness by librarians to be assessed on teaching qualities than might be vouchsafed by many a university lecturer.) Certain librarians also used conventional methods of measuring the amount of learning that had taken place, by administering pretests and post-tests. They derived support and guidance from the BLRDD research project on the evaluation of library instruction slide/tape guides that will be described later.[22] These librarians were probably the same ones who recognized the value of practical work for their students and thus received further information on the outcome of their teaching by marking the work done, adding to this picture the evidence they received from feedback, directly from students or indirectly from their tutors, solicited or not. They may not have known (or cared) that they were utilizing subjective assessment and quantitative methods to estimate the total value of their courses or to help them plan modifications, or that their data collection could be classified as formal or informal. Only later did some of them discover that their humble efforts had been directed toward *summative* or *formative* evaluation, or that they had been dipping a toe in the swirling waters of *illuminative* evaluation. From several writers,[23] however, they learned a taxonomy of evaluation and an appreciation of the different approaches possible. The library literature has also contained several expositions[24] and librarians are now being encouraged to consider the amalgam of objective and subjective assessment that constitutes illuminative evaluation. This oversimplification may be misleading but it is no part of the present writer's task to *discuss* evaluation as such, but rather to point to developments and influences. Thus it must be recorded that no results have been reported yet of the application of this composite technique, but it is known that the Travelling Workshops Experiment (TWE) at Newcastle upon Tyne Polytechnic will use this approach in assessing its workshops.[25]

PRESENT EMPHASES

It is no distortion to refer in this account of work in universities and colleges to activities in the science/technology subject areas, or to emphasize user education for undergraduates. Although increasing attention is being paid to social science and humanities fields, for well-known historical reasons instruction in information handling in these areas is still overshadowed by the progress made in reaching more and more students in life and physical sciences, in engineering, and in technological subjects. A decade ago many academic libraries offered guidance only to their postgraduate readers, but there has been a marked swing toward a major effort to equip readers studying for their first degree with the library use skills they need.

There is also a danger that the reader of this review will gain the impression that adequate reader instruction in academic institutions in Britain is not only widespread but almost universal. It must therefore be stated in conclusion that this is nowhere near the case; that many librarians have not found the enthusiasm, the resources, the staff, the support of academic colleagues, or the means to introduce teaching programs. Deficiency in only one of these factors can prevent systematic instructions being given. Evidence suggests that greater progress has been made in smaller institutions.

THE OPEN UNIVERSITY

The Open University—a "University of the Air"—began its broadcasts in 1969-1970 and 26,000 students have now graduated. While much of the information and guidance needed by these students has been provided in the form of "set books," supplemented by broadcast programs, the student in most courses has been expected to use local libraries for needed background or supportive materials. This at once throws into prominence the student's need to know how to use the local library, whatever its type, effectively and efficiently. The Open University (OU) responded to this need—in fact, anticipated it—by providing, among its printed materials for many courses, guides to the literature, to library use, and to the techniques of literature searching as part of problem-solving methodology. Visual guidance on using libraries has also been provided by making and showing to students two films, one on the use of university libraries and the other on using public library services. These films are shown on BBC television programs at intervals.

A particular feature of the OU degree course structure is the "summer school" that students attend at various universities in Britain. The staff of the libraries of these universities frequently make special efforts to orient these temporary students, sometimes by using existing resources such as printed guides or introductory films or slide/tape tours, but several of them have produced tailor-made videotape films and slide/tape presentations for this purpose. York University is one example where, interestingly, the television film was directed by a librarian who was herself a visitor from overseas and might be supposed, thereby, to have a particular affinity with the requirements of a stranger on the campus.

Senior staff in the regions that make up the OU's administrative structure have been concerned to give greater assistance to students in their areas. In the Yorkshire region, for instance, Deputy Regional Director Derek Gains has produced a register of libraries of all kinds in the region that offer facilities to OU students, drawing attention to the hours of opening and the name of the member of staff who should be approached by the student who feels the need for assistance. Derek Gains has also collaborated with Tom Wilson, of Sheffield University, in a pilot study designed to identify the information needs of students in those courses— now increasing in number—where there is an important project component demanding that the student use libraries in considerable depth. In some cases it will be demonstrated that it is not practicable for certain students to embark on such projects, because they have no easy access to the required materials. The results of this pilot study will be published shortly.

Although this investigation highlights the problems of OU students in selected courses, it had been observed that students in all courses had needs that could not be met by local libraries in a straightforward manner by stocking a finite number of identifiable books. It has become plain to many public librarians in particular that their generous provision of the official set books for OU courses has not been justified, because the students mostly obtained their own copies of these books and their real needs were for background materials and research collections. The OU staff are now well aware of this problem and have set up working groups and advisory bodies to study the problems of effective library services for their students.

At least one university—Loughborough—has acknowledged a more general commitment to provide instruction in library use for persons who are not members of the university and who are returning to studies in adult life. This is regarded as complementary to more general courses on the techniques and problems of studying, organized by a department in the university specializing in extramural activities. The courses provided by the library have included persons from many occupational backgrounds, and among them have been OU students.

TRAVELLING WORKSHOPS EXPERIMENT

Strangely, the final report of the BLRDD's Review Committee on Education for Information Use did not mention the Travelling Workshops Experiment (TWE) based at Newcastle upon Tyne Polytechnic, although in a recommendation concerned with education in the use of on-line retrieval systems, it explicitly favored the "travelling workshop approach."[26]

TWE is described in some detail in the chapter following and no attempt will be made here to duplicate that account. It is, however, one of the most important developments in Britain in the period under review and therefore merits mention and comment.

The announcement of the project was greeted with considerable skepticism by many librarians who were already actively teaching students how to retrieve and handle information and how to use their libraries. Their doubts were based on several beliefs. Courses and teaching packages designed, developed, and introduced by "outsiders" could not be tailor-made to the needs of a particular set of students. Timetable problems would be well nigh insuperable. Academics would have to be won over to accepting imported teaching. It would be difficult to squeeze any more time from lecturers who usually felt they had too little for normal subject teaching anyway. Courses of instruction provided by a travelling team would be an intrusion and a disruption of existing programs. Integration with curricular subjects would be impossible. Follow-up would be very difficult. The teaching competence of the TWE team was an unknown factor, as was the quality of their teaching materials. Students would lose opportunity to get to know the librarians of their own university or college. There was no foreseeable way of providing a future for the scheme, because there would be no funds once the grant from BLRDD was gone. Evaluation of the concept would not be possible because of the many variables and imponderables. It is not therefore surprising that the experiment has been carried out largely in institutions that had no significant programs operating before TWE provided one, supplemented by work in certain universities that were anxious to give support to the experiment rather than being in need of the help TWE could offer them.

Many of the initial doubts itemized above remained and were found to be valid and the project changed direction after the first round of teaching in the field. Two important decisions were made, one of which was to alter the presentation completely so as to emphasize learning as opposed to teaching, and the second was to retreat from the travelling workshops approach and to offer instead teaching packages that could be purchased by librarians and made available on a self-administration basis for their patrons, thus overcoming at a stroke the objections listed above.

New doubts arise, however, as TWE draws to the end of its three-year term and plans for the future. At the moment of writing, a decision is awaited as to whether or not further funds will be provided on a generous scale for a scheme that envisages the design, production, testing, and sale in Britain and North America of teaching packages covering a range of 16 subjects or more. What is at stake is the possibility of centralized production and dissemination of learning materials for library instruction purposes.

It is unfortunate that the British Library may be obliged to give its decision before the feasibility of the scheme has been demonstrated, because it is only during the present academic session (1977–1978) that librarians will be able to obtain and use the packages that are offered as samples—these are in the three original subject areas of biology, mechanical engineering, and social welfare— and during this period TWE will need the data obtained from the evaluation packages it supplies to write up its results and present its conclusions. Thus a decision to grant the substantial sum of money required for the extension of the project on the lines proposed would constitute a major act of faith by the British Library and a firm declaration of its commitment to developing a vitally important aspect of library service in a particular way and without supporting evidence, while at the same time presenting a challenge to other organized attempts to co-ordinate the production of teaching materials, such as described in the section on cooperative schemes later in this chapter. The dangers of duplication, wasted effort, and misdirection must be reckoned with.

SHORT COURSES AT THE BRITISH LIBRARY

One of the first actions of the newly formed British Library was the setting up of a discussion group, consisting of representatives from all parts of the library, to examine the role of the British Library in the provision of short courses. This group reported in November 1975[27] and recommended progressive expansion of the work already being done by each division, in recognition of the library's responsibility for the exploitation of the literature resources it contains. The British Library has uniquely comprehensive collections that can act as a base for the best possible practical instruction and also has a collective expertise that should likewise be fully exploited.

The Lending Division of the British Library (BLLD) has run short courses since its inception (as the National Lending Library for Science and Technology) at Boston Spa in 1962. Fifty such courses were provided up to 1973 for academics, librarians, and library school lecturers and more than 750 persons attended. From an initial concentration on science and technology, the courses were extended to cover the literature of the social sciences and eventually, with the participation and resources of the York University Library, including the humanities. Evaluation of the courses is now carried out routinely and charges for attendance have recently been introduced. The BLLD plans to extend its activities, always with the goal of discovering the needs of users and providing instruction that will meet those needs.

The Reference Division of the British Library (the erstwhile British Museum Library) has since 1975 acknowledged its responsibilities as the repository of unique collections and expertise by providing seminars for particular groups of librarians and others, or on particular aspects of its service or materials. Its staff have contributed to courses organized by other bodies and it has provided the facilities needed for such events.

The Bibliographic Services Division, as provider of a full cataloging service and publisher of *British National Bibliography*, has offered appropriate training courses on aspects of the service and on the use of the PRECIS indexing system. With the introduction of BLAISE for on-line cataloging and information retrieval purposes, the division will offer a wider range of appropriate instructional programs.

One of the two national libraries with a strong commitment to science and technology, the Science Reference Library (SRL) in London, itself one part of the British Library, has long been active in running courses to enable its users to exploit efficiently the large and wide-ranging stock of the library. These activities have included one-day introductory courses giving an approach to the literature of science and technology and instruction on the layout of stock and provision of catalogs.

During the past four years, series of courses have been offered on the use of literature in specific subject areas. These have included courses on the use of patents. (It should be noted that SRL had its origins in the Library of the Patent Office and still fulfills the functions of that library, as the official depository for British patent specifications.) Other areas covered by intensive, two-day seminars are chemical literature and the sources of information in physics, in engineering, and in pharmaceutical literature.

The activities of the SRL Computer Search Service have expanded considerably and demonstrations are regularly given to groups of prospective users, among them industrial information officers.

In addition, members of SRL staff serve as visiting lecturers at courses arranged by other organizations.

It is thus obvious that the British Library has given thought to its role in the field of user education in the light of the present activities of its several divisions and has made plans for the greater coordination of these activities and their expansion in the immediate future.

SPECIAL LIBRARIES AND THE NEEDS OF INDUSTRY

The opportunity for systematic or formal instruction in information handling for users of industrial, governmental, research organization, and similar libraries and information departments is understandably limited. There is a much greater expectation that the librarian or information officer will "produce the rabbit." Perhaps only with the advent of large-scale on-line information retrieval activity has the librarian been able to involve an enquirer in the search process, whereupon the need for some orientation and training has become apparent. Short courses have been offered by organizations outside the firm, not least by the providers of the service themselves and by data-base producers whose wares have been made available through the different systems.

But even before this state of affairs arose there had been formal courses, arranged by, for instance, the BLLD at Boston Spa (and its predecessor institution, the National Lending Library for Science and Technology) and by the SRL.

In one or two universities (Bradford is an example) guidance in the identification and use of sources of information and in the techniques of literature searching have been featured as an integral part of postexperience courses for engineers and managers from industry. One-day workshops have been provided by Loughborough University for managers, engineers, training officers, and research directors from firms in the region. These were jointly sponsored with a local cooperative technical information service until this was disbanded recently. There was heavy emphasis on practical work that made participants aware of many sources of information, but this led to subsequent problems when the library was unable to offer a back-up service because of severe limits on accommodation. When these have been resolved (on occupation of a new building), the library intends to reintroduce these workshops.

Aslib has recently conducted a survey of almost 700 special libraries, by postal questionnaire and selective interview, to investigate the nature and extent of any user education given. The investigator, Catherine Sullivan, found that in almost 80 percent of the organizations some measure of instruction was provided and that often this extended beyond a conducted tour and description of resources and services. Government departments were more likely to give instruction than industrial or commercial organizations and tended to use a lecture approach more frequently. There was recognition that scientific and engineering personnel had greater need for extensive in-depth instruction than had library users in a predominantly social sciences or humanities environment. It was observed that the closer personal relationships often to be found between librarians and information officers and their clients in this type of organization gave rise to a significantly different style of instruction. The survey led to a conclusion that user instruction in special libraries had probably increased considerably in the last decade. The report on this project will be published in 1978 and the present writer is indebted to Catherine Sullivan and Aslib for permission to quote from her summary of its findings.

COORDINATION AND COOPERATION

The call for coordination and cooperation has been very noticeable during the past few years and has been heard from many voices, personal and corporate, in-

cluding some with a hearing in high places. There have been several manifestations, among which the activities of the BLRDD Review Committee have already
been described at length.

National organizations like SCONUL have given effect to their views by setting
up new groups or by supporting existing ones. The Information Services Group
of SCONUL is a good example of a group of librarians who spontaneously came
together for the purposes of effecting service improvements in university libraries
and of fostering cooperative activities such as conferences, seminars, information
dissemination. The group has always shown concern about user education and
this interest is reflected in the coverage given to descriptive accounts of work in
different institutions in its official organ, the *I.S.G. Newsletter*. The group has
lately formally taken under its wing as a section the erstwhile Tape/Slide Group
of SCONUL whose work is described elsewhere in this chapter. The section has at
the same time changed its title to reflect its wider ambitions, albeit in a clumsy and
inelegant title, the Section for Cooperative Production of Packages for User
Education.

It is hoped that greater cooperation will take place, some measure of coordination be achieved, and wider and systematic dissemination of information become
possible through the activities of an Information Officer for User Education,
sponsored by the BLRDD as another consequence of the recommendations of its
Review Committee. This information Officer, Ian Malley, took up his post in February 1977, based at Loughborough University of Technology. His activities
concentrate on the following areas: (1) regular visits to libraries and information
services throughout the United Kingdom to collect information on user education developments in each and to advise on possible extensions or improvements;
(2) production of a newsletter, *INFUSE*, in which reports on all relevant activities
in the United Kingdom and overseas, information on new courses, new ideas,
research, conferences, and the current literature of user education are included;
(3) attendance at, speaking to, and promotion of courses, conferences, seminars
relevant to user education; (4) liaison with individuals and institutions overseas
and initiating of new contacts (links with clearinghouses for library instruction
are particulary stressed); (5) close contact with relevant research projects; (6) provision of a freely available enquiry service; (7) assembly, maintenance, and operation of a computerized materials bank for library instruction, to which access is
free (this includes guides and other publications); and (8) commissioning of
special projects (one such current project is a review of user education work in
the biological sciences).

After one year it can be seen that this post is very valuable. Ian Malley has been
active in all the areas listed and the importance of having a focus for work in user
education of all kinds has been amply demonstrated. Permanent funding and support are not, however, guaranteed and must be obtained.

A chapter by Frank Earnshaw in the predecessor of this book[28] described the
inauguration and operation of a cooperative scheme for the production of slide/
tape guides for use in courses of information-handling instruction and referred to
the evaluation and testing procedures employed. Out of these procedures developed a research project, sponsored by OSTI (now the BLRDD), whereby the
implementation of the procedures could themselves be evaluated. The investigation was carried out by Phil Hills and a team at the University of Surrey during

the period 1973–1975. The report of the work was published in 1977.[29] In the description of the project and its findings will be found details of the methodology for evaluating the effectiveness of slide/tape material, which uses a mixture of testing the achievement of instructional objectives and obtaining students' assessment of the material by diagnostic test and interview.

In addition, the report outlines procedures for preparing slide/tape materials for library instruction and for doing this in a cooperative scheme involving several different institutions. A necessary part of this is to bring together not only the small groups of librarians (working parties) who together design and produce the material, but also all who are taking part in such activities in seminars and conferences, so as to give guidance and expert assistance on a wider scale and ensure that the cooperative element of the program is encouraged and emphasized.

Arrangements for this coordination of effort were in the hands of the SCONUL Tape/Slide Group. Its successor, the Section on Cooperative Production of Packages for User Education, has aims that will, as its title implies, ensure that the production of effective teaching packages is promoted on a cooperative basis. In addition the section will provide a forum for discussion that will specifically include "educational technologists and others engaged in this work" as well as librarians, and will seek to disseminate information by all appropriate means.

Librarians have long recognized the value of printed and duplicated guides to their premises, collections, services, and information sources and most continue to produce publications aimed at providing point-of-use guidance. They range, obviously, from the all-embracing printed guide to the library as a whole, to leaflets introducing readers to the use of a particular reference work. They may be conceived as independent aids, to be used in isolation from any other form of assistance, such as formal courses of instruction; with the growth of self-directed study and emphasis on project work the student may reasonably expect the library to provide such publications. Alternatively, these guides may be designed and produced as handouts to accompany and supplement instructional programs.

Two factors have accelerated the production of such guides in Britain during the present decade. These are the expansion in user education work at all levels of education and the development of the subject specialization concept in university and college libraries. The factors are interdependent, in that teaching the use of the library and its resources has been clearly identified as a specific responsibility of the subject specialist librarian.[30] Interest in the materials produced has also grown and surveys have been made and published. These include a comparative study by Peter Fox[31] of English-language publications from Britain, the United States, and Canada, and a select number produced in East and West Germany. Fox's survey is restricted to one class of publication: general guides to libraries in academic institutions. It is an extension of his earlier examination of the role of printed guides in user education work.[32]

A wide-ranging and systematic survey, backed up by tabulated statistical data, has been produced by Peter Taylor for the BLRDD.[33] This study covered libraries in industry and commerce, in government, in research and trade associations, in learned societies, in universities, polytechnics, and colleges of education or further education, from which 978 replies were received. The survey was restricted to subject guides to sources of information and sought to discover the characteristics of such publications in relation to methods of production, overlap of subject coverage, format, standards of design, content, etc. Taylor's report is concerned with more than recording the results of the investigation: It explores the possibilities for cooperative production of guides and the reduction of duplication; it makes recommendations for the coordination of efforts in this field of activity by the introduction of materials banks, centralized inventory, and publicity (Taylor appends comprehensive indexes of producers and subjects covered as a starter); and it encourages initiation of further studies aimed at identifying the most effective model for future guides.

Librarians in the United Kingdom have been concerned to give assistance to colleagues overseas and, through the international organizations, have made contributions of lasting value. This is as true for user education as for other aspects of the library service and development. One such example is the work done for UNISIST, under the sponsorship of UNESCO, to organize courses, seminars, or workshops aimed at training users of scientific and technical information.[34] The methodology and suggestions for course content should be particularly useful in developing countries and carry the advantage of having been tried out in the field (in the Far East) by members of the team of authors.

It is safe to say that at no time in the past have there been more conferences and seminars on the subject of user education. These have been organized and sponsored by the Library Association, OSTI (or its successor, BLRDD), Aslib, SCONUL, and the Council of Polytechnic Librarians (COPOL)—evidence enough of the nationwide interest in the topic and the importance attached to it

TRAINING LIBRARIANS TO TEACH

The doubt has long nagged librarians in Britain that they might not be properly fitted to teach anybody anything. Working in an academic institution, anxious to ensure that students are trained to use their libraries and to find the information they need, and all too well aware that lecturers have frequently lacked the necessary information-handling skills themselves and have shown little or no enthusiasm for rectifying this omission in themselves or their charges, librarians have felt impelled to offer the required instruction themselves but have been painfully conscious of their shortcomings as teachers. It has been no comfort to recall that their lecturer colleagues in many universities and colleges have in most cases likewise received no formal training for the work and it is perhaps only school librarians who have needed to recognize the training gulf between themselves and their teacher associates. The survey by Stevenson[35] was only one instance in which librarians have expressed their concern about the problem but it did serve the useful purpose of giving overt expression to their views and of putting the problem before the BLRDD Review Committee on Education for Information Use. As noted earlier, that body recommended an investigation and a project, headed by Phil Hills of the University of Surrey, reported to the department in 1978.[36] The investigation sought facts and opinions from librarians engaged in reader instruction work and obtained usable results from 174 respondents. A parallel study was carried out using a version of the Delphi Exercise technique to elicit a consensus view of a group of experts among librarians and lecturers. The important conclusions derived from the investigation were that (1) a need existed for training librarians to teach; (2) those librarians might best obtain that training by attendance at short courses; (3) much more support should be forthcoming from library administrators, teaching colleagues, and fellow librarians; (4) library schools should incorporate this kind of training into their full-time courses but should also be the agent for providing the short-course training schemes for practicing librarians, if—and this was stressed—they have the requisite expertise among their own teaching staff. An informative chapter in the report reveals that in 1976 there were in Britain more than 60 appropriate courses offered by upwards of 20 institutions, besides several that had been arranged for staff of a particular institution. There were several long full-time courses also. Many courses dealt with audiovisual methods, several covered teaching and learning methods, and there were quite a few giving introduction to computerized information systems. All this suggests that there had been adequate response to a need that was felt before it was formally demonstrated, but that those who cried out for help had not in the main received it. This may well link closely with their other call for support (from their superiors) and the experience of one canceled course, quoted in the report, seemed to bear this out.

Arising from this project has come an attempt to remedy some of the problems revealed by it, notably the failure, for one good reason or another, of librarians to avail themselves of systematic training in teaching and learning techniques. This new project, also funded by BLRDD, aims to investigate the idea of designing and preparing a package that will introduce librarians to the range of teaching and learning methods currently used by academic colleagues and will indicate possible suitability of these methods for librarians' purposes in their user education programs. The project will not overlook the suitability of the package for use with students in schools of librarianship. Work has only just begun and further information may be obtained from Phil Hills of the University of Surrey.

CONCLUSION

If any attempt is to be made to predict the future of user education in Britain in the next few years, it is essential first to set the scene and consider many factors.

A significantly strong interest in information of all kinds, but particularly in science information, can be discerned at present. This interest is as yet, however, too diffuse, and it has truthfully been said that, as in the United States, science information is "everyone's concern but no one's responsibility." That remark, in its American context, was made with reference to moves to initiate a national approach to scientific and technical information in the United States and it is important to note that similar concern in the United Kingdom has led to the setting up of an enquiry into the scientific information field here too. If a "total information" policy can be devised and implemented, then surely training in the technique of retrieving and using such information must form an essential part of that policy.

It would seem that too many pronouncements from influential places about the need for information-handling instruction have been made to be ignored or forgotten.

Relevant technology is moving fast in areas such as computing, communications, and information transmission, but costs are likely to remain frustratingly high.

Trends in education will have effects on a population whose characteristics will be changing as the falling birth rate results in fewer 18-year-olds. Universities and colleges are likely to open their doors to a wider range of students and there will probably be more mature students. These students are just as unlikely to have received adequate preparation while at school for making effective use of major academic libraries, although their younger colleagues may have benefited from such teaching. This training must come from the schools, because the traditional slowness of change in universities will ensure that it will be a long time before a large number of them will reach out a helping hand in the way described earlier in this chapter. The universities themselves are, if not in a "steady state," expanding very slowly and very little; although the government's intentions have been expressed, little can be achieved without assured injections of more funds.

Universities and colleges are coming under greater pressure to establish and improve links with industry; this could result in more courses being offered for postexperience, management development, and retraining purposes. The library would have an important role in such programs.

There is likely to be a slow growth of cooperation in producing and using audiovisual aids for user education, but librarians have so far proved somewhat slow—even reluctant—to use other people's programs and materials.

The involvement of a larger number of librarians in cooperative production schemes will, as a spin-off, improve their teaching abilities and lead to a general raising of standards. Their interest and enthusiasm stimulated, more librarians will seek opportunities to improve their teaching and will support short courses for this purpose. Library schools may be persuaded to provide training in teaching, for full-time students and at postexperience level.

It seems that librarians are already taking note of the trend toward learning rather than teaching at all levels of education. They realize that they should not be teaching more when their academic colleagues are teaching less and this is going to influence the design and preparation of their instruction programs. They are likely to appreciate the possibilities of the "learning package" in this connection.

The twin banners of the user education movement at present are "integration" and "evaluation." Achievements under each are likely in the years ahead, but there is little chance of spectacular advance in the short term. Awareness of the need, understanding of the basics, and implementation of the ideas will raise the standard of instruction overall, but progress will be slow and sporadic.

There is a temptation to exhort at this point, but a seer who is to earn a reputation as a sage must resist it. This discursive account must end, then, with an expression of pleasure that so much is actually going on in the field of user education in Britain. Thanks are due to many colleagues in Britain who have generously given information and help to make this chapter possible.

NOTES

1. Malcolm Stevenson, "Education of Users of Libraries and Information Services," *Journal of Documentation* 33 (March 1977): 53–78.

2. Malcolm Stevenson, *User Education Programs: A Study of Their Development, Organization, Methods and Assessment*, British Library Research and Development Reports, no. 5320 HC (London: British Library Board, 1977).
3. Review Committee on Education for Information Use, *Review Committee on Education for Information Use—Final Report*, British Library Research and Development Reports, no. 5325 HC (London: British Library Board, 1977).
4. Malcolm Stevenson, *User Education Programs*.
5. Philip J. Hills, *An Investigation of Librarians' Needs in Relation to Training and Learning Methods*, Final Report (London: BLRDD, forthcoming).
6. Charles A. Crossley and John P. Clews, *Evaluation of the Use of Educational Technology in Information Handling Instruction: A Literature Review and Bibliography*, British Library Research and Development Reports, no. 5220 (Bradford: University of Bradford, 1974).
7. A. J. Wood, *On-Line Bibliographic Searching: Assessment of Use of On-Line in Teaching Librarianship and Information Science*, British Library Research and Development Reports, no. 5277 (London: British Library Board, 1976).
8. D. Smith, *Information Problems in the Humanities: A Report of the British Library Seminar*, British Library Research and Development Reports, no. 5259 (London: British Library Board, 1975).
9. Department of Education and Science, *A Language for Life: Report of the Committee of Enquiry*, Sir Alan Bullock, Chairman (London: H.M.S.O., 1975).
10. F. V. Winkworth, *User Education in Schools: A Survey of the Literature on Education for Library and Information Use in Schools*, British Library Research and Development Reports. To be published.
11. To be published in 1978. See Ann Irving, "User Education in Schools," *CRUS News*, 2 (1977): 1-3.
12. John Lindsay, "Information Training in Secondary Schools," *Education Libraries Bulletin* 10 (Autumn 1976): 16-21.
13. Barbara G. Smith, "How Do I Join? Initial Library Instruction in a Secondary School," *School Librarian* 24 (June 1976): 109-111.
14. Léonie E. Poole, "Library Skills for the First-Years," *School Library Association, Members' Newletter* 18 (September 1976): 7-11.
15. Personal communication.
16. Carolyn Rowlinson, "Educating the User: Schools," in *Educating the User: Papers Presented at a Course Held at the Library Association, London, November 1977*. To be published.
17. A similar one had been in operation at the University of Sussex, where staff shortages forced its termination. See "Sixth Form Library Visits," *Library Association Record* 77 (April 1975): 79-81.
18. Malcolm Stevenson, *User Education Programs*, p. 9.
19. Ibid., p. 24.
20. Phillip Cooke, *Integration of Instruction in Information Handling with Subject Curricula: Report of a Study over the Period February to April 1975*. Report to OSTI on Project S4/G/127. (Bath: University of Bath Library, 1975).
21. Malcolm Stevenson, *User Education Programs*, pp. 27-28.

22. P. J. Hills, L. Lincoln, and L. P. Turner, *Evaluation of Tape/Slide Guides for Library Instruction*, British Library Research and Development Reports, no. 5378 HC (London: British Library Board, 1977).
23. Notably M. Parlett and D. Hamilton, *Evaluation as Illumination: A New Approach to the Study of Innovating Programs* (Edinburgh: Centre for Research in Educational Sciences, University of Edinburgh, 1972).
24. See, for example, J. G. Brewer and P. J. Hills, "Evaluation of Reader Instruction," *Libri* 26 (1976) 55-65.
25. Colin Harris, "Illuminative Evaluation of User Education Programs," *Aslib Proceedings* 29 (October 1977): 348-362.
26. Review Committee on Education for Information Use, *Review Committee on Education for Information Use—Final Report*, p. 12.
27. A. G. Myatt and D. Russon, "The Development of Short Courses in the British Library," *BLL Review*, 4 (1976): 104-107.
28. Frank Earnshaw, "An Example of Cooperative Development of Library-Use Instruction Programs," in *Educating the Library User*, ed. by John Lubans, Jr. (New York: R. R. Bowker, 1974), pp. 392-400.
29. Hills, Lincoln, and Turner, *Evaluation of Tape/Slide Guides.*
30. See, for example, Charles A. Crossley, "The Subject Specialist Librarian in an Academic Library: His Role and Place," *Aslib Proceedings* 6 (June 1974): 236-249.
31. Peter Fox, "Library Handbooks: An International Viewpoint," *Libri* 27 (1977): 296-304.
32. Peter Fox, *Reader Instruction Methods in Academic Libraries*, Cambridge University Librarianship Series, no. 1. (Cambridge: University Library, 1974).
33. P. J. Taylor, *Information Guides: A Survey of Subject Guides to Sources of Information Produced by Library and Information Services in the United Kingdom: Final Report* (London: BLRDD, forthcoming).
34. A. J. Evans, R. G. Rhodes, and S. Keenan, *Educational and Training of Users of Scientific and Technical Information* (Paris: UNESCO, 1977).
35. Malcolm Stevenson, *User Education Programs.*
36. P. J. Hills, *An Investigation of Librarians' Needs.*

THE TRAVELLING WORKSHOPS EXPERIMENT

COLIN HARRIS
The Travelling Workshops Experiment, Newcastle upon Tyne Polytechnic Library, England

DAPHNE CLARK
The Travelling Workshops Experiment, Newcastle upon Tyne Polytechnic Library, England

ANNE DOUGLAS
The Travelling Workshops Experiment, Newcastle upon Tyne Polytechnic Library, England

The Travelling Workshops Experiment[1] is a major research project that, since its inception in July 1975, has generated an international interest among librarians. The ideas underlying the Travelling Workshops Experiment, its actual work, and especially its products are particularly significant in the present economic climate, since they demonstrate one way of overcoming the duplication of effort that occurs as library instruction programs proliferate. Even when money becomes more freely available, the principles of the Travelling Workshops Experiment will still be relevant, since reduction of unnecessary duplication should promote the creation of higher quality programs.

BACKGROUND

Research into user education, and its development, has taken rather different forms in Britain and the United States. There is, of course, a great deal of activity in both countries, particularly in the development of instruction programs for specific libraries. In both countries, however, there is a real concern that much effort is being duplicated in the development of basically similar programs, with the twofold result that time and other resources are wasted and that the products of the efforts are often poor in quality. The continual reinvention of the wheel results in a range of primitive wheels.

It is probably true that although there has been more activity in the United States, more progress is being made in Britain in the coordination of effort or in the development of cooperative instructional projects. This is due to two major factors. The first is that Britain is a smaller country with fewer institutions of higher education, thereby facilitating collaboration.[2] The second is the existence of the

171

British Library Research and Development Department (formerly the Office for Scientific and Technical Information), which provides substantial support for research in all aspects of library and information work. This support is not only for projects initiated independently by individual workers in the field; the department also takes research initiatives, both in the identification of areas in which research is necessary and in the formulation of specific projects. This is, in fact, how the Travelling Workshops Experiment came about.

> The Office of Scientific and Technical Information (OSTI) has instituted the practice of creating review panels for specific areas in the general field of scientific and technical information to determine where further research was felt to be necessary or desirable. One of these areas was the education of users of scientific and technical information and, before establishing the Review Panel proper, it was agreed that a multi-disciplinary group of people active in this area should make a preliminary survey and produce a report which the Review Panel could use as a basis for its discussion.[3]

Accordingly, a meeting was held at the University of Bath in September 1973. For a weekend, 18 individuals known to be heavily involved in or interested in user education held discussions about a wide range of issues and problems, including the organization of user education, its content, the relationship between library and teaching staff in the provision of instruction, and so on.

The proceedings of the meeting were published[4]; among recommendations for "short-term actions . . . to improve the quality of user education and to gather information and experience on which future actions could be based"[5] was a suggestion to conduct "an experiment to assess the value of a travelling workshop in a specific subject area."[6]

What exactly was meant initially by a "travelling workshop" is unclear.* For several years the National Lending Library for Science and Technology (later part of the British Library Lending Division [BLLD]) had run courses in literature searching for researchers and university teachers, and it is assumed that a travelling workshop was thought of as a means of making such courses more generally available by taking them to the users, rather than obliging the users to attend at Boston Spa, the location of the BLLD in northern England.

Eleven of the 18 participants at the Bath meeting became members of a Review Panel established by the British Library Research and Development Department (BLRDD)—known formally as the Review Committee on Education for Information Use[7]—and the idea of a travelling workshop was carried forward. In 1974 the BLRDD called for proposals to run an experimental travelling workshop in information handling in three areas: biology, mechanical engineering, and social welfare. These three subjects were selected, not only because they would provide some representation of the needs and practices in information handling in the pure, applied, and social sciences, but also because professional organizations in those areas were currently demonstrating an awareness of the information problems facing their practitioners and students, and, it was expected, would be committed to, and cooperative with, the proposed project. Newcastle upon Tyne Polytechnic Library was awarded the research grant for a period of three years from July 1975.

Note: For internal consistency, the word "travelling," in accordance with the experiment's proper name Travelling Workshops, has been retained within this chapter.

OBJECTIVES

The basic concept of a travelling workshop and the basic objectives, both of the project and of individual workshops, were determined by the British Library:

A Travelling Workshop is envisaged as a "teaching laboratory," which may be set up at the appropriate institutions (generally universities and polytechnics) to provide information, source materials, teaching aids, demonstrations and examples. It should be staffed by a multi-disciplinary team of experts working closely with the institution's own teaching and library staff, who will be encouraged to follow up the demonstration of principles by the workshop.[8]

Project Objectives
To implement and run pilot workshops in three different subject areas.
To assess the impact of the workshop on the host institutions and the participating individuals.
To make recommendations for further work to educational institutions and national bodies with an interest in this area.

Objectives of a Travelling Workshop
To demonstrate to teaching and library staff how various aspects of information handling may be taught and incorporated into the student's curriculum.
To encourage a continuing educational program in the institution and to further library-departmental co-operation to this end.
To make students aware of sources of information in their field and to show how to use them effectively.
To outline and illustrate the basic principles of communication and scientific writing in the chosen subject.[9]

In practice, the Travelling Workshops Experiment was concerned as much with investigation as with demonstration. Underlying the objectives set by the British Library are the familiar themes of course-related library instruction, and of the involvement of teaching staff in library instruction. The latter is probably the most commonly expressed problem in user education. The problems of persuading teaching staff to recognize the *need* for library instruction, of persuading them to make teaching time available for it, of persuading them to become involved in it, are serious. The task of the Travelling Workshops Experiment was not simply to "demonstrate" to teaching and library staff how various aspects of information handling may be taught and incorporated into the student's curriculum, for example, but to *find out* how they might be taught and incorporated and to *find out* how to demonstrate it.

The basic aim of the project was to set up and run a total of 32 workshops in three subject areas, with the additional aims of attempting to influence the attitudes and behavior of library and teaching staffs, to suggest ways in which instruction in information handling might be taught, and to assess the overall effects of the workshop's presence.

The fact that the teaching staff ranked equally with librarians as the project's audience was kept firmly in mind. In the appointment of the project team, for example, academic qualifications in the subject concerned or in a cognate area were required in addition to professional qualifications and experience in library and information work; it was hoped that this would allow for an understanding of the needs of the subject and therefore prevent an obsessive concern with "librarianship" in the development of courses or materials, and, of course, it was expected that some academic background in the subject would help in establishing good relations with the teaching staff. (It is not easy to assess the validity of this assumption; certainly some familiarity with the subject, whether by training or by experience, is essential. Perhaps what is most important is that an academic background in the subject gives a librarian more confidence in his dealings with the teaching staff.)

The interpretation of the project's objectives suggested a program in which actions would be continuously evaluated and revised, in a long-term effort to find the best solution. It will be seen later that the Travelling Workshop's team gradually revised the workshops. Revisions were the outcome of an evaluation program in which *all* aspects of workshops were examined to identify reasons for "success" or "failure." The evaluation strategy used, called "illuminative evaluation," has been developed and used with curriculum innovation and development projects, particularly in Britain. This strategy seemed appropriate for the evaluation of travelling workshops, since it recognizes that evaluation should not focus solely upon "intended outcomes." The aims of illuminative evaluation are:

> to study the innovatory project: how it operates; how it is influenced by the various school situations in which it is applied; what those directly concerned regard as its advantages and disadvantages; and how students' intellectual tasks and academic experiences are most affected. It aims to discover and document what it is like to be participating in the scheme, whether as teacher or pupil; and, in addition, to discern and discuss the innovation's most significant features, recurring concomitants and critical processes. In short, it seeks to address and to illuminate a complex array of questions.[10]

In addition, there is the explicit objective of assessing the impact of the workshop upon the host institution and upon the participants. Much of this is now being undertaken by an external assessment of the entire Travelling Workshops Experiment, being conducted by Aslib. This project provides the Travelling Workshops team with valuable feedback.[11]

THE ORIGINAL WORKSHOP FORMAT

The team's first task was to design a course in information handling; the courses developed for each of the three subjects had basically the same structure, but they differed in detail. (Early "workshops" will be described as "courses," since, as will be seen, they were more formal and structured than later workshops.) It was known that the content and methods of the course would probably change during the project, but the basic design was carefully undertaken, and resulted in a course (not unlike those offered by BLLD in Boston Spa) that typically lasted three days and consisted of a number of lectures complemented by practical exercise sessions, a supervised rudimentary literature search by each student, and a final discussion/ evaluation session. The basic features and rationale of the course are as follows:

1. The course was designed for a block of three days, simply because it was not feasible for the project's team—travelling tutors—to organize a course in the way that a librarian or teacher might normally do, such as an hour or two a week for a number of weeks. Also, the original conception of the travelling workshop was not in terms of the familiar teaching pattern, but precisely as a visiting, temporary service.

2. As far as possible, the course was to be presented to students who were about to start preparing for a final year (senior year) project or dissertation. It was thought that this piece of work was significant enough (sometimes 20 or 40 percent of the student's final year grade) to motivate students to attend the course, which would usually be voluntary. This fact of voluntary attendance underlined the development of the entire course; students could only be expected to attend if they believed it was relevant.

3. In determining the content of the course, the team felt that students were being prepared not only for their project or dissertation, but also for their future professional careers. This meant that some of the sources or types of sources included (such as reports or conference proceedings) might not necessarily be those of immediate relevance to the student, but it was hoped that students would understand their place in the information system. This was another principle underlying the course design. Students were not simply to learn how to use sources but to understand the working of the information system, and how each type of information source fits into the overall system.

4. Each course was to be conducted with a demonstration set of materials—sources needed for practical exercises and displays of information sources in the subject—but it was felt essential that the link between course content and the "real world" of the students own library should be firmly made. In addition, it was desirable that students should see how the various parts of the course fit together into a meaningful, systematic approach to literature searching. It was intended that both of these requirements would be met by assigning time during the course for a rudimentary literature search on the project topic. This, it was thought, would enable students to appreciate the notion of search strategy, to become familiar with the complete range of sources and services in their own library, and to establish contact with the library staff.

5. The broad content of the course can be seen from the schedule in Table 1.

6. The decision to organize the course on the basis of types of information source was not as obvious as it might appear to be. It does reflect a "librarian's" perception of the literature, and could be criticized on that ground, but any other basis of organization did not seem to be obviously superior. In addition, an approach was necessary that would allow the course to be structured in discrete parts.

7. In each part of the course instruction was given by lecture, each lecture being illustrated by a large number of slides. Notes to support the lectures were prepared and bound into a "student handbook." This handbook amounted basically to a series of lecture handouts, including some specimen entries from sources, and some lists of sources, but it was substantial—around one hundred pages. Each student received a handbook to keep, the cost being borne by the project.

8. Lectures were used, not because it was thought to be the ideal teaching method, but because it seemed to be a logical place to start in the search for the right method. Using live lectures (rather than prepackaged ones) allowed the tutor to adapt to students' needs and to local conditions where necessary, to respond to

Table 1. Schedule for Information-handling Course

Day	Time	Presentation/Activity
1st day	9:00–10:00 A.M.	Convene academic and library staff involved, Aslib assessors; finalize displays of material, equipment, etc.
	10:00–10:30 A.M.	Introduction to course; educational objectives; motivation; outline of course; pretest.
	10:30–10:45 A.M.	Coffee
	10:45–1:00 P.M.	I: The subject and its information system
	1:00–2:00 P.M.	Lunch
	2:00–5:00 P.M.	II: Access to information—reference books; books and bibliographies; periodicals, abstracts, and indexes
2nd day	9:30–12:30 P.M.	II: Access to information (cont.)—periodicals, abstracts, indexes and (cont.); official publications and statistics; other sources (reports, theses, etc.)
	12:30–1:30 P.M.	Lunch
	1:30–2:30 P.M.	III: Introduction to literature searching
	2:30–5:00 P.M.	IV: Practical literature searching
3rd day	9:30–12:30 P.M. (incl. coffee break)	IV: Practical literature searching (cont.)
	12:30–1:30 P.M.	Lunch
	1:30–3:00 P.M.	V: Discussion of literature searching; practical difficulties, etc.; evaluation of sources and presentation of information
	3:00–3:15 P.M.	Tea
	3:15–4:30 P.M.	Aslib Assessment. Post-test

problems of timing in the course, and to get immediate reactions from participants to the lecture content. It was understood at the beginning that lectures were probably prototype scripts for media presentations to be developed later.

9. Each lecture was complemented by a practical exercise session, during which students solved problems prepared by the project team, using sources discussed in the lecture. Exercises were prepared that reflected the kinds of problems students might actually experience in their literature search or in looking for specific information in their broad subject area. Practical work was included because it was felt crucial that students actually handle and use sources, rather than just learn *about* them.

MODIFICATION OF WORKSHOP FORMAT

Nine workshops were presented in this original format; the experience of these nine workshops suggested that a number of changes were necessary. The overwhelming impression was that students had not enjoyed the lectures but had, by contrast, enjoyed the practical work sessions. Apparently the lecture approach had made the workshops too formal; the content of the lectures had been too detailed and had focused too much on bibliographic aspects (one student thought that "this is what library school must be like") and not upon practical relevance to students' needs. The practical work sessions had been agreeably informal, and, for the most part, had demonstrated to students both the relevance of the sources to their subjects of study and the techniques and problems of using sources of information. It is not necessarily the fault of the lecture *method*, of course, that the lectures were not satisfactory, but, nevertheless, it appeared that practical, hands-on, self-instruction was the preferred method.

One of the key features of the original workshops proved to be the handbook, described earlier. Although this was essentially a bound collection of lecture-support handouts, it was nevertheless substantial as a guide to sources of information in each subject and their use. The handbook was received extremely well, to the extent that many students believed that given the handbook, the lectures and perhaps even the workshops were unnecessary.

Finally, although the project team still believe in the usefulness of the rudimentary literature search (and it is still occasionally used), it did not fulfil its purpose, because students were rarely at quite the right stage in their own work to make a start on their search and, even when students *did* start their search, they often tended to make directly for novel sources (such as *Dissertation Abstracts*), rather than follow a search strategy, thus defeating the object of the exercise. Also, it became clear during the first nine workshops that three whole days would not be made available for every workshop, so the literature search would need to go.

In response to these observations, a new workshop format was developed. Lectures were virtually abandoned. The handbook was developed to be more self-sufficient, both as a guide to information sources in the subject and as instruction in their use. The handbook would be used in conjunction with practical exercises as the basis for a self-accessed, self-paced, self-instruction workshop.

In the new workshop, students would be given a general introduction to the workshop, its purpose, content and organization, and would then work, individually or in pairs or small groups, through the various sections of the workshop. Each section had a "station" at which exercises, exercise sources, and displays of other relevant material were located. Using the handbook for descriptions, exercises for hands-on instruction, and answer sheets that indicated any "tricks" necessary to complete the exercises successfully, students would get a thorough and practical introduction to all major bibliographic sources in their subject. The workshop tutor (the Travelling Workshops Experiment team member) would still be available to provide guidance and assistance where necessary and, more important, to obtain feedback on the usefulness of the project's materials; this would be used gradually to modify the materials so that in the long term most of the difficulties that students had might be overcome.

Twenty-four workshops were conducted using the new format. In the course of these workshops, various other adjustments were made. The introductory lecture was developed into a slide/tape program that could be viewed by individuals or groups, and additional audiotape and slide/tape programs were developed (also out of the original lectures) to provide instruction either on types of source, such as patents, or on a specific tool, such as *Engineering Index*. Some of these, such as the *Biological Abstracts* program, involve listening or viewing by the student; others, such as the slide/tape program on *Chemical Abstracts*, are interactive programs, requiring the student to use material for practical exercises in the course of the program.

In addition, a series of posters, designed by a graphic designer in conjunction with members of the team, have been used to provide a simple reminder and to serve as point-of-use instruction to students on how to use the more complicated sources, such as the citation indexes.

The new form of workshop seemed to solve most of the problems mentioned earlier. The practical exercises, used in conjunction with the handbook and audio or audiovisual programs, enabled the students to be active and to work on materials relevant to them. Clearly not all practical questions were of direct interest to every student; most students, however, saw the purpose of the questions and even accepted the artificial nature of the workshop (having immediately available the prepared questions and the tools needed to answer them). Students were encouraged throughout to assess the value or use or approach of each source in relation to their own interests, thus preparing them at least partially for their later library search.

The new format, not surprisingly, posed its own problems. It was much less structured than the old style, and students were expected to direct themselves and to determine for themselves how much time to spend. One feature of the new workshop was that it was less time-consuming than before, so a hard-working student could complete all the assignments, including reading the relevant sections of the handbook, in five or six hours. Some students would spend more time than this, especially if they were examining items in relation to their own needs; many students, however, would spend less time, although again the quality and comprehensiveness of the handbook was frequently offered as a reason for not needing to complete the workshop.

LEARNING PACKAGES: A BENEFIT
OF THE EXPERIMENT

The transformation of the experiment from a conventional, lecture-based course into a self-contained, self-instructional, practicable workshop is important, as the implications are wider than is perhaps immediately apparent.

First, formally organized, classroom-based courses that include practical work are feasible only for small numbers of students, whereas the self-instructional approach can be used for almost an infinite number of students, especially if multiple sets of practical exercises are developed.[12] Of course, some kind of assistance must be available, but constant instruction or even supervision is unnecessary.

The second and most important implication is for librarians and teaching staff who may eventually use the materials developed by the Travelling Workshops Experiment. Teaching staff who are convinced of the value of instruction in information handling and who wish to incorporate such instruction into an existing or proposed course might feel justifiably hesitant about attempting to teach it themselves, as they probably lack sufficient bibliographic expertise; on the other hand, there is some evidence that librarians do not generally feel confident as teachers and do not wish to undertake teaching in the formal sense.[13] Both of these problems can be alleviated by the same set of appropriate teaching materials.

From its outset, the Travelling Workshops Experiment has given much attention to the question of whether the travelling workshop mode could be used as a means of providing routine library instruction for students. Early in the project's life it seemed reasonable to conclude that this would not be feasible, primarily because of the costs if travelling workshops were to be self-sufficient. This is not to say that the travelling workshop concept does not have application in limited cases, for example in large library systems with a number of proximate libraries, or in on-line information systems in which users may be prepared to pay for the training facility.

Apart from the problem of cost, however, there are two basic shortcomings to the travelling workshops mode, and these both concern the status of the workshop tutor as an "outsider." First, the workshop tutor cannot possibly be as familiar with students and their courses, and therefore their needs, as can local teachers and librarians, nor can he or she be as familiar with the local department or library's resources, strengths, and weaknesses. It is logical that if instruction will be effective only when given by someone familiar with all the local factors, then it cannot be provided by outsiders. Second, and more important, is the view held by the "inside" librarian of the workshop tutor as an outsider. Rarely did any workshop tutor encounter hostility from host librarians—quite the reverse was the case; but in a sense the temporary presence of the outsider made the librarian's life difficult. The outcomes of a workshop have favorable and unfavorable aspects. If, for example, demands for reference service or for interlibrary loans increase, the librarian may see this as an added burden on staff; if these are to be taken to be manifestations of a favorable outcome—simply increased use of the library—then the librarian does not get the credit. Indeed, the academic department could well be of the opinion that the outsider achieved something that the librarian could not achieve. (In fact, relations between teaching staffs and librarians generally improved following common commitment to a workshop.)

What was most beneficial to librarians and to teaching staff was the opportunity to use the materials developed by the Travelling Workshops Experiment. Many felt that the materials, prepared for specific subjects and to a professional standard, would (modified if necessary) form the basis of a program that they would develop. In particular, librarians felt that learning materials, developed and tested elsewhere and carrying an objective estimate of the time and resources required to run a course using them, might make teaching staff more willing to make time available.

In the course of the project there was an evident demand that the materials should be available to others to offer their own courses. As a result, it was decided to spend much of the project's final year making experimental packages of the materials available to a limited number of users. The primary aim here was to discover whether centrally produced packages of instructional materials are a feasible solution to the user education problem in individual libraries.

Each package of materials contained multiple sets of the student handbook, exercises and answers to exercises, and a copy of each poster and audiovisual program relevant to the subject. Every student received a copy of the handbook to retain, but the audiovisual programs were returned to the project. Each participating institution paid a token contribution toward the cost of a package and each agreed to undertake a predesigned evaluation. This often meant a visit from a member of the project team and/or the Aslib evaluator, but the major device was an "evaluation pack" in each package. The evaluation pack consisted of a test of knowledge of information sources, to be administered before and after a course, a postcourse questionnaire to elicit reactions from students, and a lengthy, semi-structured questionnaire designed to enable librarians or teachers using a package to gather the right sort of data to enable them to assess and explain the degree of success of the course.

Over 30 individuals used such packages during this phase. As intended, the range of ways in which they were used was broad. Several users had seen the materials being used by the project team, and tended to copy that method; some other users asked the team for advice, and this was provided to the best of the team's ability. Most users, however, devised their own courses using the packaged material, ranging from total integration with the teaching of a subject (usually by teachers) to little more than displays or exhibits.

The feedback from this phase will help assess the potential contribution that such packages can make in user education internationally and will help to make any necessary modifications to existing packages so that a wide range of potential users can use them effectively and as effortlessly as possible.

CONCLUSION

The Travelling Workshops Experiment, through teaching courses in information handling to students in a wide range of subjects, courses, and institutions, has been able to develop teaching or learning packages for use in any similar instruction program. In the near future it is hoped that the pattern already set for production of such packages can be extended, both to information handling in other subjects and to other countries. The opportunity exists to cease duplication of effort in the production of almost identical programs and instead to devote the increasingly scarce personnel and other resources to the enhancement of centrally produced programs to suit local conditions and particular student groups.

NOTES

1. The opinions expressed in this paper are those of the authors and not necessarily those of the British Library Research and Development Department. We would like to thank Peter Taylor, Aslib, for his valuable comments upon a draft of this chapter.
2. For an account of one such cooperative project, see Frank Earnshaw, "An Example of Cooperative Development of Library-Use Instruction Programs,"

in *Educating the Library User*, ed. by John Lubans, Jr. (New York: R. R. Bowker, 1974), pp. 392–400.

3. *The Education of Users of Scientific and Technical Information: Report from a Workshop Held at the University of Bath, 14–16 September, 1973* (Bath: Bath University Library, 1973), p. 1.

4. Ibid.

5. Ibid., p. 3.

6. Ibid., p. 3.

7. The committee's final report was published as British Library Research and Development Department, *Review Committee on Education for Information Use—Final Report*, BLRDD Report, No. 5325HC (London: BLRDD, 1977).

8. British Library Research and Development Department, *Specification for a Travelling Workshops Experiment* (unpublished).

9. Ibid.

10. Malcolm Parlett and David Hamilton, "Evaluation as Illumination: A New Approach to the Study of Innovatory Programs," *Evaluation Studies Review Annual: Volume 1: 1976*, ed. by Gene V. Glass (Beverly Hills: Sage, 1976), pp. 140–157.

11. Colin Harris, "Illuminative Evaluation of User Education Programmes," *Aslib Proceedings* 29 (October 1977): 348–362.

12. As Miriam Dudley points out: ". . . one hundred sets of question and answer sheets . . . can be adapted by any library; this means that in a class of one hundred, no two students will have the same set of questions. In a class of 6,700 students, there would be 67 students floating around with the same workbook, but their chances of finding each other are not good." Miriam Dudley, "The State of Library Instruction Credit Courses and the State of the Use of Library Skills Workbooks," in *Library Instruction in the Seventies: State of the Art*, ed. by Hannelore B. Rader (Ann Arbor, Mich.: Pierian Press, 1977), p. 83.

13. See, for example, Sue Galloway, "Nobody Is Teaching the Teachers," *Booklegger Magazine* 13; *Emergency Librarian* 3 (January/February 1976): 29–31.

PROGRESS AND RECENT DEVELOPMENTS IN SCANDINAVIAN LIBRARIES

Nancy Fjällbrant
*Deputy Librarian, Chalmers University of
Technology, Gothenburg, Sweden*

There is, at present, a growing realization among Scandinavian librarians that it is necessary to provide training for users in the use of libraries and literature and information resources. This has resulted, particularly in academic libraries, in the development and establishment of a number of user education programs. Interest in this field has also been shown in other ways: by surveys and organized discussions on library user education, by the introduction of the subject of user instruction into the curricula of Swedish library schools, and by the fact that aspects of user education have been the themes of papers at many library conferences during recent years. This chapter will attempt to provide an overview of library user education in the Scandinavian nations of Denmark, Finland, Norway, and Sweden in the 1970s. Emphasis will be placed on recent developments, and examples of programs established at a number of libraries will be given to illustrate the present state of the art.

ACADEMIC LIBRARIES

Interest in user education has been particularly marked, during the last five years, in Scandinavian university and academic libraries. A comparative survey of user instruction in Scandinavian and British academic libraries, carried out by Fjällbrant in 1975, showed that most of the Scandinavian academic libraries provided some form of user education.[1] The courses provided, however, showed considerable variations with regard to length and content and the number and percentage of students attending them.

Many libraries provided *library orientation* programs of about half an hour to an hour. The most common method used for orientation was the guided tour given to groups of varying size, from 5 to 40 students. The percentage attendance of potential new users varied widely. A number of libraries made use of audiovisual orientation programs; for example, slide/tape introductions have been produced at the Danish University of Technology Library, Copenhagen, at the University of Bergen Library, Norway, and at the University Libraries of Linköping and Örebro, Sweden.[2] Videotape programs designed to provide an introduction to the use of the library have been made at the Central Medical Library, Helsinki,[3] at the Helsinki University of Technology Library, Finland,[4] and at the University Library of Örebro, Sweden.[5] At Chalmers University of Technology Library, Gothenburg, Sweden, an attempt has been made to provide library orientation largely by the use of self-instructional material—color/shape coding systems and signposting, colored tracks, and a slide/tape introductory program.[6]

There has been a considerable increase in courses of library/bibliographic instruction provided by Scandinavian libraries during the last five years. The courses offered showed a great deal of variation with regard to length, timing, content, and number of potential users attending. It is not possible to describe what is being done in each individual institution; therefore examples have been chosen to epitomize Scandinavian programs of library instruction. These examples represent developments at institutions where user education has received a high priority. More detailed accounts of individual Scandinavian user instruction programs are to be found in *Proceedings of the NVBF Anglo-Scandinavian Seminar on Library User Education, November 2-4, 1976*[7] and in a recent report by Fjällbrant, "User Education Programmes in Swedish Academic Libraries: A Study of Developments in the Years 1973-1977."[8]

ROSKILDE UNIVERSITY CENTRE, DENMARK

The University Centre at Roskilde, Denmark, which was opened in 1972, is a new university experimenting with a type of educational pattern based on problem-oriented project studies. Project work is integrated into the general educational framework, and the library is used as a resource and information center. Roskilde University Library was planned as a decentralized library consisting of several branch libraries spread throughout the campus. In 1974, it was decided to develop a course for humanities students on elementary research methodology designed to support project work. The five modules of the course correspond to the major processes in the development of a project: problem formulation, literature search, argumentation, documentation, and report writing. Since 1975, a Roskilde team of three teachers and a librarian has spent considerable time on investigating problems linked to literature searching.[9]

The course on literature searching consists of four three-hour sessions. This is supplemented by practical work and experience in connection with the students' own project work. The course starts directly after the student groups have begun their work with preliminary problem formulation. The teaching group follows the development of the literature search for the project. They are interested not only in the fact that students find some literature, but also in *how* they find it and how the relevance of the material found is assessed. In the final session of the course, the students are taught how to set out references and construct bibliographies. A textbook or manual has been prepared for use during the course.

One of the main aims of the instruction given at Roskilde has been to bring a greater insight on the part of the students—and possibly their teachers—into the relationships between literature searching and research methodology. It has been pointed out by Bermann that "in teaching students to search literature, the bibliographical search is viewed and presented as only one of many types of work patterns."[10] One of the aims of the course is to get students to analyze their own project search programs and decide whether or not the programs require a systematic bibliographic search, and, if so, what types of information tools will be needed. It is hoped that this will enable the students to become increasingly independent in their work, particularly in their future projects.

HELSINKI UNIVERSITY OF TECHNOLOGY LIBRARY, FINLAND

Helsinki University of Technology Library is the national central library for technology in Finland. User surveys carried out by Erkko, in 1970,[11] and Törnudd, in 1973,[12] clearly showed the need for library user education. This has resulted in a regular teaching program consisting of a compulsory orientation course for freshmen and an elective subject-oriented course (for credit) for third- and fourth-year students.[13] Subject-oriented courses on information resources are offered in the following fields: physics and mathematics; chemistry and chemical engineering; civil engineering, surveying, and architecture; electrical and electronic engineering; forest products; mining engineering, metallurgy, and geology.

The aim of these courses is to enable students, during their studies and later during their careers, to carry out literature searches, to retrieve data, to utilize libraries and their services, and to use both manual and computer-based information services. Students are also taught how to write reports. The courses consist of 12 lectures held over a six-week period with the number of students attending each course varying from 15 to 40. Each lecture is followed by practical assignments, and the grade obtained is dependent on the number of assignments successfully carried out. The program for each course consists of the following: use of libraries; general information sources; classification and indexing; computer-based information systems; subject-related abstracting and indexing journals; subject-related reference works; the techniques of a manual literature search, including the recording of results; on-line searching; the use of report literature; the use of patents, statutes, standards, etc.; how to write a report.

A textbook and a guide to report writing have been prepared for use during these courses. Use is also made of audiovisual media—18 videotape programs have been recorded, and slide/tape presentations produced in Britain and the United States are also utilized.

In 1977, 15–20 percent of potential third- and fourth-year students took the elective courses. It is hoped that this percentage will be considerably increased in the future. User education is regarded as an important function of the library, and it is considered that this function shows a good cost/benefit ratio, that is, the increase in use and knowledge of the library is achieved at a low cost relative to other library activities.

THE LIBRARY OF THE FACULTY OF THE SOCIAL SCIENCES, OSLO UNIVERSITY, NORWAY

This library serves the Institutes of Social Anthropology, Mass Communication Research, Sociology, Political Science, Economics, Educational Research, and Psychology at Oslo University. The faculty library is integrated with the main university library in Oslo by means of direct telephone links and special cars for the transport of library materials between the main downtown building and the faculty library.

A two-level user instruction program is offered to students within the various disciplines in social sciences.[14] It consists of instruction to new students with relatively little experience in using a university library and a course for advanced students who have already learned the basic library routines, and who need to learn how to obtain materials in connection with projects and theses. The aim of the first course is to familiarize the students with the practical arrangement of the library and with basic library techniques. Teaching is given to small groups with a maximum of 12 students. The advanced course aims to enable students to carry out an information search, using the reference collection and tools for information retrieval.

It was found that most of the students knew very little about library use before they attended the courses in user instruction. Studies on student use of the library also showed that of students that had been studying at the Faculty of Social Sciences for one year, only 55 percent had been using the faculty library. Less than 10 percent had been users of the main university library in addition to the faculty library, according to a study by Kvam.[15] The findings of these studies showed that, in general, contact between students and the library was poor. The development of the courses in library instruction at the Faculty of the Social Sciences Library has concentrated on the establishment of good contact with the users. This has been achieved partly by producing small bibliographies on current topics at times when they are needed, such as in connection with seminars. Kvam pointed out that, in this situation, timing is frequently more important than making a perfectly complete bibliography. She also described the difficulties concerned with the selection of the material to be included in the library education program—how many details of bibliographical terms, abbreviations, modes of library application, and the various catalogs and reference systems to include or not to include—"Looking back on my own experience, or remembering the enthusiastic and devoted colleagues presenting detailed information to the small and bewildered audience, one can only wonder that none of the students join Eliza in Pygmalion 'Words, words, words . . . give me love.' "[16]

CHALMERS UNIVERSITY OF TECHNOLOGY LIBRARY, GOTHENBURG, SWEDEN

Chalmers University of Technology in Gothenburg has about 4,000 undergraduates and some 600 postgraduate students, who study in one of the six schools: Architecture, Chemical Engineering, Civil Engineering, Electrical Engineering, Engineering Physics, and Mechanical Engineering. During the years 1973–1977, a systematic program of user education has been developed at Chalmers University Library.[17] This program consists of four parts: (1) orientation for approximately 900 new users per year, (2) introductory courses in information retrieval for third- and fourth-year engineering students (about 800 students per year), (3) advanced courses in information retrieval for doctoral students, and (4) seminars on methods of information retrieval for nonuniversity users, such as practicing industrial engineers.

A basic plan was drawn up for the 14-hour introductory course in information retrieval for the third- and fourth-year students to cover the following topics: a brief description of the rapid increase in scientific and technical publications; scientific communication—the different channels; the forms for printed communication—with division into primary and secondary information sources; different types of literature search—current awareness, retrospective searches, factual searches, browsing; methods of information retrieval; use of different tools for different information retrieval purposes; a practical information search centered on the student's own particular topic of interest; the presentation of the results of the practical search in the form of an annotated list of references; an introduction to computer-based information retrieval.

The course starts with two introductory "stimulus" lectures—"Patterns of Scientific Communication" and "Methods of Information Retrieval." These lectures are followed by two five-hour laboratory search sessions, which start with demonstrations for small groups of students (5–7), followed by practical use of the tools shown. In the first session the students learn to use the conventional tools for information retrieval—catalogs, indexes, and abstracts. In the second session, use is made of references obtained in the first session as a starting point for work with Science Citation Index.

This introductory course has been designed to provide an economical and efficient staff/student teaching ratio. Emphasis is placed on the practical work—learning by doing—in which students search on a topic that is part of their general program of engineering studies. The students are highly motivated and often carry out searches in connection with their undergraduate theses. Evaluation of the introductory course has been carried out in five different ways: by means of studies of student attitudes, performance results, and prestructured interviews designed to provide information with regard to achievement of specific course objectives, by means of illuminative evaluation, and by long-term library use studies. These different approaches enabled "triangulation" of the results, thereby giving an overall picture of the functioning of the course. A detailed account of this evaluation work is given in a recent book by Fjällbrant and Stevenson.[18]

Advanced courses in information retrieval are offered at a number of institutions for higher education in Scandinavia. These courses are particularly common in specialized academic libraries such as medical libraries and technological university libraries. The advanced courses usually include training in the use of computer-based information retrieval systems for current awareness and retrospective searching.

SCHOOL LIBRARIES AND PUBLIC LIBRARIES

Much less emphasis has been placed on user education in Scandinavian school and public libraries, than in their American counterparts.

During the 1950s the Swedish "Bibliotekstjänst" [The Swedish Central Organization for Library Services Ltd.] began to produce a series of materials designed to teach basic library techniques primarily to school classes. The latest products of this type are *Hitta i böckerna* [How to find out from books] published in 1973 and *Hitta i biblioteket* [How to find out in the library] published in 1976.

The latter series, which is intended as an introduction packet for senior high school students, is particularly popular. The material can also be used for adult study circles at the public libraries. The aim of the series is to enable the pupils to learn how to find the literature that they require themselves. The package consists of five basic practical exercises and three more-advanced exercises. In order to avoid the situation where a whole class crowds around one part of the card catalog, the first exercise has been produced in six variations. The five basic exercises are calculated

Figure 1. *How to Find Your Books.* Pictorial Version of Library Classification Scheme. Reproduced with the kind permission of Bibliotekstjänst, Lund, Sweden.

to take up a normal 45-minute lesson period. In addition, Bibliotekstjänst produces a whole range of instructional material ranging from pictorial versions of the classification scheme (see Figure 1) and explanatory posters on how to use the catalogs to bookmarks and series describing books within different subject fields and competitions, for use in school and public libraries. Similar types of material are produced by the Danish Library Bureau.

However, there has been a change in attitude toward school library user instruction during recent years. The importance of the use of libraries as an integral part of the education pattern has now been realized. Thus, in a project carried out under the auspices of "Skolöverstyrelsen" [The Central Swedish School Board], it has been pointed out that, from the first grades, students should be taught to use their libraries as resource centers, where they can go to find out things as and when needed.[19] This ideal is, however, far from being realized in actual practice. All too often children are taught "library use" as a separate small package bearing little relationship to their other school work.

In Norway an attempt is under way to encourage this integration of the use of the library with other studies. A textbook, *Skolbiblioteken i undervisning* [The school library in education] by Aase Hvidsten-Einarsen, is based on a project carried out at the Norwegian College of Librarianship. The manual, which will be published by "Statens Bibliotekstilsyn" [The Norwegian Directorate for Public and School Libraries], is designed for teachers and explains, with examples, how use can be made of school libraries in the regular teaching program.

In 1977, an experimental course in "Information-knowledge" was held at the Royal School of Librarians in Copenhagen. One of the most interesting lectures of this course was the study of the user-librarian negotiation process and the problems associated with this interaction.

An example of the production of audiovisual material for library instruction in technical high schools and colleges can be seen in a tape/slide/handbook package produced by Norsk Senter for Informatikk (NSI). This material shows the integrated use of several media.

At the Swedish College of Librarianship, Borås, the idea of the "Pathfinders" developed in connection with the Model Library Program of Project Intrex at the Massachusetts Institute of Technology.[20] Students carry out projects in which they design Pathfinders or "Läselots" for guiding users through different subject fields. These have proved so successful that the best of the projects are collected together and sold, by the College of Librarianship, to subscribers to the series. Over a third of the *public* libraries now subscribe to Pathfinders.

PROBLEMS, LIMITATIONS, AND SOLUTIONS

In spite of recent efforts toward the development of user education in the Scandinavian libraries, significant problems remain to be faced.

The development of programs of user education is very uneven. There is not only considerable variation among the different types of library, but even within libraries of the same general type such as academic libraries. In the latter group, libraries showing the greatest commitment to user education are the specialized libraries such as the technological university libraries and the medical libraries.

User education is often regarded as a separate, and low-priority, function of the library. All too often the development of programs depends on the energy and enthusiasm of one or two staff members. If they move to other jobs, the courses they have initiated are allowed to drop.

Perhaps the most obvious problem in library user education is how to reach the *potential* user. Students who take part in elective courses in user instruction usually find these worthwhile. How do we attract the even larger numbers of potential users who never come into the building?

What do we know about the expectations, needs, and attitudes of the potential users? As Vogel expressed this[21]:

1. Do librarians know what the student (user) perceives about the services of the library?
2. Do librarians know what the student (user) really needs to know (or perceives as necessary to know) about the library?
3. Do librarians know who the student (user) is most likely to approach if he has an informational need?

Most of the contemporary user instruction courses are far more closely concerned with *cognitive* goals (knowing, conceptualizing, and comprehending) than with *affective* goals (feelings, attitudes, and values). This suggests the existence of severe limitations in our programs and the need to pay attention to all aspects of the use of libraries, which will result in *both* affective and cognitive goals and objectives for our education programs.

In order to tackle the problem of uneven development and dependence on individual efforts, it will be necessary to achieve cooperation among different libraries, types of libraries, and the schools of librarianship. In connection with this, it is interesting to note that at the Anglo-Scandinavian Seminar on Library User Education, sponsored by the Scandinavian Research Librarians Association in 1976, it was recommended that steps should be taken to encourage cooperation among libraries in this endeavor.

Library user education should not be an isolated function in the library. It needs to be closely integrated into the general pattern of the other library functions.[22] Through user education programs librarians can become aware of the needs of users. This can, in turn, affect other functions such as the acquisition policy and the details of the classification system—when the hundredth student has questioned the position of solar energy according to the systematic classification system, one can begin to suspect that modification in the system might be necessary.

If we are to attract potential users into the library, we must study their needs and expectations. In those cases where some attempt has been made to study user needs and use of the library—as at Helsinki University of Technology Library, Finland, the Faculty Library of the Social Sciences, Oslo, Norway, and Chalmers University of Technology Library, Gothenburg, Sweden—it has been possible to develop extensive programs of user education. It is necessary to try to find out as much as possible about the needs of the various user groups in order to design programs geared to the needs of potential users.

So far not many studies have been carried out on the views of different groups—students, academic staff, administrative staff, and library staff—as to students' needs with regard to the library. The few studies that have been carried out, such as those by Roy at Surrey University[23] and Fjällbrant[24] at Chalmers University reveal that attitudes and expectations vary considerably among the different groups, as do theory and practice. For example, academic staff might well say that they thought that the use of the library in connection with studies was "a very good thing"; yet when asked by the library staff for help in scheduling a short course of library instruction, say that they could not possibly spare any time from their own essential lectures.

The ideal approach is to integrate library use into the general pattern of studies, teaching students to find information as and when they need it. This need for integration into the general pattern of studies suggests close cooperation with the teachers and course organizers as well as the students.

It is to be hoped that the future will see more research into the problems of library user education: the needs and expectations of the users, the suitability of teaching methods, the design of courses. More attention should be paid to the evaluation of the work carried out, and in this connection it is important to remember that we learn more from our failures than our successes. It is also to be hoped that the subject of user education will play an increasingly important role in the curricula of the library schools—after all, if library school students are to spend two years learning how to acquire, register, and store material, it seems sensible to spend a few hours on learning how to enable users to make use of this material.

NOTES

1. Nancy Fjällbrant, *A Comparison of User Instruction in Scandinavian and British Academic Libraries;* Chalmers University of Technology Transactions, no. 337 (Gothenburg, Sweden: Chalmers University, 1975).
2. Annika Lindberg, "Planning for a Tape-Slide Programme about Linköping University Library and Its Services," in *Proceedings of the NVBF Anglo-Scandinavian Seminar on Library User Education, November 2-4, 1976. Gothenburg, Sweden,* CTHB-Publikation, no. 12 (Gothenburg, Sweden: Chalmers University Library, 1977), pp. 92-95.
3. Irja L. Öberg, "Use of Videotape Material in Library Instruction," in *Proceedings of the NVBF Anglo-Scandinavian Seminar on Library User Education, November 2-4, 1976. Gothenburg, Sweden,* CTHB-Publikation, no. 12 (Gothenburg, Sweden: Chalmers University Library, 1977), pp. 86-89.
4. T. Kivelä, "Erfarenheter från Videobandning och TV-undervisning av Användare vid Tekniska Högskolans i Helsingfors Bibliotek" [Experience of video and TV instruction of users at the Helsinki University of Technology Library], paper presented at NORDDOK's Scandinavian Symposium on User Instruction, Oslo, 1974.
5. Elisabeth Andersson, "Audio-Visual Material at Örebro University Library," in *Proceedings of the NVBF Anglo-Scandinavian Seminar on Library User Education, November 2-4, 1976. Gothenburg, Sweden,* CTHB-Publikation, no. 12 (Gothenburg, Sweden: Chalmers University Library, 1977), pp. 90-91.
6. Nancy Fjällbrant, "The Need for Library User Orientation and the Design and Development of Material and Methods to Meet This Need," in *The Spread of*

Educational Technology, ed. by Philip Hills and John Gilbert, Aspects of Educational Technology, no. 11 (London: Kogan Page, 1977), pp. 99–108.

7. *Proceedings of the NVBF Anglo-Scandinavian Seminar on Library User Education, November 2–4, 1976. Gothenburg, Sweden*, CTHB-Publikation, no. 12 (Gothenburg, Sweden: Chalmers University Library, 1977).

8. Nancy Fjällbrant, *User Education Programmes in Swedish Academic Libraries: A Study of Developments in the Years 1973–1977*, CTHB-Publikation, no. 14 (Gothenburg, Sweden: Chalmers University Library, 1977).

9. Tamar Bermann, et al., *Library User Instruction in the Framework of Project Studies: Teaching Humanities Students Literature Search during the Basic Studies Programme at Roskilde University Centre* (Roskilde, Denmark: Roskilde Universitetscenter, Institut for Sprogbrugs-, socialisations- og videnskabsforskning, 1977).

10. Ibid.

11. Kristina Erkko, *Teknillisen korkeakoulun kirjaston käyttö selvitys* [Survey of the use of Helsinki University of Technology Library], mimeographed (Helsinki, Finland: 1970).

12. Elin Törnudd, *Selvitys opiskelijoiden suhtautumisesta Helsingin teknillisen korkeakoulun kirjastoon* [Survey on student attitudes to the library], Helsinki University of Technology Library Occasional Paper, no. 10 (Helsinki, Finland: 1973).

13. Leena-Kaarina Uuttu, "User Instruction at Helsinki University of Technology Library: A Case Study," *IATUL Proceedings* 9 (1977): 70–75.

14. Brita Lysne Kvam, "Library Instruction in Norway: A Specific Example from the Library of the Faculty of the Social Sciences, Oslo University," in *Proceedings of the NVBF Anglo-Scandinavian Seminar on Library User Education, November 2–4, 1976. Gothenburg, Sweden*, CTHB-Publikation, no. 12 (Gothenburg, Sweden: Chalmers University Library, 1977), pp. 26–30.

15. Brita Lysne Kvam, "Brukerundervisning: en undersökelse fra bibliotekstjenesten ved Det Samfunnsvitenskaplige Fakultet, UB Oslo" [User instruction: an investigation from the Library of Social Sciences, Oslo University Library], *Bok og Bibliotek* 42 (1975): 80–84.

16. Kvam, "Library Instruction in Norway."

17. Nancy Fjällbrant, "The Development of a Programme of User Education at Chalmers University of Technology Library" (Ph.D. thesis, University of Surrey, Guildford, 1976).

18. Nancy Fjällbrant and Malcolm Stevenson, *Library User Education: Problems and Practice* (London: Bingley, forthcoming).

19. Gunnel Odenstam, Gunnel Svensson, and Eva Trotzig, *Lärare—bibliotekarie i samverkan: Rapport från ett ut-vecklingsarbete inom LBS-projektet* [Teacher-librarian in co-operation: report from a development project], Sektionen för Läromedelsutveckling, Skriftserie, no. 1977: 1 (Stockholm: Skolöverstyrelsen, 1977).

20. Marie P. Canfield, "Library Pathfinders," *Drexel Library Quarterly* 8 (1972): 287–300.

21. J. Thomas Vogel, "A Critical Overview of the Evaluation of Library Instruction," *Drexel Library Quarterly* 8 (1972): 315–323.

22. Fjällbrant, "The Development of a Programme of User Education."
23. B. Roy, *The Needs of the Student Library User as Seen by Academic Staff, Library Staff and Students: A Report of the Pilot Study at the University of Surrey* (Guildford: University of Surrey, Institute of Educational Technology, 1974).
24. Fjällbrant, "The Development of a Programme of User Education."

PROGRESS AND RECENT DEVELOPMENTS IN CANADIAN LIBRARIES

SHEILA M. LAIDLAW
Librarian, Sigmund Samuel Library, University of Toronto Library

This chapter will attempt a glance at instructional activities and publications in representative examples of the various types of libraries in Canada, noting any published references to these programs. However, there has been very little published specifically on the topic of library instruction in Canadian libraries. For example, the annotated *Bibliography on Library Instruction*[1] produced by the Canadian Association of College and University Libraries for their Workshop on Library Instruction at the Canadian Library Association Conference in 1975 includes only one token Canadian item in the form of an evaluation sheet summarizing viewer response to "Audiscan" programs at the University of British Columbia. The majority of recent references to library instruction programs are in annual reports and in newsnotes in *Feliciter, Quill and Quire,* and the various provincial library publications.

Some of the major recent developments in library instruction, as in other areas of librarianship, have been in sharing expertise and experience and in planning cooperative programs and conducting regional workshops. Some of these will be detailed more fully in this search for signs of progress in library instruction in Canada.

When one speaks of progress, however, there is a built-in assumption that there is a starting point from which this progression has occurred—or at least a future direction to which a subject is headed from the present vantage point. Speaking of library instruction in Canadian libraries, the ability to establish the benchmark from which progression should be measured is questionable if not impossible. This chapter will, however, refer to a variety of starting points and hopefully identify some of the directions toward which further progression seems likely in the next few years.

A variety of methods have been used to collect the data on which the comments and assumptions on the next few pages are based. For one type of library the questionnaires completed in the spring of 1976 for the report "Library Instruction in the 70's: The State of the Art in Canadian Academic Libraries" were used.[2] At that time reports were received from all ten provinces—from 90 percent of the university libraries in the country and from a representative sampling of college and special libraries. This material has been supplemented with follow-up conversations and correspondence with a number of the people whose cooperation had been sought in 1976. To obtain a clearer picture of the trends that seem to be developing material has been reviewed from the reports compiled in 1973 for the first workshop, "Instruction in Library Use in Academic Libraries in Ontario & Quebec," by librarians in 16 universities, nine colleges, and nine subject or division libraries within university libraries in these two provinces.

To expand from "Canadian *academic* libraries" to "Canadian libraries" has presented a challenge. A number of personal contacts were made to identify libraries involved in library instruction, and there was a fairly wide sampling of librarians in public, school, special, and government libraries to acquire the material on which the discussion is based. Recent annual reports and other writings were also reviewed. It would, obviously, be more satisfactory to conduct a full survey of each of these types of libraries similar to the one completed for academic libraries. Perhaps this could be initiated for a future publication.

The real starting point in developments in library instruction varies from library to library. Fortunately few Canadian libraries began with the purely custodial role that was prevelant in early European libraries. In fact, early Canadian libraries began with the service element paramount. It was, however, the kind of service that was based on a "come-and-get-it" philosophy—*if* you could find it you were welcome to use it. In recent years there has been a much greater emphasis on teaching the library user *and* the potential user about how to use the library and its resources to the fullest extent, though it is interesting to note that Canadian public libraries that have produced statements of their goals and objectives do not seem to include the goal of instructing the library user in the way that academic libraries have begun to.

LIBRARY INSTRUCTION FOR CHILDREN

As schools began to develop library service, they also began to develop library instruction programs—but the initial efforts were strictly limited. As in many U.S. schools, the emphasis was on how the material was arranged on the shelves and how the catalogs could lead to individual books. Since then, the developments have centered around developing a greater awareness on the part of both pupils and teachers of how the contents of books and audiovisual materials can enrich the school curriculum. A number of exciting programs have been and are being developed in Canadian schools, and for school-age children in other types of libraries.

Books such as *Lise et Bruno dans l'universe des livres* by Marcel Mignault[3] aid teachers and parents in presenting books to children in a favorable light, leading to the development of a taste for reading, an awareness of various media, and a growth of the curiosity and skills that will later lead to the ability to conduct research. By means of games, stories, cartoons, and other illustrations, a year's course is fully laid out, leading pupils to a much greater knowledge of library use. The need to teach children first how to handle physical volumes and then how to shelve them is well illustrated by Normand St.-Cyr in Mignault's book in one of a series of cartoon strips[4] (see Figure 1).

That this is a real concern of many librarians in Canadian elementary schools was stressed by Cicely Chibnall from Etobicoke Board of Education (in Metropolitan Toronto) when she spoke at the inaugural meeting of the Library Instruction Round Table at the American Library Association Conference in Detroit in June 1977. She also reiterated the need to instill a basic understanding of the whole idea of classification systems at this stage, and to emphasize too-often forgotten aspects of using libraries.

One example of this is her insistence that teaching youngsters how to shelve books begins with teaching them how to hold the book, especially if they are right-handed. When a left-handed youngster closes a book and goes to the shelf, the book is automatically held by the spine; this is not automatic for the right-handed person until the mechanics of shelf arrangement are understood. Visualize taking a large-size picture book to the shelf holding it by the fore-edge and the problem is clear.

Figure 1. Cartoon by Normand St.-Cyr in *Lise et Bruno dans l'universe des livres* by Marcel Mignault (La Pocatiere: Societe du stage en bibliotheconomie; Montreal: Centrale des bibliotheques, 1976). Reproduced with the kind permission of the publisher and Normand St.-Cyr.

The responsibility for both education and public libraries in Canada lies in the hands of the provinces and there is a wide variation from community to community in the way library service is provided to school-age children. David Jenkinson describes it as "Canada-wide disparity in school library development. . . . Rather than a unified national policy for education, Canada has at least ten distinct and separate policies. At any given time within a province, school libraries will be assigned varying degrees of priorities and support by the department of educa- tion."[5] Library service for children may be provided by libraries in schools or by the local public library or by a combination of both. The general pattern with school library service includes visits to and presentations in the local public/adult library around grade seven or eight to supplement the school resources.

Several public libraries, such as Lethbridge, Alberta, and Mississauga, Ontario, have developed coordinated programs that reach various age groups from pre- school to adult with different services appropriate to each age level, though they usually omit special tours for grade eight as by then they expect a fairly good familiarity with the library and its resources. Classes that come to the library regularly usually receive some instruction at the start of the first (or each) visit and are then encouraged to browse and/or listen to readings and do crafts related to books or libraries, e.g., making bookmarks. A similar pattern appears in school and public libraries, with some variation depending on how closely programs are tied to the school curriculum.

In Mississauga, from grade six up, classes usually come to the public library for orientation and to research a specific topic on which the librarian will have done some preliminary work in conjunction with the classroom teacher. The instruction will, therefore, include reference tools and other material directly related to the topic. From grades 2–5 the Mississauga program provides generalized introduction to the use of COM catalogs—which the librarians find are easier to explain than card catalogs—and also to the types of material housed in reference collections, as children who have earlier begun to browse in the general collections need some persuasion to tackle this area. On all visits these age groups will also have a definite time set aside for browsing.

For preschoolers, the librarians in Mississauga do not explain the collection in detail though they do demonstrate use of the COM catalogs, letting youngsters push the buttons on the microfilm readers and assuring them that when they learn to read they will find all the books listed there. A "walk-around" is conducted to explain where various types of books are housed before an extended story hour– craft session. In many cases, even preschool groups visit the library once a month and soon assimilate the other major message—"librarians don't bite!"[6]

Many communities, such as Chatham, Ontario, and Flin Flon, Manitoba, also maintain a close liaison with schools at all levels. A few years ago staff from Edmonton Public Library were making almost one thousand visits to classrooms in a year and welcoming a further six hundred classes to the library. Calgary Public Library has instructional programs for various community groups by staff from the main branch and also from the Boys' and Girls' Department, which arranges talks on how to use the library for the Alberta Children's Hospital Speech and Hearing Parent Groups and several similar groups. Waterloo Public Library in

Ontario regularly arranges group visits for elementary schools, the Crippled Children's Centre, playground groups, children's aid supervisors, and children, and, at the initial visit by each group, instruction in library use is provided by an orientation talk, a guided tour and "hands-on" experience.

One way in which school librarians extend their ability to teach library use is by first teaching a group of volunteers what services the library offers and how material is arranged. Kingsview Village School in Etobicoke has a slide/tape presentation for this purpose and a recent issue of *Moccasin Telegraph*[7] outlines other programs for teaching volunteers how to use and explain school libraries. Halton County (Ontario) Board of Education has developed a "Parent Volunteers Training Course" and the Manitoba Teachers' Society has issued a "Teachers Handbook in the Use of Auxiliary Personnel" for staff whose main task is carrying out library routines but who also help youngsters use libraries.

Some of the most exciting developments in library service for school children extend beyond "library instruction" and lead toward the complete integration of the library program with regular classroom teaching. There are more and more examples of Canadian school boards under which libraries in elementary and secondary schools are conducting and participating in integrated programs, e.g., Etobicoke, Metropolitan Toronto, North York, and Aurora, Ontario. One of the main justifications for this type of emphasis is that skills taught in classrooms or in the library are not necessarily transferred between the two situations, whereas the regular application of library skills in the classroom and vice versa will help make this transfer automatic and may produce lifelong benefits for youngsters.

A similarly exciting development in library instruction at the high school level is one in Brantford, Ontario, involving close communication between teacher and librarian.[8] High school students have an "independent study" component, which allows and encourages them to come to the public library at any hour of day. Several times a year the reference librarians give special instruction on specific reference works to the entire class before they continue independent study.

Two other developments throughout Canada are exemplified by programs in Ontario and British Columbia. In Etobicoke, there are regular in-service training programs for staff in school libraries. One such event brought together librarians in elementary, junior high, and high schools to hear panel presentations and share in small-group discussions. The panel consisted of a librarian from each educational level—elementary school, secondary school, community college, and university— in addition to one from the local public library. Panel members describe their libraries' programs of library instruction and the expectations librarians have of new users at each level. It is reported that several changes were made in individual programs after that evening's discussions. In North York, another suburb of Toronto, there have recently been informal meetings between individual high school librarians and university librarians in an attempt to reassess the library instruction being given in the high school, particularly to college-bound students. In New Westminister, British Columbia, the librarian of the public library also gives talks to school librarians on what the public library can do for them.[9]

With these programs there seems to be a common trend that is also occurring in public and academic libraries—a growing willingness among librarians to consult with one another and share the benefits—and problems—of one another's learning experience. I believe there has been a reduction in the number of librarians trying to reinvent the wheel in a vacuum of isolation.

In summary, therefore, the main trends that have recently been identified in library instruction for Canadian children include: making beginning instruction more basic and more realistic; integrating library instruction into classroom teaching and, hence, laying a real basis for lifelong use of books and libraries; initiating and consolidating cooperation *and consultation* among librarians in various types of libraries; developing imaginative coordinated programs that meet the differing needs of various age levels.

PUBLIC LIBRARIES

Public libraries also report a wide range of instructional activities, though one's ability to draw the line between instruction per se and publicity and public relations is somewhat shaky at times. In Chatham, Ontario, the 1976 annual report of the Public Library is itself a potential teaching device, providing as it does a detailed chronicle of one day's activities with the questions, answers, and sources or reasons for choice of answer.[10] This is an imaginative way to provide a lesson, not only in the services the library provides but also in using them—to say nothing of the reinforcement it gives to the role of the library staff in these processes.

Another library that uses its annual report to fill an instructional function about the services and resources of the library is the Greater Victoria Public Library in British Columbia, where for the past few years the report has appeared as the March issue of *LINK*, the tabloid newspaper the library circulates to its public.[11] Victoria also publishes a number of leaflets giving specific instructions on various services. Many other public libraries have been developing vigorous publishing programs in recent years, much of which has an instructional content. I imagine that few are as prolific as the Metropolitan Toronto Library, which produced approximately 500,000 pieces of literature in 1976, including such items as *The Compleat Library Guide to Toronto* and *Guide to Periodicals and Newspapers*.[12]

The media play a great role in explaining the services of a number of public libraries to their potential patrons. Many libraries use newspaper columns and time spots on radio and television to announce upcoming events. These encourage use, however incidental it may be to the announced event. Others produce television programs such as Lethbridge Public Library's "Libraries Unlimited," which runs for half an hour at 4:30 P.M. and at 8:00 P.M. on the same day and provides library staff with an opportunity to discuss and announce library services and programs to a wide audience.[13]

Mississauga, Ontario, Public Library also has a regular time slot on local cable television and usually uses this to publicize library programs. It has, however, also begun to sponsor library "commercials," based on the work of the Construction Safety Association, that deliver instructional messages with a punch. This library also works closely with other community groups and, besides sending speakers and displays to group meetings, has taken advantage of the television programs sponsored by these groups to get more "air time" for the library. For example, library staff were delighted to respond to an invitation from senior citizens to have a librarian appear on their interview show to explain how senior citizens could best use the library.

Fort Frances, Ontario, Public Library finds that it can obtain generous coverage for library information in the *Fort Frances Times*[14]; Kingston, Ontario, Public Library uses a weekly column in the *Whig Standard* and daily spot announcements are recorded by students of St. Lawrence Community College for radio broadcast in Kingston[15]; Halifax City Regional Library, Nova Scotia, provides regular information on library services to all media,[16] as do Chatham, Ontario, and Burnaby, British Columbia, among many others.

Burnaby also publishes a monthly checklist of events in branches and information flyers on using various library services, besides producing a number of television programs and running a *Storybus* to day-care centers and kindergartens.[17] The main vehicle through which it has provided both information and instruction has, however, been a tabloid newspaper delivered to 47,000 households.

There are also some examples of public libraries that do not attempt to disguise the instructional purpose of programs, though some have had wide fluctuations in the number of registrants from year to year. Kingston, Ontario, has provided a "Learn to Use Your Public Library" course for over 20 registrants each year, but the number registering for Calgary's six-week series, "Learn to Use Your Library," has varied each year.[18] This course is conducted by staff volunteers for library patrons.

In St. Catharine's, Ontario, the public library has gone the route of the slide/tape show. This has been used successfully with a number of community groups to publicize both materials and services.[19]

In addition, there are some places where instruction in library use provided by public libraries extends far beyond the immediate borrowers. In New Westminister, British Columbia, for example, the public library conducted one-day workshops (sponsored by the British Columbia Library Development Commission) for community librarians from the interior and northern parts of the province.[20] In these workshops the various reference services, resources, and tools available in New Westminister were explained.

It is often difficult to assess the value of instructional programs to the library or to the library user. Public libraries in most parts of the country, however, seem to be continually reporting increased use of collections and services and—perhaps more significant—some, such as Kamloops, British Columbia,[21] have noted an increased demand for information across the desk and by telephone or an increase in reference questions and problems, as in Scarborough, Ontario.

The increase in the number of people participating in structured and self-directed learning experiences in recent years will account for much of this. It is, however, hard to believe that the increase in the time and money being devoted by public libraries to instructional activities is not having some effect both in library use figures and in beneficial adult learning experiences.

For many years public libraries, in Vancouver, Brampton, and many other cities have provided many specialized services for the business community and other special interest groups and have provided both publicity about and instruction in these services and resources. Recently, however, in various parts of Canada, public libraries have also begun to use computerized information services providing online access to information in specific subject areas.

Libraries usually subscribe to the user training workshops sponsored by the government or commercial agencies marketing the on-line service. These provide initial staff training for the library, after which librarians use a variety of methods to encourage library patrons to make constructive use of these sophisticated services. The main method, of course, is a one-on-one session when librarian and patron together negotiate the terms appropriate for an individual search or the profile that best fits the user's needs for continuing service. There are also other situations where it is possible for patrons to have hands-on experience with the library's terminal, at least in initial stages of a new service. The opportunity for library instruction is present both during the formulation of a computer search and after its completion, especially in tracing the cited materials.

In summary, a brief list of highlights in recent developments in public library programs of library instruction would include: innovative cooperative programs for school children; production of many new instructional publications; imaginative use of media to explain library services and resources; provision of special instruction and tours to meet specific needs of community groups; shared programs involving cooperation and consultation with special and academic libraries, such as computer-based reference service.

SPECIAL LIBRARIES

The range of instructional activities in special libraries is probably as diverse as the types of libraries themselves, so only a few examples of programs that have been recently developed or have aroused recent interest will be mentioned. One of the main problems faced by special librarians attempting to provide instruction in library use is the image that has been created in the minds of their patrons—more so than in any other kind of library—that the librarian is there to do the work and to provide readers with all the information they need.

As Agnes Schryer described her task at the Statistics Canada Library in Ottawa: "It seemed we were treading new ground since organized orientation courses are given, almost exclusively, by university libraries as part of their undergraduate curriculum. . . . Catering to a specialized clientele, we had to re-think the traditional method of presentation."[22] She did, however, persevere and is still conducting the sessions begun in 1975. These take the form of a one and one-half hour program for all new staff and are advertised through the training section for the whole department (of which the library is a small part). Both professional and nonprofessional staff participate in each session, which seems to generate good discussions. The session includes a slide/tape show and is followed by a tour of the library and distribution of various publications such as handbooks and worksheets. The staff are constantly reviewing these sessions, which are offered once a month (separately in French and English), and have begun to add other informal sessions such as coffee break demonstrations on bibliographic searching and the use of on-line services.[23]

Most special libraries have always offered specialized instruction on a one-to-one basis in the use of indexes, abstracts, and so forth, in the relevant fields and are now also heavily involved in explaining the use of computerized data bases with an on-line searching capability. In addition, many offer tours and instructional sessions on their services and collections to special interest groups within the community as well as to their immediate constituency. For example, the library of the Law Society of Upper Canada conducts sessions for school groups and the librarians at the Osborne Collection in Boys' and Girls' House at the Toronto Public Library welcome groups from the Friends of the Osborne Collection and from community organizations as well as from a wide range of educational institutions.

On Prince Edward Island there are a number of interesting cooperative ventures planned or already in progress among college, university, provincial, public and special libraries. In one, a hospital librarian visits Holland College Library to give special instruction to those in the medical secretary training program in using medical literature, including material beyond the present scope of the college library. In fact, the college library itself should probably be included here with special libraries because of its unique role and function. The four main libraries in the island province each collect in areas different from the other three and the public has full access to the combined collections. Holland College, however, probably comes closer to the library-college idea than most other Canadian institutions, though Jane Armstrong is also "operating the College Library as an industrial library." She not only provides the students with instruction in how to use the library on their own, but also suggests when to call on the librarian for special research services normally provided by libraries to business communities. Much of the library instruction in the college is directed to the needs of individuals or small special interest groups. There is a separate library guide prepared for each program, augmented by a slide/tape show (which is more often used without the tape so that the commentary can be tailored to the particular audience). Academic departments such as English, mathematics, and physics/science do not offer courses in this college but provide skills training on an individual basis directly related to a student's other courses in business, commercial design, electronics, resource planning, and similar subjects—often after referral by the instructor in these courses. Library instruction, therefore, provides a unique challenge for the librarians at Holland College—as must classroom instruction for the faculty members in that college.[24]

This is a very minute glance at the mosaic of special librarianship in Canada, but it does point out some of the same trends as in other types of library: Even in library instruction there is a greater sharing of resources from library to library than in previous years, and, in many special libraries, a greater amount of instructional activity than in the past.

ACADEMIC LIBRARIES

The main trends in library instruction in Canadian academic libraries that were identified in the 1976 report[25] have continued in the past two years. These include the development of repeatable courses (usually noncredit) in specific aspects of library instruction, an increased emphasis on the teaching component of library instruction and on the place of library instruction in the university or college curriculum, more frequent analyses of user needs and production of programs to meet these needs, and more frequent reports of cooperation and consultation among libraries. From one side of the country to the other, these still seem to be high on the list of concerns of those involved in library instruction in academic libraries, though to them must now be added teaching about the use of on-line data services and microcatalogs.

One of the other developments mentioned in 1976 was the number of institutions where coordinated programs of library instruction were being designed and implemented. As recently as 1974, Anne Passarelli and Millicent Abell had been lamenting that "there is very little evidence . . . that institutions with variety in their instructional program are acting in accordance with a master plan."[26] In 1976, Laurentian, Toronto, and Sherbrooke were working on coordinated plans. To them we should add the University of British Columbia (UBC), Calgary, and a number of others. A similar approach has recently been mapped out for Erindale College Library in Mississauga, where funding has been obtained to hire extra staff to help "set up essay clinics, prepare instructional packages for students and hold a workshop on communication skills for library staff."[27]

From a growing number of university and college libraries there are reports of highly successful essay and term-paper clinics and reference consultation services. At UBC the term-paper clinics are coordinated by the Division of Library Information and Orientation, but are actually organized and conducted in the Sedgewick Undergraduate Library by the staff there, in conjunction with the School of Librarianship.[28] Students from the school provide most of the staff to create the one-on-one teaching situation that is one of the more original aspects of the program. For three weeks in both fall and spring terms, the library advertises widely in the student newspaper, encouraging undergraduates to sign up for initial interviews with library science students. Interviews include a discussion of the topic, when the paper is due, and how much has already been done. The library school students then carry out literature searches and later lead the undergraduates through the strategy before letting them proceed on their own to choose which directions to pursue. The Sigmund Samuel Library at the University of Toronto has been carrying out a similar program in a much more limited way, staffed by the librarians in the undergraduate library. This special service supplements the regular two-session essay and paper clinics for those who need further individual assistance. The Toronto clinics are planned by the interdepartmental Committee on Instruction in Library Use, in conjunction with the Coordinator of Library Instruction, and are staffed by librarians from the reference department, the science and medicine department, and the Sigmund Samuel Library.

Interest expressed in 1976 in credit courses has continued to grow. Jeanne Guillaume, the librarian in New College, Toronto, has now successfully conducted a one-term course, "Information Skills," within the Faculty of Arts and Science. It is likely that this course will be expanded in 1978–1979, and that materials used in the course will be published and sold commercially within the next year. A credit course that is taken by approximately 20 students a year[29] is offered at the Acadia University Library. Library staff at several institutions conduct parts of credit courses given by other academic departments, e.g., "Credit Course on Study Skills" at the University of Victoria, British Columbia, or the legal bibliography section of the "Legal Process Course" at the University of Alberta in Edmonton.[30] It appears, however, that the only other institution offering a full credit course is still Wilfrid Laurier University, Ontario, which was mentioned in 1976.[31]

In the past few years, many more individual sessions have been offered in relation to or as part of regular university teaching programs. At places such as UBC, Calgary, Concordia, Dalhousie, McGill, Memorial, Toronto, Winnipeg, Western Ontario, and York universities, librarians are working directly with faculty members in designing projects or instructional presentations for academic subjects as diverse as biology, botany, nursing, physical and health education, psychology, and zoology. One of the interesting ways in which these courses are produced is that used in the Science and Medicine Library at the University of Toronto. The presentation for a particular subject is worked out by one or more librarians and faculty members. Required material is put together in a package, with a list of all transparencies, posters and samples, and so forth, that are required. In this way, librarians can pick up the appropriate package, including visual aids, and use it with a minimum of further preparation. For large courses, often subdivided into many sections, this method provides a great deal of flexibility in the scheduling of librarians, as, once the package is prepared, any of the librarians can make the presentation. There is a separate, clearly indexed file of the various component parts of these packages as some parts are interchangeable, for example, transparencies on "what to do when the book you want is not on the shelf." The distinct parts on the use of reference tools that are relevant for one particular course are less likely to be interchangeable.

Devising such courses has meant librarians' establishing closer contacts with the teaching faculty, with resulting mutual benefits. In some cases student papers also show signs of an enhanced level of library use.

This is only one aspect of the new emphasis on the teaching role of the librarian that is evident on a number of campuses. Dalhousie's Committee on Improving Teaching has expressed interest in library instruction programs; at Laurentian, the university's Committee on Teaching and Learning is chaired by a librarian; in Winnipeg, University of Manitoba librarians have attended a half-day, two-week program, "In-service for University Professors," given each May and June by the Faculty of Education.[32]

The prediction, in the 1976 report,[33] that Ontario university libraries were likely to benefit from the new funding arrangements for the Ontario Universities Program of Instructional Development (OUPID) has been borne out. As mentioned earlier, Erindale College Library has received a grant from the Toronto Committee to work on a coordinated program that will include a workshop on communications' skills for library staff. The reader services' area of the University of Toronto Library has so far received two grants, one of which paid for a workshop series for library instruction personnel from all campus libraries. The four sessions of the workshop as originally planned were conducted by Professor Richard Tiberius, who devotes half time to the work of the university's Advisory Committee on Educational Development. These sessions dealt with the characteristics of effective teaching and a fifth session was added, at the request of participants, to allow them to describe and discuss a number of their own programs. As a result of this, Carolyn Murray, coordinator of library instruction, has been able to compile a directory of people on campus who can contribute to a Library Skills Exchange.[34] The improvement of teaching in library instruction programs has also been the topic of several recent workshops and conference programs described later in this chapter.

Various universities have established other funding sources from which library programs may benefit. The University of Calgary Library has used a grant from the university's Radio and Television Committee to allow them to buy services from the Department of Communications Media to prepare a series of self-instructional slide/tape programs that will assist patrons in the use of specific library resources such as catalogs, government publications, and so on.[35]

Mention has been made of a number of instances where academic librarians are working jointly with librarians in other types of libraries on improving library instruction. There is also increasing evidence of cooperation and sharing of resources between individual academic libraries. The most common area in relation to library instruction is in the discussion of on-line searching and of microcatalogs. For example, before Wilfrid Laurier University subscribed to any computerized data bases, it sponsored a number of workshops for faculty members at which Ellen Pearson, a librarian from the University of Guelph, explained the use of on-line searching services available through Guelph.[36] Similarly, both Carole Weiss and Carolyn Murray from the University of Toronto have spoken at a number of other institutions on the use of catalogs on microfilm and microfiche. This is in addition to workshops held at Toronto for staff from other libraries to share in the experience that has been gained.

A further sign of increased cooperation in library instruction is the number of "visiting firemen" who are traveling, both in Canada and other countries, to discuss and view library instruction programs. Recent visitors to Ontario libraries have been from England, Australia, Hong Kong, and the United States. Despite the title "U.S. by Bus," the descriptions of Sister M. Dennis Lynch's travels in 1977 include one article mostly devoted to observations on part of her Canadian side trip.[37]

The number and variety of publications relating to library instruction is even greater now than at the time of the earlier report, and there seem to be two trends developing that will, I am sure, continue in the present tight budget situation. More people are developing colorful one-page flyers, often turning them into attractive folders by unusual machine-folded arrangements. Many of these are now acquiring a professional look by use of transfer lettering, etc., though it would appear that UBC and Concordia are still the only two libraries with graphic artists on the staff. The newest group of publications can be typified by a Toronto example entitled *Consultation and Computer Searching Services*, which gives a simple description of all data bases available in this rapidly expanding area of library service.

Displays tied into programs of orientation and instruction "demonstrating the processes by which information may be found, by utilizing the various collections and services offered by the library" are reported from Newfoundland to British Columbia,[38] and are clearly contributing to the effectiveness of the programs themselves.

The number of libraries with staff members employed full time for library instruction is still limited. The University of British Columbia was one of the first to head in this direction when it established a Division of Library Information and Orientation in the mid-1960s, but the most recent developments have been in Ontario and Quebec where the few "library instruction librarians" have been in contact with one another to pool ideas. Some have also met as a group with faculty members involved in educational or instructional development. I believe this sharing of expertise and experience is an important development at this particular time when all must strive to make the most effective use of limited financial resources. Also, as library resources and services become more sophisticated, patrons deserve the most professional instruction that can be devised.

A summary of trends in library instruction in academic libraries would include many of the same directions noted two years ago: increased relationship of library instruction programs to the academic curriculum; development of courses and instructional packages; great stress on improving effectiveness of teaching; increased availability of nonlibrary funds for library instruction purposes; growth of computer searching and catalog services; and development of cooperation and consultation among various libraries, librarians, and faculty members.

WORKSHOPS AND CONFERENCES

It would also be appropriate to note the increased activity of library organizations and various *ad hoc* groups in the area of library instruction. From time to time the Canadian Library Association (CLA) through its divisions has sponsored "Show and Tell" workshops. The recent events have placed more emphasis on improvement of programs and of their teaching components; for example, the preconference workshop of the Canadian School Library Association in 1975 was devoted to the study of curriculum planning and development and focused on the "process" of systematic curriculum design. It stressed that the "implications of systematic curriculum design are crucial for the school librarian . . . and will enable the school librarian to plan with teachers for the most effective use of the Library Resource Centre facilities."[39]

The Canadian Association of College and University Libraries sponsored a preconference instruction workshop in 1976 and the topic was also on the CLA program in 1977. A joint program in November 1977 was sponsored by the New York and Ontario Library Associations and the spring 1978 program of the Western New York/Ontario Chapter of the Association of College and Research Libraries is also a workshop on library instruction.

The annual Ontario/Quebec Workshop on Library Instruction in academic libraries has recently been concentrating on the effectiveness of library instruction and includes a miniworkshop on instructional techniques in the 1978 program. It has been interesting to see further workshops develop and to see greater involvement by library schools. Western librarians sponsored a workshop in Calgary in June 1978; British Columbia librarians formed the British Columbia Clearing House on Library Instruction; and Dalhousie University School of Library Service sponsored a weekend workshop on instruction in February 1977.

The York University Conference, "Canadian Libraries in Their Changing Environment," also looked at library instruction from a number of vantage points. At least one of the speakers at that conference drew attention to one factor that should be kept in mind as one looks at the positive trends and developments noted in this chapter. Beryl Anderson's survey of library priorities conducted in special libraries clearly shows that orientation and public relations ranked lowest for most special libraries.[40] Fortunately it would appear that this is not true for other types of libraries, and, so far, they have been able to justify spending on library instruction because of its effects on use of the collections. One can but hope that this is the real direction for the future.

NOTES

1. Canadian Association of College and University Libraries, *Bibliography on Library Instruction* (Ottawa: 1975).
2. Sheila M. Laidlaw, "Library Instruction in the 70's: The State of the Art in Canadian Academic Libraries," in *Library Instruction in the Seventies: State of the Art,* ed. by Hannelore B. Rader (Ann Arbor, Mich.: Pierian Press, 1977), pp. 1–23.
3. Marcel Mignault, *Lise et Bruno dans l'universe des livres* (La Pocatiere: Societe du Stage en bibliotheconomie, 1976).
4. Ibid, pp. 21–22.
5. David Jenkinson, "School Libraries," in *Canadian Libraries in Their Changing Environment,* ed. by Loraine Spencer Garry and Carl Garry (Toronto: York University Centre for Continuing Education, 1977), pp. 203–204.
6. Conversation with Helen McIntosh, Mississauga Public Library, April 1978.
7. *Moccasin Telegraph* 18 (1), Autumn 1975.
8. Brantford, Ontario, Public Library, Annual Report 1969, p. 3.
9. New Westminister, British Columbia, Public Library, Annual Report 1976, p. 6.
10. Chatham, Ontario, Public Library, Annual Report 1976.
11. Greater Victoria Public Library, "Annual Report," *LINK* 3 (March 1977); 2 (March 1976).
12. Metropolitan Toronto Public Library Board, Annual Report 1977, p. 11.
13. Lethbridge, Alberta, Public Library, Annual Report 1976, p. 11.
14. Fort Frances, Ontario, Public Library, Annual Report 1976, p. 8.
15. Kingston, Ontario, Public Library, Annual Report 1976, p. 3.
16. Halifax, Nova Scotia, City Regional Library, Annual Report 1975, p. 11.
17. Burnaby, British Columbia, Public Library, "Annual Report," *Booknews* 5 (1974).
18. Calgary, Alberta, Public Library, Annual Report 1973, p. 19; Annual Report 1975, p. 15.
19. Conversation with June Munro, June 1977.
20. New Westminister, British Columbia, Public Library, Annual Report 1976, p. 6.
21. Kamloops, British Columbia, Public Library, Annual Report 1972, p. 2.
22. Agnes Schryer, "Library Orientation at Statistics Canada Library," *Feliciter* 21 (September 1975): 6–7.
23. Conversation with Agnes Schryer, March 1978.
24. Conversations with Jane Armstrong, February 1976 and April 1978.
25. Laidlaw, "Library Instruction in the 70's."
26. Anne B. Passarelli and Millicent Abell, "Undergraduate Programs and Problems," in *Educating the Library User,* ed. by John Lubans, Jr. (New York: R. R. Bowker, 1974), p. 123.

27. Toronto University, *Bulletin* 31 (April 17, 1978): 1.
28. Conversation with Joan Sandilands, March 1978, and correspondence from her, March 1976.
29. Questionnaire from John Mercer, March 1976.
30. Questionnaire completed March 1976.
31. Laidlaw, "Library Instruction in the 70's," p. 13.
32. Questionnaire completed March 1976.
33. Laidlaw, "Library Instruction in the 70's," p. 18.
34. Carolyn Murray, "Workshop Series for Library Instruction Personnel—An Assessment," report submitted to Advisory Committee on Educational Development (Toronto: ACED, University of Toronto, 1978).
35. Calgary University, Alberta, University Library, Annual Report 1977, p. 44.
36. Wilfrid Laurier University, Library, Annual Report 1975, p. 12.
37. Sister M. Dennis Lynch, "U.S. by Bus: 4," *Catholic Library World* 49 (February 1978): 309–310.
38. Irene Bennell, "An Approach to Displays in an Academic Library," *APLA Bulletin* 37 (Summer 1973): 43–45.
39. Doreen Bertrand, "Principles of Instructional Design," *Moccasin Telegraph* 18 (Winter 1975): 12.
40. Beryl Anderson, "Special Libraries," in *Canadian Libraries in Their Changing Environment*, pp. 249–250.

BIBLIOGRAPHY

This list of relevant literature began to evolve shortly after the publication of *Educating the Library User* in 1974. It is made up of items gleaned from current professional journals and issues of *Library Literature* and *Library and Information Science Abstracts*. A number of colleagues have made suggestions of items for inclusion. Also, bibliographies distributed at conferences on instruction have been culled for representative materials. The reader should note that this bibliography does not strive to duplicate all of the items referred to in individual chapters, several of which have substantial bibliographies addressing specialized areas in the field of user education. Appended is a listing of a recent phenomenon: library instruction clearinghouses, directories, and newsletters.—Ed.

ARL Member Libraries Using Audiovisual Materials for Point-of-Use Library Instruction. Washington: Association of Research Libraries, September, 1977.

Adams, Golden V., Jr. "A Study: Library Attitudes, Usage, Skill and Knowledge of Junior High School Age Students Enrolled at Lincoln Junior High School and Burns Union High School, Burns, Harney County, Oregon 1971-1972." Provo Utah: Brigham Young University, Graduate Department of Library and Information Sciences, 1972. ERIC ED 077 538.

Aluri, Rao. *Library-Use Instruction for Engineering Students.* 1977. ERIC ED 143 367.

Ball, Howard G. "Adventures of Captain Media; or How to Find the Campus Media Center." *Library Scene* 4 (July 1975): 16-20.

Bate, John. "An L-Test for Library Users." *SLA News* 122 (July 1974): 103-105.

Beam, Karen G. "Library Instruction: Teaching a Survival Skill." *Hoosier School Libraries* 14 (April 1975): 18-19.

Beck, R. J., and Norris, L. "Communication Graphics in Library Orientation." *Catholic Library World* 47 (December 1975): 218-219.

Beeler, Richard J., ed. *Evaluating Library Use Instruction: Papers Presented at the University of Denver Conference on the Evaluation of Library Use Instruction, December 13-14, 1973.* Ann Arbor, Mich.: Pierian Press, 1975.

✓ Bellardo, Trudi, and Waldhart, Thomas J. "Marketing Products and Services in Academic Libraries." *Libri* 27 (1977): 181-194.

Blackwell, E. M., et al., "Sequence of Library Skills." *Hoosier School Libraries* 14 (Fall 1975): 18-21.

Blazek, Ron. *Influencing Students toward Media Center Use: An Experimental Investigation in Mathematics.* Chicago: American Library Association, 1975.

Bodner, Deborah Huntington. "A Descriptive Analysis of the Council on Library Resources' College-Library Programs." Paper for the School of Library Science of the University of North Carolina, May 1975.

Boehm, Eric H. "On the Second Knowledge: A Manifesto for the Humanities." *Libri* 22 (1972): 312-323.

Borda, Eva. "Introduction to Library Services for Allied Health Personnel." *Medical Library Association Bulletin* 62 (October 1974): 363-366.

Breivik, Patricia Senn. *Open Admissions and the Academic Library.* Chicago: American Library Association, 1977.

Brewer, J. G., and Hills, P. J. "Evaluation of Reader Instruction." *Libri* 26 (1976): 55-65.

Brittain, Michael, and Irving, Ann. *Trends in the Education of Users of Libraries and Information Services in the USA: A Report Submitted to the British Library Research and Development Department.* Loughborough, England: Loughborough University, Department of Library and Information Studies, 1976.

Brown, Jean. "The Missing Link in Teacher Education." *Moccasin Telegraph* 17 (1974): 50-55.

Bryson, J. A. "Library Orientation and Instruction in North Carolina Academic Libraries." *North Carolina Libraries* 33 (Summer/Fall 1975): 19-23.

Butler, Elizabeth, et al. "Toward Guidelines for Bibliographic Instruction in Academic Libraries." Draft no. 3 by the ACRL Bibliographic Instruction Task Force, September 1974.

Capen, Betty. "Rock Springs High School Library Revises Sophomore Orientation." *Wyoming Library Roundup* 29 (December 1974): 31.

Coleman, Kathleen. *Directory of Library Instruction Media: Produced by California Academic Libraries.* San Diego: California Clearinghouse on Library Instruction, 1976.

————, and Dintrone, Charles. *How to Use the Library.* San Diego: San Diego State University, 1974.

Colorado Council on Library Development. Committee on Instruction in the Use of Libraries, compiled and written by the committee, Margaret Knox Goggin, chairperson. *Instruction in the Use of Libraries in Colorado.* Denver: Colorado State Library, 1974. Photocopied.

A Comprehensive Program of User Education for the General Libraries: The University of Texas at Austin. Austin: University of Texas at Austin, The General Libraries, 1977.

Corlett, Donna. "Library Skills, Study Habits and Attitudes and Sex as Related to Academic Achievement." *Educational and Psychological Measurement* 34 (1974): 967-969.

Cottam, Keith, "Library Use Instruction in Tennessee's Academic Libraries: An Analysis and Directory." *Tennessee Librarian* 26 (Summer/Fall 1974): 73–79.

Crawford, Richard, "The Place of the Library in Open University Preparation Courses." *Assistant Librarian* 67 (September 1974): 143–144.

Crossley, Charles A., and Clews, John P. "Evaluation of the Use of Educational Technology in Information Handling Instruction." A literature review and bibliography submitted to the British Library, September 1974. Bradford: University of Bradford, 1974. BLRDD Report No. 5220.

Crump, Diana. "Card Catalog Bingo." *Hoosier School Libraries* 14 (Fall 1975): 21+.

De Somogyl, A. "Make Your Point: Library Skills Now or Never." *School Library Journal* 22 (November 1975): 37.

Doyle, Carol. "Library Media Center Skills: Supplement." *Booklist* 71 (June 1, 1975): 1001–1003.

Dudley, Miriam. *Workbook in Library Skills: A Self-Directed Course in the Use of UCLA's College Library.* Los Angeles: College Library, University of California Library, 1973.

Dyson, Allan J. "Organizing Undergraduate Library Instruction: The English and American Experience." *The Journal of Academic Librarianship* 1 (March 1975): 9–13.

The Education of Users of Scientific and Technical Information: Report from a Workshop Held at the University of Bath, 14–16 September 1973. Somerset, England: University of Bath, 1973.

Elkins, Elizabeth A., et al. *Developing Printed Materials for Library Instruction.* Annual New York Library Association meeting, Lake Placid, N.Y., October 16, 1976. n.p.: New York Library Instruction Clearinghouse, 1976.

Essary, K., and Parker, S. "Educating Your Patrons." *Arkansas Librarian* 32 (1975): 26–29.

Evans, Al. "From A to V: Audio Tour of the Library." *Kentucky Library Association Bulletin* 38 (Fall 1974): 18–21.

Everything You Ever Wanted to Know about Library Instruction But Didn't Have Time to Ask. San Diego: California Clearinghouse on Library Instruction, 1974.

Farber, Evan Ira, and Kirk, Thomas G., Jr. "Instruction in Library Use." *ALA Yearbook* 1976: 59.

Fast, Betty. "Mediacentric." *Wilson Library Bulletin* 51 (May 1977): 732–733.

Fiction Friction. Osterville, Mass.: Cellar Door Cinema, 1973. 16mm film.

Finley, Robert. "No Two Are Alike." *Learning Today* 8 (Winter 1975): 39–47.

Fjällbrant, Nancy. "A Comparison of User Instruction in Scandinavian and British Academic Libraries." *Transactions of Chalmers University of Technology* 337 (1975): 1–37.

_____. "Evaluation in a User Education Programme." *Journal of Librarianship* 9 (April 1977): 83–95.

_____. "Evaluation of Introductory Courses in Information Retrieval at Chalmers University of Technology Library, by Means of Studies of Student Attitudes." *Tidskrift för Dokumentation* 32 (1976): 109–114+.

_____. "Library Instruction for Students in Universities in Britain." *Transactions of Chalmers University of Technology* 335 (1974): 3–34.

———. "Planning a Programme of Library User Education." *Journal of Librarianship* 9 (July 1977): 197–211.

———. *A Study of User Behaviour and Needs at Chalmers University of Technology Library.* Gothenburg, Sweden: Chalmers Tekniska Hogskola, Biblioteket, 1976. CTHB-Publication No. 10.

———. "Teaching Methods for the Education of the Library User." *Libri* 26 (1976): 252–267.

———. "The Use of Audio-Visual Material in Library Instruction." In *Ikkeboklig Materialei Bibliotekene* (Proceedings of the fourth meeting of the Scandinavian Research Librarians Association, June 24–26, 1974), pp. 63–80. Trondheim, Norway, 1975.

———. "User Education and Its Integration into the Functioning of the Academic Library." *Nordisk Tidskrift för Bok-och Biblioteksväsen* 64 (1977): 44–51.

———. *User Education Programmes in Swedish Academic Libraries: A Study of Developments in the Years 1973–1977.* Gothenburg, Sweden: Chalmers Tekniska Hogskola, Biblioteket, 1977. CTHB-Publication No. 14.

———."User Instruction in the Libraries of the Technological Universities in Scandinavia: Some Recent Developments." *IATUL Proceedings* 7 (December 1974): 54–59.

Foster, B. "Do-It-Yourself Videotape for Library Orientation Based on a Term Project." *Wilson Library Bulletin* 48 (February 1974): 476–481.

"Freshman English Teachers and Librarians. . . ." *College & Research Libraries News* 38 (December 1977): 332.

Freudenthal, Juan R. "Bibliographic Instruction: A New Library Movement." *The Library Scene* 3 (December 1974): 18–19.

Galloway, Sue. "Nobody Is Teaching the Teachers." *Booklegger Magazine* 3 (January/February 1976): 29–31.

———, and Sherwood, Virginia. "Essentials for an Academic Library's Instructional Service Program." *California Librarian* 37 (April 1976): 44–49.

Gebhard, Patricia. "How to Evaluate Library Instructional Programs." *California Librarian* 37 (April 1976): 36–43.

Geiser, Cherie. "Individualized School Library Orientation." *Wyoming Library Roundup* 29 (December 1974): 32–33.

Gillespie, Mary, et al. *Curriculum Guide for Teaching Library Media Skills, Kindergarten–8th Grade.* Toledo, Ohio: Toledo Board of Education, 1974.

Givens, Johnnie. "The Use of Resources in the Learning Experience." *Advances in Librarianship* 4 (1974): 149–174.

Glogoff, Stuart J., and Seeds, Robert A. "Interest among Librarians to Participate in Library-Related Instruction at the Pennsylvania State University Libraries." *Pennsylvania Library Association Bulletin* 31 (May 1976): 55–56.

Greig, J. S., et al. "Reader Education for Engineers: A Progress Report." *Australian Academic and Research Libraries* 6 (September 1975): 133–134.

Guss, Margaret, et al. "Advice on Making a College Orientation Video-Tape." 1973. ERIC ED 082 781.

Harris, Colin. "Educating the User: Travelling Workshops Experiment." *Library Association Record* 79 (July 1977): 359–360.

———. "Illuminative Evaluation of User Education Programmes," *Aslib Proceedings* 29 (October 1977): 348–362.

Hartley, Audrey A. "Hey That's *Love Story.*" *North Carolina Libraries* 34 (Spring 1976): 23-24.

Heard, Marlene. "First Graders Use the Catalog: Happy Accident at Dixon School, Brookfield." *Wisconsin Library Bulletin* 70 (September/October 1974): 225-226.

Horton, Allan. "Early Attempts at Reader Education at the University of New South Wales." *IATUL Proceedings* 5 (December 1970): 54-60.

Houston, Shirley. "Atrisco Elementary, Albuquerque: Our Latest Project Is Attempting to Breathe Some Life into the Dewey Decimal System for Fifth Graders." *New Mexico Libraries Newsletter* 4 (February 1976): 3.

Jeffries, John. "TV Can Teach Readers Best." *Library Association Record* 78 (January 1976): 18.

Jones, Anona M., and Thielding, Ernie C. "Reference Skills On-Line: A Computer Assists Individually Planned Instruction." *Wisconsin Library Bulletin* 72 (May 1976): 103-104.

✓ Joseph, Margaret A., and Schmelzle, Joan C. *Library Instruction Workbook: A Basic Introduction to the Use of the UTSA Library.* San Antonio, Tex.: University of Texas at San Antonio, 1976.

Keever, Ellen H., and Raymond, James C. "Integrated Library Instruction on the University Campus: Experiment at the University of Alabama." *Journal of Academic Librarianship* 2 (September 1976): 185-187.

Kirk, Thomas, "Bibliographic Instruction—A Review of Research." In *Evaluating Library Use Instruction: Papers Presented at the University of Denver Conference on the Evaluation of Library Instruction, December 13-14, 1973,* ed. by Richard J. Beeler, pp. 1-29. Ann Arbor, Mich.: Pierian Press, 1975.

————, and Freudenthal, Juan. *Annotated Bibliography on Bibliographic Instruction for Undergraduate Students.* Chicago: American Library Association, July 1976.

Kirkendall, Carolyn, ed. "Library Instruction: A Column of Opinion." *Journal of Academic Librarianship* 2 (November 1976): 188-189.

Krier, Maureen. "Bibliographic Instruction: A Checklist of the Literature, 1931-1975." *Reference Service Review* (January/March 1976): 7-31.

Lee, Sul H., ed. *A Challenge for Academic Libraries: How to Motivate Students to Use the Library.* Ann Arbor, Mich.: Pierian Press, 1973.

Library Instruction Programs 1975: A Wisconsin Directory. Madison: Wisconsin Library Association, 1975.

"Library Orientation and Use Instruction." *Alabama Librarian* 26 (September 1975): 8+.

"Library Use Instruction in Academic and Research Libraries." *ARL Management Supplement* 5 (September 1977): 1-6.

Lindgren, Jon. "The College of Wooster Bibliographic Assistantship Program." Wooster, Ohio: College of Wooster, July 1, 1975. Photocopied.

Lolley, John L. "Educating the Library User." *Texas Library Journal* 51 (Spring 1975): 30-32.

Long, Carol. "A Comparison Between Tutor-Librarianship in Great Britain and the Library-College in the United States." Master's degree research paper, Kent State University, 1972.

Lubans, John, Jr. "Colorado Library Association Annual Meeting Presidential Address, October 18, 1976." *Colorado Libraries* 2 (December 1976): 4-7.

————. "Evaluation Attempts of Library Use Instruction Programs at the University of Colorado Libraries." In *Evaluating Library Use Instruction: Papers Presented at the University of Denver Conference on the Evaluation of Library Instruction, December 13-14, 1973*, ed. by Richard J. Beeler, pp. 67-73. Ann Arbor, Mich.: Pierian Press, 1975.

————. *First Annual Progress Report to the Council on Library Resources and the National Endowment for the Humanities for the Year September 1, 1973-August 31, 1974: Program to Improve and Increase Student and Faculty Involvement in Library Use.* Boulder: University of Colorado Libraries, 1974. Photocopied. ERIC ED 097 864.

————. "Library User Studies." *Encyclopedia of Library and Information Science.* New York: Marcel Dekker, Inc., 1975.

————. "In Pursuit of the Educated Library User: A Dilemma." *Ohio Association of School Librarians and Educational Media Council of Ohio Bulletin* (joint issue) 28 (October 1976): 7-9.

————. *Reference Statistics, 1975-1976: An Analysis and Recommendations.* Boulder: University of Colorado, 1977. ERIC ED 139 408.

————, moderator. "Educating Librarians and Users for a New Model of Library Services." Program given at the American Library Association Annual Conference, San Francisco, Calif., July 1, 1975. 2 audiotapes. Los Angeles: Development Digest, 1975. Includes address by Marcia Bates.

————, et al. *Second Annual Progress Report to the Council on Library Resources and the National Endowment for the Humanities for the Year 1974-1975: Program to Improve and Increase Student and Faculty Involvement in Library Use.* Boulder: University of Colorado Libraries, 1975. Photocopied.

Manning, D. J. "Report of a Committee of the University and College Libraries Section of the Library Association of Australia Appointed to Examine the Requirements for Reader Education Activities in Universities and Colleges." *Australian Academic and Research Libraries* 4 (December 1973, Monograph Supplement): 1-19.

Margrabe, Mary. *The "Now" Library: A Stations Approach Media Center Teaching Kit.* Washington, D.C.: Acropolis Books, Ltd., 1973.

Miller, N. L. "Remote Control Tour; or, How to Escape the Beginning-of-School Library Orientation." *Hoosier School Libraries* 15 (December 1975): 43.

Miller, Rosalind. "Curriculum Delusions." *Library Journal* 99 (November 15, 1974): 3028-3029.

Miller, Stuart. "Library Use Instruction Programs in American Colleges." Ph.D. diss., University of Chicago, 1976. Microfilm.

Mitchell, Rosemary. "Academic Achievement and Use of the Secondary School Library." Paper delivered for Graduate Diploma in Librarianship, Tasmanian (Australia) College of Advanced Education, 1973.

Morris, Jacquelyn M., and Webster, Donald F. *Developing Objectives for Library Instruction.* Annual New York Library Association meeting, Lake Placid, N.Y., October 16, 1976. n.p.: New York Library Instruction Clearinghouse, 1976.

Noack, Andreas. "Nutzerschulung für Schüler der Erweiterten Oberschulen ein Experiment." *Zentralblatt für Bibliothekswesen* 87 (September 1973): 539-541.

Nordling, Jo Anne. *Dear Faculty: A Discovery Method Guidebook to the High School Library.* Westwood, Mass.: F. W. Faxon Co., 1976.

Palmer, Roger C. "Project Report: Audiovisual Orientation for Freshmen, Summer Program." State University of New York–Buffalo, University Libraries, 1973. ERIC ED 081 455.

"Past, Present, and Future of Library Instruction: Bibliography." Southeastern Library Association, November 1976. Photocopied.

Perry, Emma Bradford. "A Study to Determine the Effectiveness of a Library Instruction Course in Teaching the Use of the Library to Upward Bound Students." A project report submitted to the Graduate College, Western Michigan University, April 1974.

Peterson, Violet E. *Library Instruction Guide (Junior & Senior High Schools),* 4th ed. Hamden, Conn.: Shoe String Press, 1974.

Pila, Moritz. "The Mistaken Panacea." *Learning Today* 8 (Winter 1975): 58–59.

Pollet, Dorothy. "New Directions in Library Signage." *Wilson Library Bulletin* 50 (February 1976): 456–462.

Poole, Jay Martin. "Minutes from Meeting of ACRL Undergraduate Librarians Discussion Group San Francisco, American Library Association, Annual Meeting, July 2, 1975." *UGLI Newsletter* 8 (November 1975): 4–9.

"Programming for Reference Service." Wayne State University, Detroit, Michigan, University Libraries, 1973. ERIC ED 077 532.

Rader, Hannelore B. "An Assessment of Ten Academic Library Instruction Programs in the United States and Canada." A Council on Library Resources Fellowship Report, Eastern Michigan University, Ypsilanti, 1976. Photocopied.

Rappaport, Jean. *School Library Journal* 22 (February 1976): 3. Letter to the Editor.

"Reader Education, Two Comments." *Australian Academic and Research Libraries* 6 (June 1975): 92–95.

Robson, John, et al. "Plato IV Comes of Age." *Network: International Communication in Library Automation* 1 (July 1974): 12–14.

Sable, Martin H. "Needed: Library Skills; Teaching Bibliography in Academic Libraries." *Wisconsin Library Bulletin* 70 (November 1974): 305–306.

Sadow, Sandra, and Beede, Benjamin. "Library Instruction in American Law Schools." *Law Library Journal* 68 (1975): 27–32.

Schryer, Agnes. "Library Orientation at Statistics Canada Library." *Feliciter* 21 (September 1975): 6–7.

"A Sequence of Library Skills." *Hoosier School Libraries* 14 (Fall 1975): 18–21.

Sevier, Nancy. "How to Organize the Team-Taught Library Skills Course." February 1974. [University of California at Los Angeles. College Library.] Mimeo.

Shapiro, E. L. "Logical Schemes for Teaching User. . . ." *Nauchnye I Tekhnicheskie Biblioteki SSSR. Moscow* 1 (1975): 36–42.

Sharplin, C. D. "Library Orientation: What Is It Worth in Alberta?" *Library Association of Alberta Bulletin* 5 (October 1974): 110–112.

Shelton, John L. "Project Uplift: Cultivating the Library Habit." *Wilson Library Bulletin* 50 (September 1975): 59–62.

Sisley, Janice M. "Whadayado in the IMC? Or Videotape Visits." *Wisconsin Library Bulletin* 70 (November 1974): 312–313.

"Sixth-Form Library Visits." *Library Association Record* 77 (April 1975): 79–81.

Smalley, Topsy N. "Bibliographic Instruction in Academic Libraries: Questioning Some Assumptions." *Journal of Academic Librarianship* 3 (November 1977): 280–283.

Smith, Barbara G. "How Do I Join, Please? Initial Library Instruction in a Secondary School." *School Librarian* 24 (June 1976): 109–111.

Stamps, Margaret, and Phelps, Eloise. *Library Roundup Program for Learning Library Skills.* Pueblo: University of Southern Colorado, 1975.

Stevenson, Malcolm. "Progress in Documentation: Education of Users of Libraries and Information Services." *Journal of Documentation* 33 (March 1977): 53–79.

Stewart, Barbara C. *An Evaluation of a Course in Library Instruction at Ball State University.* 1976. ERIC ED 138 246.

Stoffle, C. M. "How Much Time for Library Instruction." *Wisconsin Library Bulletin* 69 (June 1973): 176.

✓ Sullivan, Peggy. "What Do They Need to Know." (A review of *Educating the Library User*, ed. by John Lubans, Jr., R. R. Bowker, 1974). *The Review of Education* (May/June 1976): 279–284.

Thomas, Lucille C., and Kirk, Thomas. *Annotated Bibliography on Library Instruction in Elementary, Middle, and Secondary Schools.* Chicago: American Library Association, July 1976.

Tietjen, Mildred C. "Library Instruction Improvement Association." *Library Scene* 4 (June 1975): 12–13.

Tucker, John Mark. "An Experiment in Bibliographic Instruction at Wabash College." *College and Research Libraries* 38 (May 1977): 203–209.

Valley, Ruth R. "If Learning Is Fun, Can Success Be Far Behind?" *Hoosier School Libraries* 14 (April 1975): 34+.

Vuturo, Robert. "Beyond the Library Tour: Those Who *Can*, Must Teach." *Wilson Library Bulletin* 51 (May 1977): 736–740.

Walker, Maxine. "Teaching or Learning." *Australian Library Journal* 23 (June 1974): 177–181.

Whildin, Sara L. "Library Instruction in Pennsylvania Academic Libraries: A Survey Summary." *Pennsylvania Library Association Bulletin* 31 (January 1976): 8.

Wilkinson, E. H., et al. *The Use of a University Library's Subject Catalogue: Report of a Research Project.* North Ryde, New South Wales: Macquarie University, 1977.

Windell, John T. *The Practice of Biology.* Sarasota, Fla.: Omni Press, Inc., 1975, pp. 29–51.

✓ *Writing Objectives for Bibliographic Instruction in Academic Libraries: A Summary of the Proceedings of Sessions of the Midwest Federation of Library Associations, Detroit, October 1–2, 1975.* Kenosha, Wis.: Director's Office, Library-Learning Center, University of Wisconsin-Parkside, 1976.

Yaple, Henry M., comp. "Programmed Instruction in Librarianship: A Classified Bibliography of Programmed Texts and Other Materials 1960–1974." University of Illinois Graduate School of Library Science *Occasional Papers*, no. 124. July 1976.

⌐○\

LIBRARY INSTRUCTION CLEARINGHOUSES, DIRECTORIES, AND NEWSLETTERS

This welcome addition to the Bibliography was compiled in July 1978 by William Prince (Virginia Polytechnic Institute and State University), Linda Lester (Findlay College) and James Ward (David Lipscomb College) for the Committee on Cooperation of the ALA-ACRL Bibliographic Instruction Section. It is appreciatively printed here through the courtesy and permission of Carolyn Dusenbury (University of Utah), chairperson of the Committee on Cooperation.—Ed.

CLEARINGHOUSES

California Clearinghouse on Library Instruction. Southern section—contact person: Nancy Sevier, College Library, UCLA, Los Angeles, CA 90024, (213) 825-2138. Northern section—contact person: Carol Rominger, Shields Library, University of California, Davis, CA 95616, (916) 752-1126.

Clearinghouse on Bibliographic Instruction. Contact person: Jane Fowler, Bates College Library, Lewiston, ME 04240, (207) 784-2949.

Florida Library Orientation & Bibliographic Instruction Clearinghouse. Contact person: June Stillman, Box 25000, Florida Technological University Library, Orlando, FL 32816, (305) 275-2485.

Illinois Clearinghouse on Academic Libraries (ICALI). Contact person: Melissa Cain, Undergraduate Library, University of Illinois, Urbana, IL 61801, (217) 333-3503.

Library Orientation—Instruction Exchange (LOEX). Contact person: Carolyn Kirkendall, Center for Educational Resources, Eastern Michigan University, Ypsilanti, MI 48197, (313) 487-0168.

New England Bibliographic Instruction Center (NEBIC). Contact person: Joy McPherson. Library Science Librarian or Dorrie Senghas, Library Director, Simmons College Library, Simmons College, 300 The Fenway, Boston, MA 02115, (617) 738-2226 or 738-2241.

New York Library Instruction Clearinghouse (NYLIC). Contact person: Jacquelyn Morris or Betsy Elkins, Moon Library, SUNY College of Environmental Science & Forestry, Syracuse, NY 13210, (315) 473-8615.

Southeastern Library Association (SELA), Southeastern Bibliographic Instruction Clearinghouse (SEBIC). Contact person: James Ward, Box 4146, David Lipscomb College Library, Nashville, TN 37203, (615) 385-3855, ext. 283.

British Columbia Clearinghouse on Library Instruction. Contact person: Virginia Chisholm, Box 2503, New Westminister, British Columbia V3L 5B2, (604) 521-4851.

Library Instruction Materials Bank (LIMB). Contact person: Ian Malley, Information Officer for User Education, Library, Loughborough University of Technology, Loughborough, Leicestershire LE11 3TU, United Kingdom, Loughborough (UK) 0509-63171, ext. 243.

CLEARINGHOUSES IN THE PLANNING STAGES

Australia. Reader Education Data Base (working name—to start in Jan. 1979). Contact person: Patrick Condon, Caulfield Institute of Technology Library, Box 197, Caulfield East, Victoria 3145, Australia, (03) 211-7722, ext. 157.

New Jersey. Contact person: Marion L. Smitherman, Library, Burlington County College, Pemberton-Browns Mills Rd., Pemberton, NJ 08068, (609) 894-9311, ext. 482.

Specialized. Industrial Relations Bibliographic Instruction Materials. Contact person: Laura Carchia, Industrial Relations Collection, Building E53-238, Massachusetts Institute of Technology, Cambridge, MA 02139, (617) 253-5658.

DIRECTORIES

Illinois. *Library Instruction Programs in Illinois Academic Libraries: A Directory and Survey Report.* Melissa Cain and Lois Pausch, comp. Illinois Library Association and Illinois Association of College and Research Libraries, 1978. $2.00. Available from: Illinois Library Association, John Coyne, Exec. Secretary, 425 N. Michigan Ave., Chicago, IL 60611.

Maryland. *Directory of Library Orientation and Instruction Programs in Maryland.* Maryland Library Association, Academic and Research Libraries Division, Library Orientation & Exchange Committee, Fall 1976 (will be updated). Free. Available from: R. Merikangas, Undergraduate Library, University of Maryland, College Park, MD 20742.

New York. *New York Library Instruction Programs: A Directory.* Jacquelyn Morris, Betsy Elkins, Ray Murray, comp. New York Library Instruction Clearinghouse, 1976 (will be updated). $2.00 (make checks payable to SUNY Research Foundation). Available from: New York Library Instruction Clearinghouse, Moon Library, SUNY College of Environmental Science & Forestry, Syracuse, NY 13210.

Ohio. *Directory of Library Instruction Programs in Ohio Academic Libraries.* Linda L. Lester and Lorrine M. Novak, comp. Academic Library Association of Ohio. Project Team on Bibliographic Instruction, 1977. $1.50 (ED 145 862). Available from: Linda Lester, Shafer Library, Findlay College, Findlay, Ohio 45840.

Pennsylvania. *A Directory of Library Instruction Programs in Pennsylvania Academic Libraries.* Sara Lou Whildin, comp. Pennsylvania Library Association, College and Research Library Division, 1975. $3.00 (ED 118 071). Available from: Sara Lou Whildin, Delaware Campus, Pennsylvania State University, Media, PA 19603.

Virginia. *Directory of Academic Library Instruction Programs in Virginia.* William W. Prince, comp. Virginia Library Association. Library Instruction Forum, 1977. $2.25; free for Virginia librarians (make checks payable to Virginia Library Association). Available from: William W. Prince, Carol M. Newman Library, VPI & SU, Blacksburg, VA 24061.

Southeastern Library Association (SELA). *Southeastern Bibliographic Instruction Directory: Academic Libraries.* James E. Ward, Jane A. Albright, and Kathleen Phillips, comp. Southeastern Library Association, 1978. $6.00 (make checks payable to Southeastern Library Association). Available from: Southeastern Library Association, Box 987, Tucker, GA 30084.

Southwestern Library Association (SWLA). *Academic Library Instruction in the Southwest.* Ann Brooke, et al., comp. Southwestern Library Association, 1976. $2.00. Available from: Ms. Marion Mitchell, SWLA Task Force on Library Instruction, Southwestern Library Association, 7371 Paldao Dr., Dallas, TX 75240.

Wisconsin. *Library Instruction Programs 1975: A Wisconsin Directory.* Carla Stoffle, Johanna Herrick, and Suzanne Chernik, comp. Wisconsin Library Association and Wisconsin Association of Academic Librarians. Task Force on Instruction in Academic Libraries, 1975. $3.00 WLA members; $4.00 nonmembers (ED 118 057). Available from: Mrs. Elizabeth Bohmrich, Wisconsin Library Association, c/o Madison Public Library, 201 Mifflin St., Madison, WI 53703.

DIRECTORIES TO BE PUBLISHED

Florida. *Library Orientation/Instruction in Florida Academic Libraries: A Directory.* 1978. Contact person: June Stillman, Box 25000, Florida Technological University Library, Orlando, FL 32816.

Maryland. *Directory of Library Orientation and Instruction Programs in Maryland.* Contact person: Bruce Sajdak, Undergraduate Library, University of Maryland, College Park, MD 20742.

Michigan (will be published in Oct. 1978). Contact person: Hannelore Rader, Educational & Psychology Division, Center for Educational Resources, Eastern Michigan University, Ypsilanti, MI 48197.

New England. *Directory of Bibliographic Instruction Programs in New England Academic Libraries.* Contact person: Joan Stockard, Wellesly College Library, Wellesly, MA 02181.

New York. *New York Library Instruction Programs: A Directory.* Contact person: Jacquelyn Morris, Moon Library, SUNY College of Environmental Science & Forestry, Syracuse, NY 13210.

NEWSLETTERS

American Library Association (ALA). *Library Instruction Round Table Newsletter,* 1978. Available free to round table members. Contact person: Linda Dougherty, editor, Clearing Branch Library, Chicago Public Library, 5643 W. 63 St., Chicago, IL 60639.

California. *CCLI Newsletter,* semi-annually (published alternately Northern & Southern section, California Clearinghouse on Library Instruction), October 1977- . Contact person: Mandy Paulson, University of California/San Diego, Box 109, LaJolla, CA 92037.

Illinois. *Illinois Clearinghouse on Academic Library Instruction Newsletter,* quarterly, Spring 1977- . Contact person: Melissa Cain, Clearinghouse Coordinator, Undergraduate Library, University of Illinois, Urbana, IL 61801.

Library Orientation—Instruction Exchange (LOEX). *LOEX News,* quarterly, 1974- . Contact person: Carolyn Kirkendall, editor, Project LOEX, Center of Educational Resources, Eastern Michigan University, Ypsilanti, MI 48197.

New York. *New York Library Instruction Clearinghouse Newsletter,* March 1976. Contact person: Jacquelyn Morris, NYLIC, Moon Library, SUNY College of Environmental Science & Forestry, Syracuse, NY 13210.

Virginia. *VLA Library Instruction Forum Newsletter,* quarterly, 1977- . Available free to Virginia librarians. Contact person: William Prince, editor, Newman Library, VPI & SU, Blacksburg, VA 24061.

/

Wisconsin. *Library Instruction News Communique (LINC)*, 3/year, 1973- . Contact person: Julie Czisny, editor, University of Wisconsin-Milwaukee, Milwaukee, WI 53201.

Great Britain. *Infuse*, bimonthly, 1977- . Cost: £7.00 overseas; £5.00 UK. Contact person: Ian Malley, Information Officer for User Education, Library, Loughborough University of Technology, Loughborough, Leicestershire LE11 3TU, England.

Library-College. *The Library-College Experimenter: A Clearinghouse.* Norman, Oklahoma, no. 1, February, 1975- .

Ohio. *Bio-feedback; Newsletter of the ALAO Project Team on Bibliographic Instruction*, Academic Library Association of Ohio, no. 1, June 1976- .

INDEX

Birdsall, Douglas, 10
BLAISE, 161
Bonn, Galeriella, 19
Breivik, Patricia S., 16, 62, 64
Brennan, Exir B., 13
British libraries, 147-169, 171-181,
 183. *See also* Travelling Work-
 shops Experiment (TWE)
British Library Lending Division. *See*
 Lending Division of the British
 Library
British Library Research and Develop-
 ment Department (BLRDD), 147-
 148, 149, 150, 151, 157, 159, 163,
 164, 165, 166, 172
Budgets, 10, 14, 29, 30, 46, 51, 94, 109,
 110
Bullock Report, 149
Burton, Susan, 5, 7, 11
Bushnell, David, 64

Cain, Melissa, 8, 9, 10
Cammack, Floyd M., 6, 7, 9, 10
Canadian Association of College and
 University Libraries, 195, 207
Canadian libraries, 94, 195-209
"Canadian Libraries in Their Chang-
 ing Environment," 207
Canadian Library Association (CLA),
 207
Canadian Library Association
 Conference, 195
Canadian School Library Association,
 207
Case study, Colorado State University
 Libraries, 111-123
Center for Research on User Studies
 (British), 149
Central Swedish School Board, 189
Certification of media personnel, 30-31
Chemical Abstracts. See Workshops
Chibnall, Cicely, 197
Clark, Daphne, 171
Classrooms and the high school library,
 45-55
Clayton, Howard, 17

Clearinghouses for libraries. *See*
 Library clearinghouses
Clews, John P., 14, 148
Cohen, Arthur, 64
Cole, Jane B., 16
College courses in library skills, 63, 99,
 142-145, 156, 158-159, 160, 161,
 185-186, 187, 204-205
College libraries, 57-69, 71-91. *See
 also* University libraries
Commission on Education in Library
 Use. *See* Wisconsin Association of
 Academic Libraries (WAAL)
Commission on Instruction, ALA, 140
Community college libraries, 57-69
*The Compleat Library Guide to
 Toronto*, 200
Compton, Christopher, 133
Computer-assisted instruction (CAI)
 and computers, 109, 131
Computer Search Service (British), 161
Conferences (Canadian), 207-208
Conferences on Library Orientation,
 14, 22
*Consultation and Computer Searching
 Services* (Canadian), 206
Cooke, Phillip, 156
Cooperation among libraries, 131-132
Corlett, Donna, 15
Cottam, Keith M., 5, 6, 7
Council for National Academic
 Awards, 155-156
Council of Polytechnic Librarians
 (COPOL), 165
Council on Library Resources, 19, 73,
 93, 96, 106
Cross, Patricia, 59, 65
Crossley, Charles A., 14, 147, 148
CSU Office of Educational Media.
 See Case study, Colorado State
 University Libraries
CSU Office of Instructional Develop-
 ment. *See* Case study, Colorado
 State University Libraries
Curricular developments, 30-31, 34-35,
 38-44, 46, 140-142
Curriculum guides, 29, 31, 34, 45